MICROFOUNDATIONS

All economists are familiar with the division of the subject into micro-economics and macroeconomics. However, few economists are able to give an accurate account of what distinguishes micro and macro and what the relationship between them is. The increasing interest in the 'microfoundations of macroeconomics' has typically been regarded as a consequence of the view that economics is about the rational behaviour of individuals and that macro propositions are a result of the inter-actions of individuals. Accordingly, the usual interpretation of the microfoundations literature is that it provides macroeconomics with a foundation in theories of individual behaviour.

However, in *Microfoundations: A Critical Inquiry* Maarten Janssen argues that it is really microeconomics' concern with the functioning of markets (rather than its concern with rational individual behaviour) that underlies the theories which attempt to provide macroeconomics with microfoundations. This claim is substantiated by an analysis of the aggregation problem, of the individualistic foundations of equilibrium theories, of the rational expectations hypothesis and of some models from the New Classical and New Keynesian microfoundations litera-ture. It combines a thorough treatment of the technical aspects of these subjects with a critical discussion of the philosophical issues they raise.

The author

Maarten C.W. Janssen is an Associate Professor of Microeconomics at Erasmus University, Rotterdam and has been a visiting scholar at Duke University, North Carolina and at the Université Catholique de Louvain, Belgium. He has written on microfoundations in *Journal of Macroeconomics* and *History of Political Economy*. Other publications include an article on Milton Friedman in *Economics and Philosophy*. Amongst his current research interest is the interaction between rational behaviour and social norms.

MICROFOUNDATIONS

A Critical Inquiry

Maarten C. W. Janssen

London and New York

First published 1993
by Routledge
11 New Fetter Lane, London EC4P 4EE

Simultaneously published in the USA and Canada
by Routledge
29 West 35th Street, New York, NY 10001

Typeset in 10pt September Roman by Leaper & Gard Ltd, Bristol
Printed and bound in Great Britain by Biddles Ltd, Guildford and King's Lynn

British Library Cataloguing in Publication Data
A catalogue record for this book is available from the British Library
ISBN 0-415-08631-0

Library of Congress Cataloging-in-Publication Data
Janssen, Maarten Christiaan Wilhelmus, 1962–
Microfoundations : a critical inquiry / Maarten C. W. Janssen.
p.   cm.
Includes bibliographical references and index.
ISBN 0-415-08631-0
1. Microeconomics.   2. Macroeconomics.   3. Equilibrium (Economics)
I. Title
HB172.J35   1993
338.5—dc20   92-32043
                                                  CIP

CONTENTS

Preface   ix
Introduction   xiii

Part I Micro and macro in economics: definitions and relations

1 THE MEANING OF MICRO AND MACRO IN
   ECONOMICS   3
   Two ways to distinguish micro from macro   3
   Alternative definitions   6
   The terminology used in this book   8

2 INDIVIDUAL BEHAVIOUR AND AGGREGATE
   RELATIONS   10
   Explaining individual behaviour   11
   Explaining aggregate relations   15
   Explaining aggregate relations in terms of individual
        behaviour: two examples from other sciences   17
   Explaining aggregate relations in terms of individual
        behaviour: the theory of reduction   21
   Methodological individualism and reduction in economic
        theory   26
   An introduction to some game theoretic concepts   29
   Methodological individualism and game theory   35

3 GENERAL EQUILIBRIUM ANALYSIS AND
   MACROECONOMICS: ALTERNATIVE
   PROGRAMMES   41
   General equilibrium analysis   42
   Mainstream macroeconomics   44
   'Micro' foundations of macroeconomics: interacting
        programmes?   48

v

Intermezzo: Methodology

4 ECONOMICS AND THE REAL WORLD   57
Economic models as approximations of the real world   58
Economic models as caricatures of the real world   63
Economics without the real world   65

Part II Aggregation issues

5 AGGREGATION, ANALOGY AND THE
REPRESENTATIVE AGENT   71
The Klein/Nataf approach   75
The May/Pu approach   77
The two approaches reconsidered   79
Empirical restrictions on aggregate excess demand functions   82
On the differences between individual and aggregate
    relations: against reductionism?   84
Aggregate relations and the representative agent   92

6 ON THE PROBABILITY DISTRIBUTION OF
AGGREGATE DEMAND   94
Individual demand   96
The distribution of aggregate demand   96
Discussion and conclusion   100
Appendix   102

Part III Equilibrium and expectations

7 INDIVIDUALISTIC FOUNDATIONS FOR
MARKET EQUILIBRIUM   107
An individualistic explanation of competitive equilibrium
    prices?   110
An auctioneer with an objective function   113
The limit points of the core   114
Strategic market games   119
Competitive equilibria and Bertrand competition   122
The limit points of Cournot competition   124
Discussion and conclusion   129

8 THE INDIVIDUAL RATIONALITY OF
RATIONAL EXPECTATIONS   131
The government and the public as two rational agents   135

'Rational' expectations as an equilibrium assumption   137
Rationalizable expectations of other agents' expectations   140
Discussion and conclusion   142

Part IV Microfoundations

9 WHAT IS THIS THING CALLED
MICROFOUNDATIONS?   147
New classical microfoundations   148
New Keynesian microfoundations   152
Cooperating and competing programmes   156

10 RATIONALIZABLE ANIMAL SPIRITS   160
A model   162
Nash equilibria and rationalizable strategies   165
Welfare implications   167
Government policy   168
Discussion and conclusion   173

Conclusion   174
Notes   177
References   185
Author index   194
Subject index   197

PREFACE

The relation between microeconomics and macroeconomics is one of the most intriguing topics in contemporary economic theory. Many mainstream economists are working on what they call 'microfoundations of macroeconomics'. Outside the mainstream, there are economists who claim that microeconomics is in need of a 'macrofoundation'. Finally, some philosophers of economics have critically examined the relation between 'micro' and 'macro' in economics.

However central the issue of the relation between micro and macro theory might be, there are few economists who have given a systematic account of the relation. Consequently, the distinction between micro and macro theory and the relation between them is rather unclear. This study is an attempt at clarification. Its aim is partially of a theoretical and partially of a more methodological nature. Most methodological studies are either exclusively normative or exclusively descriptive. Normative methodologies urge economists to adopt methods in conformity with the standards set by the methodology. Descriptive methodologies, on the other hand, try to account for developments that actually take place in economics. This study is neither exclusively normative nor exclusively descriptive in nature. The point of departure is that economists themselves are normative and the question this study addresses is whether economists actually build theories that are in conformity with the norms that are set by themselves. Applying this idea to the present topic – the relation between microeconomics and macroeconomics – one can argue that mainstream economists are normative in the sense that they want to build macroeconomics on theories of individual behaviour. I think there are good reasons to obey this norm and these reasons are outlined in the introduction below. But the main aim of the book is *not* to argue in favour of the norm. Instead, the study is devoted to the question of whether mainstream economists obey the norm, i.e.

whether the macroeconomic models that we have at the moment actually are based on theories of individual behaviour. Of course, the question would not be an interesting one if the answer were positive. Indeed, the argument developed in the book will result in the claim that the microfoundations literature does *not* provide macroeconomics with individualistic foundations.

At the moment many economists are sceptical about the fruitfulness of most methodological studies. To them, I would say that I share this scepticism. This might seem to be an odd position given the above methodological stance. So, let me then also say that ideally speaking good theoretical (and empirical) research should be combined with some methodological reflection (and vice versa). In this study I therefore try to illustrate the general methodological ideas with a detailed analysis of the economic theories in question. Moreover, I attempt to make a contribution to economic theory whenever the analysis shows that currently available theories do not meet the existing norms. The potential danger for the present endeavour is that economic theorists might find the methodological reflections too vague and more philo-sophically inclined economists might find the details too cumbersome. I have tried to find the middle ground. Accordingly, I have not included very technical material in the book; the contributions to economic theory take more the form of examples than of overall theories, the idea of the examples being that they bring home the general notions discussed in the book.

This book is a completely revised version of my PhD dissertation. I am deeply indebted to my two advisors, Theo Kuipers and Ad Pikkemaat, who each in their own way were of invaluable help during the period I worked on my dissertation. Theo Kuipers was supervisor of a paper on 'reduction in economics' which I wrote as an undergraduate student and he stimulated me to think of a dissertation project. Ad Pikkemaat became involved in the project as early as 1985. His careful reading of almost every word that I wrote before finishing the dissertation was of great help in structuring my thoughts. Apart from them, I want to express a special word of thanks to Neil de Marchi. His open-mindedness in personal and professional matters has helped me a great deal over the past years.

Several other persons and some institutions have also contributed in important ways to the finishing of this book. The Department of Econo-metrics at the University of Groningen is gratefully acknowledged for giving me the opportunity to carry out my own research project. Of the many people in Groningen who were important to the finishing of my dissertation, I want to mention especially Harry Garretsen for all the time that we spent together discussing our work. The Department of Microeconomics and the Department of Philosophy at the Erasmus University, Rotterdam provided the possibility to pursue my combined interest in economic theory and the philosophy of economics. During the past two years in Rotterdam I have had the opportunity to share many experiences with Sanjeev Goyal. I wish to thank him for his understanding on many occasions. The Netherlands Organization for Scientific Research (NWO) is gratefully acknowledged for the financial support they gave me for a stay at Duke University in the autumn of 1989. The Department of Economics at Duke provided a pleasant environment for doing research. During the spring of 1991 and 1992 I stayed at the Université Catholique de Louvain. The Department of Economics in Louvain provided the right kind of atmosphere to rewrite my dissertation into its present form.

More important than institutions are the persons who have contributed through discussions in some way or another to the present shape of the study. Here, I would like to mention in particular: Marina Bianchi, Tilman Börgers, Willem Buiter, Theo Dijkstra, Hans van Ees, Bert Hamminga, Dan Hausman, Kevin Hoover, Simon Kuipers, Uskali Mäki, Philippe Mongin, Hervé Moulin, Alan Nelson, Maarten van 't Riet, Alexander Rosenberg, Michel de Vroey, Jack Vromen, Bernard Walliser and Roy Weintraub, Ernst Koesveld and Maurits Pino helped to prepare the final version of the text.

Finally, I wish to thank Wolkens-Noordhoff for permission to use parts of my PhD dissertation; Duke University Press for permission to use my article 'What is This Thing Called Microfoundations?', *History of Political Economy* 23: 687–712 as a basis for chapter 3; and Louisiana State University Press for permission to use my article, 'The Alleged Necessity of Microfoundations', *Journal of Macroeconomics* 13: 619–39.

Rotterdam

INTRODUCTION

Macroeconomics should be built upon a microeconomic foundation. Nowadays, this is a widely accepted doctrine in the economics profession. Most economists take the necessity for a microeconomic foundation for granted. If arguments in favour of the necessity for microfoundations are cited, they are often of the following reductionist form. Society consists of individuals who are the *only* subjects that make economic decisions. So, in order to explain what is going on in the economy as a whole — e.g. unemployment, inflation, business cycles – we have to understand the individual decisions from which a particular situation originates. I think that this 'reductionist credo' itself is *largely* correct. However, if it is used as an argument in favour of the necessity for microeconomic foundations it is presupposed either that microeconomics is only concerned with individual behaviour or that all microeconomic propositions can be derived from statements concerning individual decision making. In this book I claim that both presuppositions are not correct: the microeconomic techniques that are used in the microfoundations literature themselves lack individualistic foundations. Accordingly, the above rationale for microfoundations breaks down.

There are good reasons why economists might like to stick to the reductionist credo of *methodological individualism* (MI) according to which theories about the economy as a whole should be built on assumptions concerning individual behaviour. (A more detailed definition of MI is given in chapter 2.) An important argument, I think, is that when the principle of individualism is kept in mind, one does not fall easily into the trap of postulating a suspect entity that behaves independently of individual members of a group and that serves the interest of the group. If the principle is not adhered to one might, for example, 'explain' the existence of a certain component (institution) of the economy as a whole by referring to the function it performs in the system. But this would assume what needs to be explained, namely how that particular component is able to perform that function. Also, it would be unclear how that particular component could have emerged.

A second reason to be interested in MI derives from considerations concerning the way economics might be used to guide policy interventions. It is true that policy makers are mainly interested in the consequences of a certain policy measure on the economy as a whole. However, most policy measures are effective at the individual level and policy makers attempt to influence individual behaviour in such a way that the desired consequences at the system level are achieved. Accordingly, an analysis that remains at the aggregate level is not useful to guide policy interventions, because it tends to neglect the fact that individuals mediate between policy measures and system-wide consequences of those policy measures. On the other hand, it should also be admitted that an analysis that focuses on the impact of policy measures on individual behaviour is not very useful either if the system-wide consequences of the interaction between individuals are not studied. What is needed is a type of research in which the system-wide consequences of different policy measures are studied with individual behaviour performing the role of mediator. The general idea behind the kind of research I have in mind will be further discussed in chapter 2. Here, an example will be given as a means to illustrate the above claims.

Suppose a government is interested in reducing the level of unemployment. It considers introducing a job-training programme and it wants to know what the impact of such a programme is. Clearly, if the programme is effective it has a positive impact on the probability of an unemployed individual getting a job. However, unemployment in society will decrease only if a new job is created or a vacant job filled. Thus, two kinds of transitions have to be studied: the impact of the (macro) policy on the behaviour of individuals and the impact of the behaviour of individuals on the (macro) variable of interest. The sociologist Coleman (1990) has called these transitions the macro-to-micro and the micro-to-macro transition, respectively.

Of course, if aggregate relationships were stable over time and under different policy regimes, the second reason for being interested in MI would not be an important one. In this case we could simply use aggregate relationships to give policy advice. However, since Lucas (1976), the question of whether traditional macroeconometric relations and models are stable under alternative policy regimes is usually answered with a simple 'no':

given that the structure of an econometric model consists of optimal decision rules of economic agents, and that optimal decision rules vary systematically with changes in the structure of series relevant to the decision-maker, it follows that any change in policy will systematically alter the structure of econometric models.

(Lucas 1976: 43)

Accordingly, traditional macroeconometric models are not able to predict the consequences of alternative policy regimes.

On the other hand, it is sometimes said that aggregate relationships are more stable than individual relationships. The argument essentially is that potential instabilities at the individual level average out at the aggregate level (see, e.g., Schlicht 1985). This view can be challenged, however. First, if the view that aggregate relationships are more stable is not restricted to stable policy situations, it contradicts the Lucas critique outlined above. But in recent years people seem to be adapting their behaviour more and more to changes in public policies thereby trying to undo the impact of the policy measure on their own welfare. There are numerous examples (tax evasion, social security) in which the intended goal of a policy measure is not reached, because of changes in individual behaviour. In those cases, it seems questionable that aggregate relationships are more stable than relationships in which the reaction of individuals on different policy measures can be taken into account. Second, the 'averaging out' argument depends on the view that individuals act independently of each other. If, however, an individual's action positively depends on the actions taken by other individuals (as, for example, in game theoretic models of strategic complementarities), individual relationships may turn out to be more stable than relationships at the aggregate level. Whatever the final answer on the issue of stability, it is clear that in order to make an argument in favour of one of the two positions a model is needed in which the internal structure of the economic system is described. Such a model would be in line with a form of individualism that is sketched above (and discussed in more detail in the chapters to follow).

The view expressed in this book is thus very much in line with Haavelmo's emphasizing the importance of modelling *autonomous relations*. In a famous example he observes that

If we should make a series of speed tests with an automobile, driving on a flat, dry road, we might be able to establish a very accurate functional relationship between the pressure on the gas throttle ... and the corresponding maximum speed of the car. And the knowledge of this relationship might be sufficient to operate the car at a prescribed speed. But if a man did not know anything about automobiles, and he wanted to understand how they work, we should not advise him to spend time and effort in measuring a relationship like that. Why? Because (1) such a relation leaves the whole inner mechanism of a car in complete mystery, and (2) such a relation might break down at any time, as soon as there is some disorder or change in any working part of the car.... We say that such a relation has very little *autonomy*, because its existence depends upon the simultaneous fulfilment of a great many other relations, some of which are of a transitory nature.

(Haavelmo 1944: 27–8)

In other words, if macroeconomic relations are stable over time, the economist might want to build a model of the inner mechanisms of society in order to enquire why this is so. Such an explanation might unravel conditions that need to hold for the macroeconomic relation to be stable. The explanation might furthermore suggest alternative macroeconomic relationships that hold if these conditions are not met.

Of course, one should not stick to MI in a dogmatic way. In many situations there is not enough information about individual agents to build a practically useful model. In such situations aggregate regularities may suffice to serve a practical purpose. Accordingly, individualism does not require the abandonment of aggregate regularities. It seems better to hold a mild point of view on the issue. So, I agree with Brodbeck that a social scientist should

keep the principle of methodological individualism firmly in mind as a devoutly to-be-wished-for consummation, an ideal to be approximated as closely as possible. This should at least help us assure that nevermore he (the social scientist) dally with suspect group-minds and impersonal 'forces', economic or otherwise.

(Brodbeck 1958: 6)

It is frequently claimed that economic theories in general, and theories (or models) with microfoundations in particular, are based on a form of individualism. Above we have seen the reasons why this would be a to-be-wished-for state of affairs. The rest of this study is mainly devoted to the question of whether the claim is justified. In the introductory paragraph I have raised some doubts. Before being able to show that the microfoundations literature does *not* provide macroeconomics with individualistic foundations, there is a long way to go. First, we have to distinguish between two different definitions of *microeconomics*. According to the first definition, microeconomics is the study of individual economic behaviour; according to the second definition, microeconomics (in particular, partial and general equilibrium theory) is the study of the functioning of economic markets. In part I of this study I will provide a discussion of the different ways in which the terms 'micro' and 'macro' are employed in economics and I demonstrate that the two terms can be contrasted in two different ways. Roughly speaking, one basic contrast associated with the two terms is between individual and aggregate behaviour; the other contrast is between, on the one hand, micro theories in which issues of market valuation and the distribution of a given quantity of resources play important roles and, on the other hand, macro theories in which the emphasis is more on the level of total output and employment. In this way part I provides the general context for the more detailed discussion given in the other three parts of the book.

Before going into details, however, a chapter on methodology is invoked. An argument against microfoundations that one hears every now and then is the following. In an empirical science one is interested in knowing the empirical regularities that govern the subject. Macroeconomics gives a reasonably accurate description of aggregate relationships in the economy. Models in the microfoundations literature might provide a theoretical justification for these aggregate relationships, but at the expense of a high degree of simplification. More importantly, as these models do not give a *better* description of empirical regularities than the traditional macroeconomic models, they do not contribute in a significant way to the process of gathering knowledge about the economy. Therefore, there is nothing to be gained by building economic models with microfoundations. As there is some truth in this criticism (especially as far as the high degree of simplification is concerned), I wanted to deal with it in an adequate way. I have toyed with the idea of not introducing a separate chapter on methodology and, instead, discussing some methodological problems whenever it was necessary in the specific context. The disadvantage of this alternative approach is that it remains unclear how the different parts form a coherent methodological view. This danger is real, particularly because of the mixed state of the art in economics. I think that some branches of economics are best regarded as part of an empirical science, whereas other branches are better considered as a form of mathematical political philosophy.[1] Both branches are important in the rest of the book. For example, empirical issues play an important role in the chapters on aggregation problems in economics (part II), whereas issues related to political philosophy are more prominent in part III on market equilibrium and expectations.[2] In order to sort out the differences in the questions involved, I have decided to take an explicit methodological stand early in the study.

Part II delves into the aggregation problem in economics. It will be argued that MI does not assume that aggregate relationships are similar to individual relationships. Requirements of analogy and representativity have been major obstacles in solving the aggregation problem. Instead of interpreting the well-known 'aggregation problem' as a severe problem, I will interpret it as showing that the a priori restrictions macroeconomists frequently impose on aggregate relationships are too severe. In particular, the requirement that aggregate relationships be of a deterministic kind has to be abandoned. In the light of the fact that aggregate statistics contain less information than individual level data (if available) it is more likely that aggregate relationships be of a probabilistic variety. The second part of the book illustrates some of the differences between individual and aggregate behaviour in cases in which strategic behaviour does not play a role.

Part III forms an important part in the chain of arguments presented in the book. It deals with the question of whether equilibrium notions that are used in economics are founded in a theory of individual behaviour. It will be shown that although market equilibrium notions are not inconsistent with notions of rational individual behaviour, they are (generally speaking) neither derivable from them. So, we arrive at the conclusion that equilibrium notions are *extra*-rational and *not* based on individual behaviour. The game theoretic approaches that have tried to give foundations for the notion of market equilibrium suffer from a similar weakness. I will demonstrate that in some cases, however, the deficiencies in the game theoretic approaches can be remedied. Furthermore, it will be shown that the concept of rational expectations as it is commonly used is also an equilibrium concept and as such equally dubious from an individualistic point of view.

Finally, part IV goes into the microfoundations literature. The first argument put forward in this part can be summarized in the following syllogism. Given that equilibrium notions are generally employed in the microfoundations literature and that these notions are not (yet) founded in a theory of individual behaviour, it follows that the microfoundations literature does not provide macroeconomics with a foundation in a theory of individual behaviour. Another interpretation of the micro-foundations literature will be provided in which the second meaning of microeconomics (theories of market valuation and distribution) plays an important role. Roughly speaking, microeconomic foundations will be regarded as synonymous with 'foundations in general equilibrium analysis', *not* with foundations in individual behaviour.

It can be argued that J.M. Keynes was the founder of the idea that macroeconomics should be studied as an autonomous discipline. New classical economists objected to the autonomous character of macro-economics:

> The most interesting developments in macroeconomic theory seem to me describable as the reincorporation of aggregative problems such as inflation and the business cycle within the general framework of 'microeconomic' theory. If these develop-ments succeed, the term 'macroeconomic' will simply disappear from use and the modifier 'micro' will be superfluous. We will simply speak, as did Smith, Ricardo, Marshall and Walras, of economic theory.
>
> (Lucas 1987: 107-8)

It is clear that traditional general equilibrium analysis is more in line with (new) classical positions. New Keynesians have got into some diffi-culties reconciling Keynesian views with general equilibrium analysis. From the above it will be clear that new Keynesian economics might abandon the equilibrium notions without abandoning the fundamental notion of rational individual behaviour. The last chapter makes a start with this project. Among other things, it shows how to make sense of the Keynesian notion of *animal spirits* in a model in which individuals behave rationally.

Part I

MICRO AND MACRO IN ECONOMICS: DEFINITIONS AND RELATIONS

1

THE MEANING OF MICRO AND MACRO IN ECONOMICS

The two major branches of economic theory are microeconomics and macroeconomics. The terms micro and macro have been commonly used for more than fifty years now and one would think that it should be clear how the two terms are to be understood, and in particular what distinguishes the one from the other. As observed by Machlup (1963) some time ago, this is, unfortunately, not the case, and this state of affairs has not changed significantly since then. The main problem that the confusion generates is that the relation between microeconomics and macroeconomics remains unclear. The present chapter sorts out different attempts to define the two terms in a coherent way. The purpose is not to arrive at 'sound' definitions, but rather to delineate a few possible ways to distinguish micro from macro. In the rest of the book, two (different) ways to make the distinction will play a crucial role. Here, these two ways are introduced and contrasted with other ways to distinguish microeconomics from macroeconomics.

TWO WAYS TO DISTINGUISH MICRO FROM MACRO

Economics is not the only science in which the terms micro and macro coexist. In other sciences the terms micro and macro are usually employed as synonyms for respectively 'small' and 'large'. This is also *one of the ways* in which the concepts are used in economics. Some economists regard microeconomics as the study of the behaviour of individual economic units, and macroeconomics as the study of relations between broad economic aggregates. One only needs to turn to the first pages of the introductory chapters of many textbooks to encounter this view. Henderson and Quandt (1980: 2), for example, posit that the major branches [of economics] are *microeconomics*, which is the study of economic actions of individuals and well-defined groups of individuals, and *macroeconomics*, which is the study of broad aggregates such as total employment and national income.

Allen (1967: 1) observes

> the term 'macro-economics' ... applies to the study of relations between broad economic aggregates, as opposed to the decision-taking process of individuals and firms which is the subject-matter of 'micro-economics'.

Individual economic units can be considered parts of the economy as a whole. In the light of the above division, the study of the parts is the domain of microeconomics, while the study of the system as a whole is the concern of macroeconomics.

The above division is, among other things, based upon the view that microeconomics confines itself to the study of individual units. However, this view has been seriously challenged. Nelson (1989: 25–6), for example, poses the question of whether microeconomic theory explains 'the behaviour of individuals *in addition to* the behaviour of entire markets' (my italics). Further, he notes that 'it is uncontroversial that microeconomics is intended to provide explanations of aggregative phenomena such as relative prices' (Nelson 1989: 26). Branson (1979: 1) begins his macroeconomic textbook by positing that

> in microeconomic theory ... the focus of the analysis is on the determination of relative prices and the allocation of scarce resources among alternative uses. On the other hand, in its now traditional form, macroeconomics focuses on the level of utilization of resources ... and the general price level.

In this view, microeconomic theory is a theory of value (relative prices) and distribution (allocation); it is about the question of how a fixed amount of pie is divided among individuals. Arguments about the working of the market play an important role in this conception of microeconomics. Macroeconomics, on the other hand, is more concerned with the size of the pie. Note that, according to this view, both disciplines analyse *aggregate* phenomena. Accordingly, it is not immediately clear what kind of notion of 'micro' underlies this use of the term 'microeconomics'.

In the second view, theories (of the whole economy) in which models of several individual units are integrated are also studied as part of microeconomics. The Arrow–Debreu model (ADM) of general equilibrium is a typical example. The method has two essential features. First, the desired actions of individual units are modelled as the optimization of an objective function subject to constraints. The individuals express these desired actions on pre-existing markets. Second, only those states of the model are considered in which the desired actions of all individuals are compatible with each other. Such states are called *equilibrium states* and the markets are supposed to function in such a way that the economy is in one of those equilibrium states. Microeconomic textbooks such as Kreps (1990) and Varian (1992) typically include a treatment of ADM.

The difference between the above two ways to distinguish between microeconomics and macroeconomics is mainly due to the confusion about the meaning of the term microeconomics, the main question being whether or not to consider ADM and the tradition of general equilibrium analysis (GEA) as part of microeconomics. The origin of this confusion can be explained as follows. Traditionally, economics was divided between the theory of value and distribution on the one hand and the theory of money on the other hand. As Varian (1987) observes, the distinction between microeconomics and macroeconomics became popular only after the publishing of Keynes' *General Theory*. Keynes (1936: 292–3) made the following observation:

> The division of Economics between the Theory of Value and Distribution on the one hand and the Theory of Money on the other hand is, I think, a false distinction. The right dichotomy is, I suggest, between the Theory of the Individual Industry or Firm ... on the one hand and the Theory of Output and Employment *as a whole* on the other hand.

The terms microeconomics and macroeconomics became associated with Keynes' distinction between the theory of the individual industry or firm and the theory of aggregate output and employment, respectively. As we will see, it is beyond doubt that the *General Theory* shaped the field of modern macroeconomics so that a change with respect to content and terminology occurred around the same time. This cannot be said of microeconomics. Microeconomics is still concerned with theories of value and distribution and not only with theories of individual households or firms.

ALTERNATIVE DEFINITIONS

The two possible ways to distinguish microeconomics and macro-economics outlined in the previous section do not exhaust the ways the two terms have been defined in the economic literature. First, it has to be mentioned that some authors have tried to reconcile the two views on microeconomics. In his textbook on microeconomic theory, Malinvaud (1972: 2) notes that

> the main object of the theory in which we are interested is the analysis of the simultaneous determination of prices and quantities produced, exchanged and consumed. It is called micro-economics because, in its abstract formulations, it respects the individuality of each good and each agent.

In this way, Malinvaud captures the 'value and distribution' as well as the 'individual behaviour' interpretation of the term 'microeconomics'. Although I think that Malinvaud's definition covers the content of 'microeconomics' to a large extent, I do not employ his definition in what follows and I will explain why. The definition *suggests* that all microeconomic propositions can be *derived* from propositions concerning the behaviour of individual agents. In the previous section, we have seen that the microeconomic method of general equilibrium analysis is concerned only with equilibrium states. At this stage of the study it is, however, an unsettled question of whether – and not a fact that – restricting attention to equilibrium states of a model can be justified in terms of propositions concerning individual behaviour. If we do not want to fall into the trap this suggestion presents and we want to address the question about the individualistic foundations of the equilibrium notion seriously, we must choose another terminology.

A somewhat similar suggestion can be found in the way Quirk and Saposnik (1968) deal with the division of microeconomics and macro-economics. They define microeconomics as the study of the behaviour of isolated economic agents and macroeconomics as the study of the behaviour of the economy as a whole (this is in line with the first way of making the distinction presented in the previous section). They go on to argue that

> General equilibrium theory forms a bridge between these two branches of economic theory, using the tools of microeconomics to analyze the behavior of the entire economy. In common with macroeconomics, general equilibrium theory is concerned with the interrelationships that exist among the markets for goods and

services in the economy; in common with microeconomics, the analysis in general equilibrium theory is carried out in terms of individual decision makers and commodities rather than in terms of aggregates.

(Quirk and Saposnik 1968: 1)

In the above quote it is also suggested that all propositions of GEA can be regarded as logical consequences of the view that individual agents are decision makers. Chapter 7 will be devoted to a detailed analysis of this question. Here, it suffices to say that the terminology that is used should be such that one is able to address this question.

There is another element in the definitions from Malinvaud (1972) and Quirk and Saposnik (1968) that needs to be discussed briefly. It can be argued that microeconomics deals with many different homogeneous goods, while macroeconomics concentrates its analysis on a few composite goods (one consumption good, one type of labour and so on). It is clear, however, that in its abstract form GEA studies an arbitrary number of goods, which can be either few or many. This suggests that a distinction between microeconomics and macroeconomics is not easily drawn according to the *number* of goods that is considered.

Beside attempts at reconciling the two ways to define microeconomics and macroeconomics presented in the previous section, a third definition has been proposed. This definition proposes to draw the dividing line between the terms micro and macro by the term *coordination*. Weintraub (1979: 74–5), for example, argues that

> *most of the traditional microeconomic concerns are embedded in models that either assume or produce coherent outcomes*

and

> macroeconomics has been involved with questions like unemployment, inflation and control of economic aggregates, and thus *its domain of discourse is system-incoherence, or the failure of the economic system to produce automatically well-coordinated outcomes.*

A similar dividing line can be found in Leijonhufvud (1976) – but, it must be said, he is more concerned with comparing general equilibrium theory and Keynesian theory – and, more recently, in Van Ees and Garretsen (1990: 124) who propose to 'classify micro and macro theories of the economy as a whole in those that assume perfect coordination and those that do not take this assumption for granted'.

7

Although coordination issues play an important role in the chapters that follow, I will not use this criterion to distinguish microeconomics from macroeconomics. The reason is threefold. First, unlike the first two criteria discussed in the previous section, this third criterion to distinguish microeconomics from macroeconomics is not widely adhered to and unless there is a good reason to do so, it seems wise not to introduce new terminology. Second, in many theories (whether they are 'micro' or 'macro', 'Keynesian' or 'classical') it is not so much an issue whether coordination is assumed or not, but rather how much coordination is assumed. Accordingly, the distinction will become quite vague if the suggestion were followed. Third, coordination failures and coordination successes can be considered as system-wide or aggregate outcomes. From the perspective of the first criterion, it is then a natural question to ask whether, and if so how, individual behaviour leads to coordinated outcomes. So, the important question is not so much whether coordinated outcomes are assumed or not, but rather what features of individual behaviour guarantee that (some form of) coordination will be achieved.

THE TERMINOLOGY USED IN THIS BOOK

In the previous two sections a few ways to distinguish between microeconomics and macroeconomics have been reviewed. The main difficulty in providing 'sound' definitions is that it is not obvious whether GEA should be regarded as part of microeconomics. Because of the possible confusion, I avoid the use of the term microeconomics altogether. Instead, I use the term 'individual behaviour' when writing about the behaviour of a single economic agent. The phrase 'general equilibrium analysis' (GEA) will be used for models that deal with the economy as a whole in terms of equilibrium states in which the desired actions of all individuals are compatible. The term 'individual behaviour' will be contrasted with 'aggregate behaviour'. This contrast will be used when dealing with a part of the economy as a whole (e.g. individual and aggregate consumption behaviour), but also when analysing how individual behaviour leads to certain aggregate properties of the economic system. The view on the economy as a whole, which we have called GEA, will be contrasted with a view in which the economy as a whole is analysed without recourse to individual behaviour. By lack of a better term, I will call this alternative view 'macroeconomics'. Thus, the basic two distinctions are then made between individual and aggregate behaviour, on the one hand, and between GEA and macroeconomics on the other hand.

One's perspective on the relation between microeconomics and macroeconomics depends to a large extent on the definitions of the terms involved. In the next chapter I discuss the connection between 'micro' and 'macro' that arises if these terms are understood as 'individual' and 'aggregate'. Questions that will arise are the following. Is it possible to describe and/or explain the way the economic system behaves in a manner that does not ultimately refer to the individual agent? Is it possible to explain the behaviour of the individual economic agent in a way that does not refer to the system of which it is a part? Is there an interpretation of the dictum 'the whole is more than the sum of its parts' such that it applies to economics? At the end of the next chapter I will discuss in detail how game theory fits into the individualistic programme of economics.

Chapter 3 provides a general background for a discussion of the relation between GEA and macroeconomics. When there are two approaches to analyse the economy as a whole, a natural question is to what extent they differ. There clearly is a difference in method, but are there other differences? Is macroeconomics more policy oriented and GEA more theory oriented? Are the two approaches consistent with each other and, if so, how should one conceive of the relation between them? These questions will be given an introductory treatment in chapter 3. A more detailed discussion has to wait until chapter 9.

2

INDIVIDUAL BEHAVIOUR AND AGGREGATE RELATIONS

The relation between individual and aggregate behaviour has been frequently studied in economics. This chapter will provide a general background to a more detailed discussion which will be given in chapters 5 to 8. The emphasis of the present chapter will be on how individual behaviour and the relation between aggregates might be explained. First, however, a terminological point has to be made, namely that the notions 'individual' and 'aggregate' are treated here *in a relative way*. Depending on the problem at hand, it may well be that corporate bodies can be regarded as 'individuals'. For example, households or firms may be regarded as 'individuals' relative to the aggregate level of the economy as a whole. However, a household (firm) will be treated as an aggregate concept with respect to the different human beings that constitute the household (firm). The notion of an aggregate relationship will be used for relationships between aggregate concepts.

There are several reasons why the concept of an 'individual' is stretched in the above way. First, it is clear that the claim that economics is based on a form of individualism only has a chance to survive potential criticism if a broad notion of 'individual' is taken: as households and firms *are* treated as basic concepts in economics, the position that economic theory is non-individualist would be a trivial one if the notion of 'individual' was taken in a more narrow way. Second, if the concept of an individual agent is defined as an actor who can be regarded as being responsible for his actions (see also the next section), then it is important to note that in many branches of modern law firms and (local) governments are held responsible for their actions and *not* the human beings that work for them. Accordingly, the broad concept of an 'individual' alluded to above is in line with a conception in law that natural persons *and* organizations can be held responsible for their actions. This argument is further examined in Coleman (1990: 534–42).

The present chapter is divided into seven sections. The first section is concerned with the way in which individual behaviour is explained in economics. In the following section I briefly discuss two ways to explain aggregate relationships: one with and one without recourse to individual behaviour. The third section presents two examples of the way aggregate relationships are explained in terms of individual behaviour in other sciences. It will turn out that there are some common elements in the structure of these types of explanations. The next section presents a general model in which these common elements are characterized. The fifth section discusses the way in which this model is used to give a precise definition of MI. The model will be used in order to be able to focus the critique (briefly discussed in the introduction) on the allegedly individualistic foundations of economic theory. Applications of the model to economics are dealt with in chapters 5, 6 and 7. It will turn out that MI is closely related to the view on society that is expressed in game theory. The sixth section will then introduce the reader to some game theoretic concepts and arguments that play an important role in parts III and IV. The last section of the chapter discusses the relation between a somewhat unorthodox view on game theory and MI in an explicit way.

EXPLAINING INDIVIDUAL BEHAVIOUR

Although the view that individual behaviour can be described as a form of rational behaviour is widely accepted in economics, there is still some discussion about what it means to behave rationally (see, e.g., Elster 1983 and Sen 1976). It is the intention of this section to clarify how the concept of rational behaviour is used in this book. A discussion of why the concept is used will be postponed until chapter 4.

I will say that individual agents behave rationally if they choose the most appropriate action to achieve a certain goal in the light of the information they possess. Some elements of this definition require further elaboration. First, the definition assumes that an agent has a preference ordering over possible consequences. This preference ordering is frequently represented by an agent's utility function, which acts as a primitive term in explaining an agent's behaviour. The question of why particular entities enter the utility function as arguments is usually left unanswered in economics.

Second, at the moment an agent decides upon an action the consequences of the action are often not completely and precisely known. The point in time when the decision is made is thus an essential ingredient for the evaluation of a rational action. *After* the action is chosen, new information may arise that destroys the reasons for which the agent has chosen the action. This, however, does no harm to the rationality of the action: rationality is an *ex ante* and not an *ex post* concept. In general, there are two kinds of uncertainty individual decision makers face. On the one hand, they may not know the exact mechanism by which an outcome (consequence) is brought about by a certain action. On the other hand, a specific outcome often depends not only on the action chosen by the particular agent, but also on the actions chosen by other agents. In this case, even if the exact mechanism that relates actions and outcomes is known, uncertainty about the actions chosen by other agents prohibits an agent from foreseeing the exact consequences of his or her intended action. In what follows, the emphasis will be on the second type of uncertainty (sometimes referred to as endogenous uncertainty), not because the first type of uncertainty is believed to be of less importance to economics, but instead because it is not intimately related to the topic of the book. The second type of uncertainty follows from the fact (which is at the core of the argument presented in this book) that an individual agent is not the only agent in the economic system.

A *third* aspect of the above definition is the difference between instrumental (or practical) and cognitive (or epistemic) rationality (see, e.g., Bicchieri 1987 and Walliser 1989). Instrumental rationality argues that an agent chooses the most preferred action *given* an expectation about the consequences of this action. Instrumental rationality does not say anything about the 'rationality' of these expectations. Cognitive rationality, on the other hand, treats the relation between available information (data) and the agent's expectations. Cognitive rationality may take on several forms, of which only two will be discussed here. The least restrictive version of cognitive rationality asserts that an agent's expectations have to be consistent with all the information he or she possesses. For example, if an agent knows that the other agents in the economy behave rationally he or she may not expect the other agents to adopt actions rational agents will never choose (see also the last two sections). In many models, this version of cognitive rationality turns out not to be a strong requirement, i.e. expectations remain largely undetermined. A stronger form of cognitive rationality asserts that an agent forms an expectation that is optimal from the point of view of a certain evaluation criterion (e.g. minimizing mean square error) taking account of a specific theory of the system and the available information. The hypothesis of 'rational expectations' (REH), which is frequently adopted in economics, is often regarded as a version of this stronger form of cognitive rationality. In its most simple form, REH asserts that the subjective expectation of an individual agent equals the objective mathematical expectation of the relevant economic theory conditioned on all the relevant data that are available up to the moment the expectation is formed. In chapter 8, I will discuss some details of the relation between cognitive rationality and REH.

Figure 2.1 illustrates the way in which cognitive and instrumental rationality are related. The middle section of the figure represents the notion of instrumental rationality: given the set of possible actions, the preference ordering and expectations about the consequences of an action, agents select their most preferred action. The left side of the figure represents the cognitive aspect of rational behaviour. If the strong form of cognitive rationality is adopted, the expectation is based on a specific theory and a specific evaluation criterion. If the weak form of cognitive rationality is chosen, the only requirement is that there is *some* theory and *some* evaluation criterion according to which the particular expectation is the best given the available information.

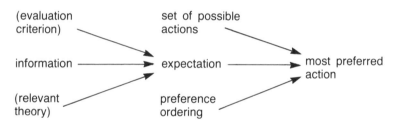

Figure 2.1 Cognitive and instrumental rationality

In what follows, I use a concept of rational behaviour that includes both instrumental and cognitive rationality. One may wonder whether one should subsume information gathering under the heading of rational behaviour. In the scheme above information is treated as a primitive term. Economists sometimes argue that rational agents gather extra information up to the point where the expected marginal benefit of a 'unit' of information equals the expected marginal cost of acquiring the extra unit (see, e.g., Boland 1982). Looking at figure 2.1 reveals, however, that this leads to an infinite regress, because expectations about possible consequences of intended actions are based upon, among other things, the available information, which in turn is based upon expectations about the costs and benefits of information gathering (see also Elster 1983 and Hoogduin and Snippe 1987). This leads to the question of where these latter expectations come from, and so on. In order to avoid a discussion of the conceptual difficulties related to this infinite regress, I will not be concerned with the information-gathering process in what follows. The analysis starts at the point where agents are assumed to possess some specified amount of information.

A final point to be considered when defining rational behaviour is 'the set of available actions'. There is an unresolved dispute about the kind of primitive terms that are acceptable in an explanation of an agent's behaviour. Above, it has been noted that an agent's preference ordering acts as a primitive term in economics. Economists widely agree that preference formation is a research domain of other social sciences, most notably psychology;[1] however, they disagree about the phenomena that are allowed to constrain the set of actions available to the agent. Essentially, two positions can be distinguished in the literature. Those holding the first position (see, e.g., Boland 1982: 30–7) assert that 'natural' conditions (e.g. the weather, production technology at a certain moment in time) are the only primitive terms that are allowed to constrain an agent's action beyond psychological states. Boland claims that neoclassical economics adheres to this position of *psychological individualism*. In contrast, others state that all kinds of institutions and the actions of other agents are also allowed to constrain the set of possible actions of an agent. The latter position has been given several names, such as 'situational logic' or 'logic of the situation' (Popper 1972 and Hands 1985) and 'situational determinism' (Latsis 1976).

In this study I adopt the position that institutions are allowed as primitive terms in an explanation of individual behaviour, for two reasons. First, it seems unnecessarily restrictive to exclude institutions as primitive terms. For example, when one is asked why someone drives a car on the right of the road, it seems to be a perfectly legitimate explanation to point at the institution that prescribes that everybody should drive on the right. One may be interested in the reasons why that institution came into existence, but that question does not directly bear upon the explanation of the particular agent's behaviour.

A second reason for adopting the 'situational logic' position is that, contrary to what Boland (1982) argues, economic explanations of individual behaviour (even the neoclassical ones) *do* adopt institutions as primitive terms. This is easily demonstrated by the following textbook example. Suppose that there are two commodities, the quantities of which are denoted by x_1 and x_2. The utility the agent under consideration derives from consuming these quantities is $U(x_1,x_2)$. The agent's endowment of the commodities is represented by ω_1 and ω_2 and the prices of the commodities are denoted by p_1 and p_2. The agent wants to maximize utility. In order to do so he or she has to exchange one of the commodities against the other. One unit of x_1 exchanges for p_2/p_1 units of x_2. The agent is thus constrained by the endowments (ω_1, ω_2) *and* the price ratio p_2/p_1. This ratio, often regarded as an institution in fully competitive markets, thus acts as a primitive term in the explanation.

EXPLAINING AGGREGATE RELATIONS

In economics individual behaviour is explained by using the rationality concept. The next question that concerns us here is how aggregate relations should be or can be explained. In particular, does an aggregate concept exist that explains aggregate relationships in a way similar to the way the rationality concept is used to explain individual behaviour?

Contrary to common wisdom, explanations of aggregate relationships in which no reference is made to individual characteristics can be found in economic theory. Aggregate concepts that are invoked in such explanations include the *natural rate of unemployment*, the *law of supply and demand* (or the Invisible Hand), and, to some extent, the notion of a *representative agent*. That these concepts are *aggregate* concepts is easily seen. For example, to say 'naturally, person X is unemployed' has quite a different meaning from saying 'the natural rate of unemployment in an economy is, say, 5 per cent' and it is not clear what is meant by 'person X is naturally unemployed'. The natural rate of unemployment is a property of an economic system (if it exists at all) which is not readily transferable to statements about individuals. The natural rate is a kind of equilibrium concept about which I have more to say in chapter 7.[2] The difficulties in providing the law of supply and demand with individualistic foundations are well known (see, e.g., Arrow 1959 or Sensat 1988). The mere fact that these difficulties exist shows that the law is an aggregate law. With respect to the notion of a representative agent the following distinction has to be made. First, an economy might be described in terms of the interaction between a representative household, a representative firm and a government. If the notion of a representative agent is used in this way, it is *not* an aggregate concept in the sense distinguished in the introduction to this chapter, because the representative agents of such an economy are 'individuals' relative to the whole economy. What this type of representative agent models claims is that the differences between households, for example, are not important for an understanding of the functioning of the economy as a whole: if households act non-strategically with respect to one another, one can say that the representative household is representative for the behaviour of all households.[3] Second, in some other models, for example some 'real business cycle models', the economy is described as if it consists of only one representative 'individual', say a Robinson Crusoe economy (see, e.g. King and Plosser 1984). The Robinson Crusoe version of a representative agent cannot be regarded as an individual with respect to the economy as a whole, because (before the arrival of Friday) Robinson Crusoe constitutes the whole economy and so the distinction between the aggregate and the individual level disappears. Another way to express this argument is to say that Robinson Crusoe is not really a representative agent, because he does not represent any individual in a modern economy. In a modern economy Robinson Crusoe is a fiction whose behaviour supposedly describes the behaviour of the entire economy. Introducing fictitious agents in this way is, however, identical to explaining aggregate phenomena directly by means of aggregate concepts.[4]

An interesting thing to note is that these aggregate concepts are used in the microfoundations literature (and also in general equilibrium models) as though they were not problematic from an individualistic point of view. This, once again, shows that there is some confusion about what the subject of microeconomics is supposed to cover (see also chapter 1).

So, aggregate concepts are used in economic explanations. It is, however, also conceivable that an explanation of an aggregate relationship runs along the following lines. Let us concentrate on an example in which the relationship between national consumption and national income is to be explained. First, we can explain the consumption behaviour of individuals using the rationality principle discussed in the previous section. This first step could result in the conclusion that the consumption behaviour of rational individuals depends on their income. Second, we can regard the functional relationship between national consumption and national income as the collective result of the consumption behaviour of all individuals taken together. The two steps taken together will constitute an individualistic explanation of the aggregate relationship (for more details, see chapters 5 and 6). It is not ruled out on a priori grounds that the above aggregate relationship can also be explained without recourse to individual behaviour. However, if such an aggregate explanation existed, we would have two different types of explanation for the same relationship. In such cases, the relation between those explanations would be unclear. As both explanations have the same implications, at least in part, one might like to 'explain' the validity of one of the explanations by the other. Due to the fact that an explanation in terms of individual behaviour has, in general, more structure to it than an aggregate explanation can provide, it is more likely that the first type of explanation is more fundamental.

In order to investigate the structure of explanations of aggregate relationships in terms of the behaviour of individuals the following two sections concentrate on explanations of this type in other sciences. The next section treats two examples and the section after that discusses a general model which accounts for the structure of explanations of this type.

EXPLAINING AGGREGATE RELATIONS IN TERMS OF INDIVIDUAL BEHAVIOUR: TWO EXAMPLES FROM OTHER SCIENCES

This section discusses some details of two studies in which aggregate relationships are explained by a theory of the behaviour of individuals. The first example is taken from physics and describes the relation between the ideal gas law (IGL) and the kinetic theory of gases (KTG). The second example comes from the domain of sociology and outlines the explanation of Mancur Olson's hypothesis by means of utility theory.

An explanation of the ideal gas law

The IGL is a description of the relation that holds between certain properties of a gas under ideal circumstances. It is an aggregate relation because it does not refer to the individual molecules that constitute the gas. The IGL is usually stated in the following form: $PV = rT$, where P is the pressure exerted at any instant by the molecules on the wall of the container, V is the volume that is occupied by the gas, r is a constant and T is the temperature of the gas.

The KTG is a theory about the behaviour of gas molecules (the individuals that constitute the gas). The theory assumes that a container of gas is composed of a large number of molecules possessing equal masses whose movements and collisions are supposed to conform to the laws of Newtonian mechanics. Note that the motion of a molecule depends on the interaction with other molecules. Physicists have shown that the IGL can be regarded as an implication of the view that the behaviour of gas molecules conforms to the KTG. In this way, the KTG provides insight on why the IGL provides an accurate description of the behaviour of gases. The following brief exposition is based upon Nagel (1961: 342–5) and Kuipers (1990).

In a first step, Newtonian laws are applied to a molecule with mass m and velocity v that collides with the wall. The following auxiliary hypotheses are used in this step: the collisions are perfectly elastic, the dimension of the gas molecules and the impact of cohesive forces are negligibly small. The individual law that is derived from this set-up is: $\Delta p = 2mv$, where Δp is the change in momentum per collision.

In a second step, these individual collisions are aggregated in a sophisticated way. The statistical assumption used in this step postulates that the molecular motions are chaotic, i.e. the molecules move in all directions, but on average there is an equal number of molecules moving in any direction and the average velocity is equal in all directions. The aggregated law that can be derived states that the pressure P on the wall times the volume V of the gas equals $2/3N\bar{u}$: $PV = 2/3N\bar{u}$, where N is Avogadro's number and $\bar{u}$ is the mean kinetic energy.

This aggregated law still differs from the IGL. However, physicists suppose that the temperature T of the gas is proportional to the mean kinetic energy. Stated in a more precise way the claim is that one obtains the IGL if, in a third step, T is *identified* with $2/3(N/r)\bar{u}$.

If asked why the IGL takes this form, i.e. if asked for an explanation of the empirical evidence expressed by the IGL, one may point at the KTG and say that the interaction of gas molecules is such that the IGL emerges. The explanation can be separated into three parts, which can be called application, aggregation and identification. One may wonder why this explanation is widely accepted as a major scientific achievement. It can be argued that some rather restrictive assumptions have been made in the first two steps and that the identification of terms is rather *ad hoc*. In the next section the first of these issues is taken up again. For a discussion on the identification step the reader is referred to Nagel (1961: 358–61).

At this stage, it can already be noted that the example illuminates the point that an explanation of an aggregate relationship in terms of individual behaviour does not presuppose that the aggregate relation is similar to the relation that holds for the individuals. It is clear that the IGL is of a different nature than the KTG. This fact, however, does not restrain physicists from asserting that the IGL can be explained in terms of the KTG.

An explanation of Olson's hypothesis in sociology

In 1965, Olson wrote *The Logic of Collective Action*. A part of the book is devoted to a discussion of the following hypothesis:

> the larger the group, the farther it will fall short of providing an optimal amount of a collective good.
>
> (Olson 1965: 35)

Olson's hypothesis describes an *aggregate* relationship relating the size of a group to the amount of a collective good that will be realized by the group. For the purposes of this study, it is of interest that this hypothesis has been derived as an implication of the notion that individuals maximize utility. The explanation of Olson's hypothesis treated here is an example of the more general programme of rational choice theory in sociology in which aggregate relationships are explained using utility theory (see, e.g., Coleman 1986 and 1990 and references therein). In this section, I will sketch the structure of the explanation, which is based upon Kuipers (1984) and Lindenberg (1987).

In a first step of the explanation of Olson's hypothesis, expected utility theory is applied to a hypothetical situation in which individual members of a group have to decide whether or not they will participate in the realization of a collective good. If the good is realized, all individuals benefit from it, but only those individuals who participate in the realization of the good pay a certain amount. We take a very simple model to illustrate the case. The group consists of n members; m will be used for the number of participants. So, suppose that the utility an individual i derives from the consumption of the collective good is positive and denoted by $U_i(g)$. The utility of the cost of participating is negative and denoted by $-U_i(c)$. Both utility levels are supposed to be independent of n and m. The subjective assessment of the chance that the good will be realized will be denoted by $R_i(n,m)$. The increase of the subjective assessment of the chance that the good will be realized because of the individual's participation will be denoted by $b_i(n,m)$ and $b_i(n,m) = R_i(n,m + 1) - R_i(n,m)$. It is assumed that $b_i(n,m)$ is independent of m (henceforth the argument m will be dropped), positive for all values of n and decreasing in n, i.e. for all n, $b_i(n) > 0$ and $b_i(n + 1) < b_i(n)$. Agents will participate if the increase in their expected utility because of participation outweighs their share of the total cost of realization: $R_i(n,m + 1)U_i(g) - U_i(c) > R_i(n,m)U_i(g)$ or $b_i(n)U_i(g) > U_i(c)$. As $b_i(n)$ is decreasing in n, we can derive the following individual regularity:

for all individuals, there is a certain size of the group beyond which she or he does not participate.[5]

The intuitive idea behind this regularity is that each individual thinks that the larger the group, the more likely the realization of the collective good remains unaffected by the individual's participation or non-participation. If the group is very large the cost of participation outweighs the increased likelihood that the good will be realized. Therefore, an agent will prefer to be a 'free rider' if the size of the group is larger than a certain number.

In the second step of the explanation we aggregate the above regularity in the behaviour of individuals. The aggregate relationship we are aiming at is of the following type: the larger the group, the lower the degree of participation. Although there is a strong resemblance between the individual regularity and this aggregate regularity, the aggregation procedure has to be carried out carefully. First, it will be clear that the aggregate regularity cannot be derived by simply comparing two *completely different* groups, because the differences between individuals might be quite large. Somehow, the individuals in the groups compared have to be similar. Likewise, it will not do to add some 'new' individuals to an existing group, because the size of the group beyond which newcomers do not participate might be very large. Instead, aggregation is performed by means of a thought experiment, in which the group of individuals is formed by uniting two subgroups. Denote by n_1 and n_2 the sizes of the two subgroups and by m_1 and m_2 the number of participants in those two subgroups. Furthermore, define n_3, the size of the united group, as $n_1 + n_2$ and m_3 as the number of individuals who participate in the realization of the collective good in the united group. With these assumptions and using the individual regularity it will be clear that $m_3 \leq m_1 + m_2$. So, the following aggregate regularity can be derived:

> If a group has been formed by uniting two subgroups, then the total number of participants in the collective good will not increase.

This aggregated relationship differs on two accounts from the aggregate regularity (Olson's hypothesis) that have to be explained. First, the formulation is somewhat more sophisticated due to the way the aggregation procedure has been performed. Second, the aggregated relationship talks about 'number of participants', whereas Olson's hypothesis is about 'the optimal amount of a collective good'. There seems to be an intimate relation, however, between the number of participants and 'the farther the group will fall short of providing an optimal amount of a collective good'. If it is postulated that this relation holds, (a sophisticated reformulation of) Olson's hypothesis can be derived.

Again, as in the previous example, one might wonder why the above explanation should be regarded as a scientific achievement. It can be argued that some rather restrictive assumptions have been made in the first two steps, that the identification of terms is rather *ad hoc* and that even with all the restrictive assumptions one is not able to arrive at Olson's hypothesis, but only at a reformulation of it. In the following section I will say more about these issues.

EXPLAINING AGGREGATE RELATIONS IN TERMS OF INDIVIDUAL BEHAVIOUR: THE THEORY OF REDUCTION

In the previous section we have discussed two examples in which an aggregate relationship is explained in terms of the postulated behaviour of individuals. The emphasis has been on the structure of the explanation. An attentive reader may have noticed that there are striking similarities between the two examples. In a first step, a theory (KTG, utility theory) is applied to the behaviour of the 'individuals' (molecules, human beings) that constitute the whole entity (the gas within the container, the group). In a second step the regularity in the behaviour of the individuals is aggregated. A final step transforms this aggregated relationship into the aggregate relationship that has to be explained.

Analyses in which aggregate relationships are explained in terms of the behaviour of individuals fall within the philosophical category of 'reduction'.[6] On the basis of the above two and other examples, Kuipers (1990) asserts that reduction is just a special type of explanation. Since Nagel (1961) it is generally acknowledged that a theory explains a law (relationship) if a *formal* and an *empirical* condition are fulfilled. In order to characterize the formal structure of an explanation Kuipers (1990) has constructed a general scheme consisting of the following five steps:

(1) application $\quad T \qquad H_1$

(2) aggregation $\qquad L_1 \qquad H_2$

(3) identification $\qquad\quad L_2 \qquad H_3$

(4) correlation $\qquad\qquad L_3 \qquad H_4$

(5) approximation $\qquad\qquad\quad \underline{L_4} \; \_ \; \_ \; \_ \; \underline{H_5}$

$$L$$

In this scheme, T is the explanatory theory (for example, KTG or utility theory), L is the regularity (law) to be explained (for example, IGL or Olson's hypothesis), L_1-L_4 are 'intermediate laws' and H_1-H_5 are auxiliary hypotheses that are made in each step.

The empirical condition requires good reasons to accept theory T and the auxiliary hypotheses H_1-H_5 as approximately true. The empirical condition prevents an explanation from being a mathematical exercise only. Of course, it is difficult to say what counts as 'approximately true' and what does not. For the moment, it suffices to say that the explanatory theory T may have proven its merits in other fields, while the auxiliary hypotheses may be treated as 'approximately true' on the basis of their being used in the explanation itself. Chapter 4 will discuss more details concerning the importance of the empirical condition for economics. The reader is also referred to Nelson (1992).

In the *application step* theory T is applied to systems L deals with. It seems that the least one should require of an explanation is that a theory be applied to a certain situation. Although from a methodological point of view this application is fairly trivial, it involves some ingenuity on the theorist's part to come up with the auxiliary assumptions that are needed to apply the theory to the case under consideration. In the *aggregation step* the resulting 'individual law' is aggregated, usually by means of a statistical assumption. Often, the law L contains one or more concepts that are absent in the vocabulary of the aggregated law. An *identification* or a *correlation step* is needed in order to relate concepts of different vocabularies to each other. One may employ the term 'identification' if the auxiliary hypotheses are identities and 'correlation' if the auxiliary hypotheses are empirically verifiable relationships. In order to arrive at law L it is frequently necessary to simplify the regularity L_4 by means of appropriate idealizations. This is done in the *approximation step* (for an example, see below).

In the philosophy of science, there is a vast number of articles and books on the notion of reduction (see, e.g., Kemeny and Oppenheim 1956, Schaffner 1967, Sklar 1967, Nickles 1973 and Balzer *et al.* 1984). Most authors agree that the main purpose of reduction is to unify a scientific discipline 'by showing a law or a theory in a new light'. Two ways to achieve this unification have attracted special attention. First, a reduction may effect an economy in vocabulary, by showing that what has been regarded as two different notions 'really' is two different expressions for the same entity (or predicate); see, for example, Causey (1977). Second, a reduction may provide the insight that the regularity to be explained makes some tacit assumptions, by showing that it is an idealization of a more general regularity that can be derived from some theory (see also chapter 4).

Kuipers' terminological diagnosis states that the notion of 'reduction' is used in the philosophical literature if at least one of the following steps is present in an explanation of a law (regularity) L: aggregation (2), identification (3) or approximation (5). As a rule, the order of appearance of the steps is as in the above scheme, but exceptions are possible. It is also clear that not every step of the above scheme appears in every example of reduction. The term *micro-reduction* is used for cases in which an aggregate relationship is explained in terms of the postulated behaviour of individuals. The two cases presented in the previous section are typical examples. In the rest of this section, both cases will be reconsidered in the light of the above general discussion.

The explanation of the IGL by means of the KTG is often regarded as the classic example of reduction. A closer look at this paradigmatic example reveals that steps (1), (2) and (3) are present with corresponding auxiliary hypotheses. The IGL can also be reduced in the following indirect way. If two of the less plausible assumptions (that the dimension of gas molecules is negligibly small and that the impact of cohesive forces can be neglected) are substituted for more plausible ones, Van der Waals' law can be obtained. Van der Waals' law reads: $(P + a/V^2)(V - b) = rT$, where a represents the impact of cohesive forces and b is the volume of the gas molecules. The IGL can subsequently be regarded as an approximation of Van der Waals' law by applying the limit operations $a \rightarrow 0$ and $b \rightarrow 0$. This indirect route to the reduction of the IGL involves steps (1), (2), (3) and (5).

It remains to be seen why the reduction of the IGL to the KTG is widely accepted as a major scientific achievement. It seems that the restrictive assumptions and the identification of terms are made just to be able to derive the IGL. From this point of view, the reduction that is accomplished does not seem to be a major scientific achievement, but a mathematical exercise only. So, why is this reduction regarded as an important contribution to physics? First, let us consider the role of the restrictive assumptions. Note that the IGL is an *ideal* law: it holds under ideal circumstances (conditions) only. From this perspective it is *not surprising* that restrictive assumptions are needed to derive the IGL. The restrictive assumptions might be interpreted as conditions under which the IGL holds. Accordingly, the reduction yields some insight into the *kind* of situations in which the IGL can be legitimately employed. In other words, the reduction illuminates some of the hidden assumptions of the IGL. More importantly, the reduction shows directions for further research: if the aggregate relationship holds only under ideal conditions, the question becomes what kind of relationship holds if these conditions are not met? We have seen that Van der Waals' law can be derived if two of the less plausible assumptions are substituted for more plausible ones. Van der Waals' law provides a better description of the behaviour of 'non-ideal' gases than the IGL. Thus, the reduction described in the previous section is not the end result of research in this field, but rather a starting point for both theoretical and empirical research.[7]

As we have seen, the explanation of Olson's hypothesis by means of utility theory involves an application and an aggregation step. Yet, the nature of the third step has been left undiscussed thus far. We must discuss how the transformation from 'the degree of participation' to 'the farther it will fall short of providing an optimal amount of a collective good' can be characterized. From the scheme above, two interpretations are possible. If the degree of participation and the optimal amount of a collective good are regarded as empirical concepts to which a value can be attached in an independent way, then the postulated relation has to be interpreted as a correlation. Empirical research may come up with the conditions under which the relation holds. Conversely, if it is not possible to regard (one of) the two concepts as empirical constructs, then the postulated relation can be regarded as an identification of terms. Lindenberg (1987: 98–9) argues that there are reasons to believe that the postulated relation is a correlation and he mentions some conditions under which it is likely to hold.

The above explanation of Olson's hypothesis illuminates some important aspects of how the reductionist approach can be applied to the social sciences. Olson's hypothesis can be illustrated as shown in figure 2.2:

aggregate level   group size  'shortage of collective good'

Figure 2.2 Olson's hypothesis

The figure shows that Olson's hypothesis is about a group as a whole; no reference is made to individual behaviour. The explanation that is given introduces an 'individual level'. This is schematized in figure 2.3:

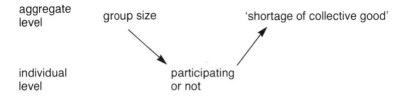

Figure 2.3 A reductive explanation of Olson's hypothesis

The figure illustrates that in the explanation of Olson's hypothesis individual behaviour mediates between two aggregate variables. Accordingly, there are two transitions to be made: a macro-to-micro and a micro-to-macro transition (using Coleman's terminology, see the introductory chapter and Coleman 1990). The micro-to-macro transition emphasizes the claim that individual behaviour has to be discussed with reference to the (social) situation in which the individual is located (cf. the remarks on the 'logic of the situation' in the first section of this chapter). Thus, a reductive account can accommodate the claim that individual behaviour is determined, at least partly, by the social situation. It is thus not so much a question of whether the individual level determines the aggregate level or vice versa. The figure shows that certain features at the aggregate level are important determinants of individual behaviour, whereas (the interaction of) individual behaviour determines certain (other) features at the aggregate level. In many of those cases the factor of time is important. At a certain point in time, there exist some aggregate variables (rules, norms, institutions), which individual agents take as given. The interactive behaviour of individuals produces new features (for example, new rules) at the aggregate level or reproduces (reinforces) the old features. These new aggregate features might be taken as given by the individuals in the next time period.

Finally, it has to be said that Olson's hypothesis is not true in many circumstances. As the IGL, it is an *ideal* regularity. Accordingly, it is not surprising that restrictive assumptions are needed in order to be able to deduce Olson's hypothesis. Restrictive assumptions include the assumption that the cost of participation is fixed and independent of the number of participants and the assumption that the utility of consuming the collective good is independent of the size of the group. These assumptions can be regarded as a set of conditions under which the hypothesis may be legitimately employed. In chapter 4, I will come back to this point.

METHODOLOGICAL INDIVIDUALISM AND REDUCTION IN ECONOMIC THEORY

The present section combines the treatment of rational behaviour and reduction in the preceding sections by discussing how the concept of methodological individualism (MI) can be employed in economic theory. MI will be regarded as a special case of micro-reduction and thus as a special type of explanation.

In this study, MI is interpreted as a view that allows only individual agents to be the decision makers in any explanation of aggregate economic regularities and aggregate economic phenomena. An explanation has to satisfy two conditions in order to conform with this definition: (*i*) it should be possible to represent it as a micro-reduction, i.e. an aggregation step has to be involved; (*ii*) the theory that is applied should be about the behaviour of individual[8] decision makers. Some of the features of this definition require further elaboration. First, it is not contrary to MI to invoke in an explanation hypotheses that cannot be derived from individual decisions. This is because a micro-reduction may involve a correlation, an identification and/or an approximation step with corresponding auxiliary hypotheses. These steps may be introduced by the economic theorist in order to relate different concepts to each other or to show that one regularity really is a limiting case of the other.

Second, the present study deals with the relation between individual behaviour and aggregate outcomes. Accordingly, MI is defined in such a way that it applies to situations in which two levels of analysis are involved. For two levels of analysis to exist, at least two individuals have to be distinguished in the analysis, because it is only in such cases that the difference between the individual and the aggregate level can be made. Two transitions are then important. The macro-to-micro transition deals with issues of how individual behaviour is influenced by macro entities; the micro-to-macro transition specifies the mechanism that shows how individual behaviour results in an aggregate outcome. Cases in which individual behaviour is explained in individualistic terms are excluded on this account. One might want to define MI in such a way that it covers such cases, but as this is not the focus of the study, I have not done so.

Third, it cannot be emphasized enough that MI does *not* argue that reduced regularities do not have any use-value. Blaug (1980: 51), for example, implicitly drawing the distinction between microeconomics and macroeconomics along the lines of our first criterion in chapter 1 –

26

that of the individual versus the aggregate level – has posed that MI 'would rule out all macroeconomic propositions that cannot be reduced to microeconomic ones'. Against this view I would argue that a reduction is only a particular form of *explanation.*[9] An adequate *description* of an aggregative regularity is not ruled out. On the contrary, an aggregate description has to exist in order to provide it with an explanation. Also, an explanation in terms of individual behaviour in no way *presupposes* that the aggregate relation is similar to the relation that holds for the individuals, although it does not preclude this possibility either (see, e.g., Schelling, 1978 for an interesting set of examples and the two cases discussed previously).

Fourth, MI requires that individuals be decision makers. In economics, the focus is on rational decision making. In principle, one could argue that MI does not restrict the theories on individual behaviour that potentially may be used to explain an aggregate regularity. However, as this study is concerned with theories that claim to use the notion of rational behaviour, I have decided to include it in the definition of MI. The first section of this chapter has dealt with the notion of rational behaviour. There, I argued that institutions are allowed as primitive terms in an explanation of individual behaviour. The notion of MI that results is thus identical to what Agassi (1960, 1975) has termed *institutional individualism.*

Below, we will discuss in more detail some interesting features of individual decision making in a world that is occupied with more individuals. It is worlds of this kind that MI is about. The notion of endogenous uncertainty, briefly referred to in the first section, plays an important role in such a world. Two issues will be focused upon here. First, in the social sciences individual behaviour may depend crucially on the way the behaviour is aggregated. Thus, aggregation is *not* a procedure a theorist may perform *after* individual behaviour is understood, but is an essential ingredient of rational individual behaviour itself. Second, the first section discussed the concepts of instrumental and cognitive rationality. Here, it is important to note that both types of rationality are affected by the fact that an agent is *only one* of the agents in an economy. Before making some general observations with respect to these issues, let us turn to the following hypothetical example.

Example 2.1 **A Guessing Game (Moulin 1986)**

Consider a group of individuals. These individuals independently and simultaneously choose a natural number between 1 and 100. The winners are those persons who have chosen the number that is closest to two-thirds of the average of the numbers mentioned. (In Keynes' famous Beauty Contest the winner is the person who is closest to the average number.) This rule of the game can be interpreted as an aggregation rule. What number should a rational individual choose? Consider these three cases.

(i) Suppose that the aggregation rule is *not known* to the individuals. In this case every number can be a rational choice, because an individual cannot know how the winning number is selected.

(ii) Suppose that the aggregation rule is known to the players. Then, the choice of a number v with $67 < v \leq 100$ *cannot* be a rational choice for the largest number the others can choose is 100. If individual i chooses a number v, while the others choose 100, the average number is $\{100(n-1) + v\}/n$, where n is the number of individuals in the group. The largest number, call it $\bar{v}$, individual i can rationally choose is $2\{100(n-1) + \bar{v}\}/ 3n$. It is easily shown that $\bar{v}$ cannot exceed 67. In general, all the other choices can be rational choices. For example, for $n = 10$, an individual expecting the other nine individuals to choose 100 should choose 64, or 1 if expecting the other nine to choose likewise.

(iii) Suppose that not only is the aggregation rule known to the players, but also that it is known that all the players are rational. In this case, a choice of a number larger than 45 ($\simeq 2/3 \cdot 67$) cannot be rational, because now all individuals know that no one will choose a number that is larger than 67. Further, suppose it is also known that all the players know that all the players are rational. Then a choice of a number larger than 30 ($= 2/3 \cdot 45$) cannot be rational. In the limit, i.e. if all players know that ... all players know that everybody is rational, 1 is the only rational choice.

The example illuminates the two points made above. The first case shows that the rationality of individual behaviour crucially depends on the way the behaviour is aggregated. The notion of rational behaviour is empty if individuals care about aggregate outcomes but do not know how their behaviour is transformed in an aggregate outcome. In chapter 7, I will discuss some economic literature (Bertrand games and strategic market games) in which a similar phenomenon occurs. The second case shows that the fact that an agent is not the only individual in the game has an impact on the *instrumental aspect* of rational decision making, because the optimal choice for an individual depends on the choices made by other individuals: if the other nine in a group of ten choose 100 or 1 the tenth person should choose 67 or 1.

The fact that each group member is only one of the individuals in the above guessing game also bears upon the *cognitive aspect* of rational behaviour. In the example, individuals simultaneously choose a number. Thus, they are unaware of the number chosen by the other individuals and they have to base their action upon the numbers they expect others to choose. If an individual has no means of excluding some numbers as nonsensical, all numbers between 1 and 67 can be regarded as rational choices. However, if the individuals expect the others to choose numbers *in a rational way*, the situation alters. In this case, individuals cannot consistently expect that the other individuals will choose numbers between 67 and 100. Accordingly, the rationale for choosing a number between 45 and 67 breaks down.

The above argument depends upon the assumption that an individual expects that the other individuals will also choose a number in a rational way. In order to link this assumption to the discussion of cognitive rationality in the first section, we have to specify the information individuals are assumed to possess. If individuals know that the others behave according to the postulates of rational choice and also know that the others know the aggregation rule, then the only consistent expectation is that the others will choose a number between 1 and 67. This is required by cognitive rationality. Given this expectation, instrumental rationality assures that individuals will choose a number between 1 and 45.

I made an assumption here about the knowledge an individual has about the knowledge of the other individuals. Also, at the end of the example I introduced assumptions about even higher levels of knowledge. In game theoretic literature agents are said to have *common knowledge* that p is the case, if not only everyone knows that p is true, but also that everyone knows that everyone knows that p is true, and so on (see, e.g., Aumann 1976 and the next section). If the rationality of individuals and the aggregation rule are common knowledge, then each individual expects the others to choose the number 1 (cognitive rationality). Given this expectation everybody will indeed choose 1 (instrumental rationality).

AN INTRODUCTION TO SOME GAME THEORETIC CONCEPTS[10]

The following lengthy quote from von Neumann and Morgenstern (1944) provides an idea of why game theory is a useful instrument to illuminate the notion of MI.

> Crusoe is given certain physical data (wants and commodities) and his task is to combine them and apply them in such a fashion as to obtain a maximum resulting satisfaction. There can be no

doubt that he controls exclusively all the variables upon which this result depends.... Thus Crusoe faces an ordinary maximum problem, the difficulties are of a purely technical – and not conceptual – nature ...

Consider now a participant in a social exchange economy. His problem has, of course, many elements in common with a maximum problem. But it also contains some, very essential, elements of an entirely different nature. He too tries to obtain an optimum result. But in order to achieve this, he must enter into relations of exchange with others. If two or more persons exchange goods with each other, then the result for each one depends in general not merely upon his own actions but on those of others as well. Thus each participant attempts to maximize a function (his above-mentioned "result") of which he does not control all variables. This is certainly no maximum problem, but a peculiar and disconcerting mixture of several conflicting maximum problems. Every participant is guided by another principle and neither determines all variables which affect his interest.

(Von Neumann and Morgenstern 1944: 10-11)

The quote illustrates quite well part of the problems we have discussed above, namely the difference between decision making in an economy with more than one individual and decision making against nature. Game theory employs mathematical models to analyse individual decision making in situations in which individuals are mutually dependent on each other. There exist games with mutual and games with conflicting interests. Game theory has two important subdisciplines, cooperative and non-cooperative game theory. A game is a *cooperative game* if agents are allowed to make binding contractual agreements with one another; it is a *non-cooperative game* if the rules of the game do not allow them to do so. Here, we will focus on non-cooperative game theory, because it is closer to MI (see the next section).[11]

There are two logically equivalent ways to represent non-cooperative games, namely the *normal form* and the *extensive form*. The analysis in non-cooperative game theory centres around the following three elements:[12]

(*i*) $N = \{1, \ldots n\}$ is the set of players.

(*ii*) $S_i \subset \mathbb{R}$ is the strategy space of player i; $s_i \in S_i$ is a strategy of player i; $S = \mathbf{X}_{i \in N} S_i$ is the Cartesian product of individual strategy spaces, $s = (s_1, \ldots, s_n) \in S$ is a strategy combination and $s_{-i} =$

30

$(s_1, \ldots, s_{i-1}, s_{i+1}, \ldots, s_n)$ is the combination of all strategies except the one of player i.

(iii) $P_i(S) \in \mathbb{R}$ is the payoff function of player i.

Nothing has been said yet about a timing element in games. In this respect one can make an important distinction. There are games in which players have to decide *simultaneously* on their strategies. Other games have a *sequential* nature in the sense that players choose their strategies one after the other. Although the two ways in which non-cooperative games can be represented are logically equivalent, there is a difference in that *normal form* games hide the sequential nature that may be present. The normal form highlights the overall strategies available to each player. It is a convenient way of representing *one-shot* games, i.e. games that are played only once and in which players simultaneously make a decision. The *extensive form* of a game, on the other hand, highlights the decision structure of the game. It exposes all the decisions individual players can made and the sequence of decisions. Simultaneous decisions are modelled using so-called *information sets*. At each moment a player has to make a decision, he or she is at a *decision node*. If the player knows all the decisions that have been made, then he or she knows exactly at which decision node he or she is situated and the single decision node constitutes his or her information set. Games in which each information set consists of one decision node are called *games of perfect information*. In the case of simultaneous decisions a player does not know the decision of the other player(s) so that his or her information set consists of two or more decision nodes.[13] In much of what follows, we will be concerned with one-shot games.

The solution concept that is frequently used in non-cooperative game theory is the *Nash equilibrium*. A Nash equilibrium is a strategy combination $s^* \in S$ for which each player maximizes his or her own payoff with respect to his or her own strategy *given* the strategies of all other players: s^* is such that $P_i(s^*) \geq P_i(s_i, s^*_{-i})$ for all $s_i \in S_i$ and for all $i \in N$. A crucial question for the discussion that is to follow is whether the Nash equilibrium is a consequence of rational individual behaviour. This is one of the issues that will be discussed in the next section.

Apart from the Nash equilibrium notion, the notions of a *dominated strategy*, a *best response strategy*, *iteratively undominated strategies* and *iterated elimination of strategies that are not best responses (point-rationalizability)* are also important in the rest of this book. There exist two different notions of dominance, 'strong' and 'weak'. A strategy s'_i is *strongly dominated* by a strategy s''_i if for all possible choices of strategies by all other players strategy s_i' gives a payoff that is smaller than the payoff that i would have obtained under s_i'', i.e. $P_i(s_i', s_{-i}) <$ $P_i(s_i'', s_{-i})$ for all $s_{-i} \in S_{-i}$. A strategy s_i' is *weakly dominated* by a strategy s_i'' if for all possible choices of strategies by all other agents strategy s_i' gives a payoff that is never larger and sometimes strictly smaller than the payoff that i would have obtained under s_i'', i.e. $P_i(s_i', s_{-i}) \leq P_i(s_i'', s_{-i})$ for all $s_{-i} \in S_{-i}$ and $P_i(s_i', s_{-i}) < P_i(s_i'', s_{-i})$ for at least one $s_{-i} \in S_{-i}$. Finally, a strategy s_i' is a best response to a strategy combination s_{-i}, written $s_i' = BR(s_{-i})$, if s_i' maximizes agent i's payoff given s_{-i}, i.e. $P_i(s_i', s_{-i}) \geq P_i(s_i, s_{-i})$ for all $s_i \in S_i$. A Nash equilibrium is a fixed point of the set of best response functions. The important difference between the notion of dominance and the notion of Nash equilibrium is that the first notion involves all strategies the other players might possibly adopt, while the second notion only involves the strategies the other players adopt in equilibrium. Instrumental rational behaviour as discussed in the first section requires that players do not choose weakly (and strongly) dominated strategies.

The notion of iteratively undominated strategies (IUS) can be defined as follows. A strategy s_i is Q_{-i}-undominated if there does not exist a strategy s_i' such that $P_i(s_i', s_{-i}) > P_i(s_i, s_{-i})$ for all $s_{-i} \in Q_{-i}$. In words, a strategy is undominated on a certain domain (a certain set of strategies Q_{-i} of the other players) if there is no other strategy that is strictly better on that domain. Let $D_i^1 = \{s_i \in S_i | s_i \text{ is } S_{-i}\text{-undominated}\}$, i.e. D_i^1 is the set of S_{-i}-undominated strategies. The definition of rationality requires that rational players will choose a strategy $s_i \in D_i^1$. The set of IUS for player i, called D_i, can be defined inductively as follows. Suppose that $(D_i^k)_{i=1}^n$ is well defined for some k and let $D_{-i}^k = \mathsf{X}_{j \neq i} D_j^k$. Then

$$D_i^{k+1} = \{s_i \in D_i^k | s_i \text{ is } D_{-i}^k\text{-undominated}\} \text{ and } D_i = \{s_i \in S_i | s_i \in D_i^k \text{ for all } k \geq 1\}.$$

The notion of point-rationalizability (henceforth simply to be called 'rationalizability') is closely related to the notion of IUS. It is inductively defined on the basis of the best response functions $BR(s_{-i})$ in the following way. Let $R_i^0 \equiv S_i$ and $R_{-i}^0 \equiv S_{-i}$. Furthermore, define the iterative procedure by $R_i^k \equiv \{s_i \in R_i^{k-1} | s_i = BR(s_{-i}) \text{ for some } s_{-i} \in R_{-i}^{k-1}\}$. Finally, the set of rationalizable strategies for player i, called R_i, can be defined as $R_i \equiv \{s_i \in S_i | s_i \in R_i^k \text{ for all } k \geq 1\}$.

The concepts that are introduced above will be illustrated by means of the following three examples.

Example 2.2 A Game of Perfect Information

Consider a sequential game with two players and perfect information. Both players have three options: (L, M, R) for player 1 and (l, m, r) for player 2. Player 1 decides first. The extensive form of the game is as shown in the following figure:

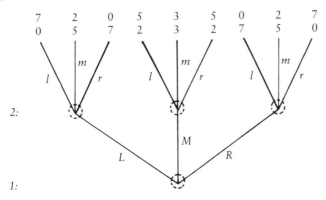

The payoff in the top (second) line is that of player 1 (2). There are four decision nodes and also four information sets (indicated by the broken symbols that encircle the nodes). It is easy to see that (M, m) is the unique Nash equilibrium: $P_1(L, m) = 2 = P_1(R, m) < P_1(M, m) = 3$ and $P_2(M, l) = 2 = P_2(M, r) < P_2(M, m) = 3$. This is also the 'natural' solution in the sense that it is a logical consequence of the two players being rational and the fact that 1 knows that 2 is rational (this being an implication of the common knowledge assumption). As 2 is rational he plays r if 1 plays L, m if 1 plays M and l if 1 plays R. Those strategies are player 2's best responses to player 1's respective strategies. Since this is known to player 1, she has the choice of getting 0, 3 or 0 by choosing L, M and R, respectively. Her rational choice is thus M. This also illustrates a more general point: in games of *perfect* information the 'natural' solution is *one* of the Nash equilibria.

Example 2.3 A Simultaneous Move Game (Bernheim 1984)

Consider the game of example 2.2 with the modification that now players decide simultaneously. The normal form and the extensive form of the game are presented in the figures below. In the normal form, the payoffs for players 1 and 2 are represented in the lower left and upper right corners, respectively.

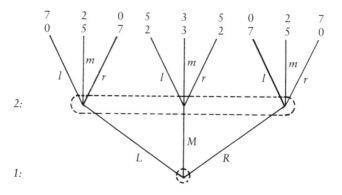

The extensive form has four decision nodes, but only two information sets: the three decision nodes of player 2 are within one information set. Because of the simultaneous decision nature of the game, player 2 does not know which decision player 1 has made, i.e. he does not know at which of the three decision nodes he is situated at the moment a decision upon a strategy is required. This is thus a game of imperfect information. The Nash equilibrium in pure strategies of this game is also (M, m). It is, however, not clear whether this is also the 'natural' solution of the game: none of the strategies is dominated. If, for example, player 2 expects 1 to choose L, then player 2's best response is r. Looking at the best responses it is easy to see that all three strategies are also rationalizable. The question of whether the Nash equilibrium is the natural solution in this game comes down to the question of whether player 1's expectation that player 2 plays m is the only expectation that is consistent with the information available to player 1 (see the first section on cognitive rationality).

Example 2.4 **A Game to Illustrate the Notion of IUS**

There are two players, called 1 and 2, who have to choose a strategy L, M or R.

2:	L_2		M_2		R_2	
1:						
L_1		2		1		0
	2		4		1	
M_1		4		3		2
	1		3		5	
R_1		1		5		4
	0		2		4	

The game is symmetric. It is easily seen that for both players strategy M dominates strategy R and L and both M are S_{-i}-undominated. So, $D_i^1 = \{L_i, M_i\}$, $i = 1, 2$. In a second stage of the iterative procedure M_i is dominated by L_i: only L_i is D_{-i}^1-undominated. This means that L_i, $i = 1, 2$, is the unique strategy that survives the iterated elimination of dominated strategy. This is also the unique Nash equilibrium. This is one of the special cases in which the implications of the two notions coincide.

METHODOLOGICAL INDIVIDUALISM AND GAME THEORY

The question that has to be faced then is how game theory precisely fits into the programme of MI and, particularly, how the macro-to-micro and the micro-to-macro transitions are made in game theory. If one concentrates on the normal form of the game, one easily neglects that individuals behave in an institutional environment. In the normal form, individual choices seem to be connected with the payoffs without interference from any institution. One might even get the impression that there is not really an aggregate level in normal form games. (The reader might like to go back to the examples of the previous section to check this.)

An important question is where the aggregate level reveals itself. I think a key term, here, is the rules of the game. The rules of the game describe the situation in which the individual players find themselves. They describe the constraints on the strategies players might choose (the set of strategies), the information the players have at the moment they have to choose a strategy (for example, whether or not they know the strategies chosen by other players; cf. examples 2.2 and 2.3) and the sequence of strategies. Some of those rules might be interpreted as a physical description of the situation in which individual players interact, while others should be interpreted as exogenous institutions. Thus, the rules of the game help to make the macro-to-micro transitions.

But for an explanation to be in line with the definition of MI given above, there should also exist an aggregate phenomenon that endogenously arises through the actions of individual players in the game. Here, the situation seems to be even more problematic, because a particular configuration of individual payoffs seems to be the only consequence of the strategies chosen by individual players (again, compare examples 2.2, 2.3 and 2.4). Fortunately, appearances can be deceptive. A normal form game is a particular representation of social interaction between individuals. The normal form representation does not tell us how the individual payoffs are arrived at and for the individual agents this information is also not really needed in order to choose their strategies (as long as they know how their payoffs depend on the chosen strategies). However, in the pre-normal form description of the social interaction there is usually a step which specifies how individual payoffs are related to individual strategies and often this step involves some form of aggregation. In order to be more concrete let us briefly reconsider the game presented in example 2.1 and the discussion surrounding that example. The winner of that game is determined by a rule that aggregates the numbers quoted by all participating individuals. The individual payoffs are in turn determined by using the notion of the winner of the game. In the normal form specification of the game, however, this intermediate step between individual strategies and payoffs is not presented. In chapter 7 we will encounter other examples (e.g. the Bertrand game) in which aggregate concepts (like market prices) are not directly reflected in the normal form description of the game. Nevertheless aggregate concepts play an important role in mediating between individual strategies and individual payoffs. So, to summarize this discussion, although aggregate phenomena usually remain implicit in the normal form description of a game, they do arise endogenously as a combined result of the rules of the game and the strategies chosen by individual players.

The above account differs considerably from the one given in Bicchieri (1987). She argues that the way collective outcomes are deduced from the solutions to the decision problems of isolated agents 'proceeds by assuming that the collective outcome will be a state of equilibrium' (Bicchieri 1987: 503). My account differs to the extent that collective outcomes (e.g. the winner of the game described in example 2.1) are determined for every combination of individual strategies, not only for equilibrium strategies. For example, the winner of the game of example 2.1 is defined for all numbers that can be chosen. In my view, the Nash equilibrium notion is *not* used to bridge the gap between individual strategies and collective (or aggregate) outcomes, but instead it is used to try to give a more determinate solution to the decision problems the individual players face.

This leads us to the question of whether individual rational players should 'play Nash'. In the rest of this section I will argue that, generally speaking, there are not very good reasons for this assumption. I will claim that an (iteratively) undominated strategy should be the basic notion in game theory and not the Nash equilibrium notion.

Until recently, the notion of Nash equilibrium was regarded as the 'natural' solution to a non-cooperative game. If players know which strategies the other players are (or will be) using (e.g. as in the game of perfect information of example 2.2) this question is easily answered.[14] In such cases the problem of cognitive rationality (see the first section) does not present itself. Knowing that the other players 'play Nash' each rational player should 'play Nash' as well, because in this case the Nash equilibrium strategy maximizes a rational player's payoff (instrumental rationality). However, the situation is different in simultaneous move games. With respect to this type of game, there seems to be a growing consensus that, in general, the notion of Nash equilibrium is *not* an 'unavoidable consequence' of the view that individuals are rational decision makers (see, e.g., Gul 1989). A Nash equilibrium gives a characterization of a state in which all players have chosen their best actions *given* the strategies adopted by other players. In simultaneous move games, players have to decide upon their action while being ignorant about the strategies chosen by other players. Thus, decision-making individuals cannot maximize payoffs given the decisions of other individuals. Instead, they make a decision that is the most appropriate one given a certain expectation (instrumental aspect). All individuals choose Nash equilibrium strategies if they all expect that a certain Nash equilibrium results. However, the expectation that a Nash equilibrium results generally is not the only expectation that is consistent with the available information (cognitive aspect). If an individual *expects* that the others do not choose equilibrium strategies it is likely that this individual will not choose an equilibrium strategy either. The notion of Nash equilibrium is thus not an unavoidable consequence of the view that individuals are decision makers.

Other notions that are better founded in the theory of rational behaviour have been proposed: sophistication or iteratively undominated strategies (Moulin 1979), rationalizability (Bernheim 1984 and Pearce 1984) and correlated equilibrium (Aumann 1987). In general, the set of strategies that is predicted by each of these notions is strictly larger than the set of Nash equilibria. In some special cases, however, all these notions coincide. I do not go into the details of the notion of correlated equilibrium, referring readers to the original paper. A general characterization of the relations between the four notions as provided by Bernheim (1986) and Tan and Werlang (1988) suffices for our purposes. They argue that all notions involve the requirements of what I have called instrumental rationality and common knowledge of this rationality. Correlated equilibrium further requires that players have a 'common prior', while rationalizability additionally requires that each player conceives of the choices of the other players as independent events. The independence requirement excludes the possibility that a player believes that other players' behaviour is correlated. If these latter two requirements are both added to the two requirements underlying all notions, then the notion of Nash equilibrium is obtained. This is illustrated in the following figure, which is taken from Bernheim (1986).

	distinct priors	common priors
unrestricted beliefs	IUS	correlated equilibrium
independence	rationalizability	Nash equilibrium

It is widely accepted that in simultaneous move games rational players should play an iteratively undominated strategy. The concept of IUS is a logical consequence of the view that individual players are rational and that this rationality is common knowledge. Intuitively, the argument runs as follows. Instrumental rational players choose strategies $s_i \in D_i^1$; see the previous section for the notation used. As this is known to all players, all players know that all other players $j \neq i$ choose a strategy $s_j \in D_j^1$ (cognitive rationality). Players may find additional strategies that are dominated given that the other players choose a strategy $s_j \in D_j^1$: instrumental rational players choose a strategy $s_i \in D_i^2$. Subsequent applications of the same argument lead to the conclusion that players choose a strategy $s_i \in D_i$.

In contrast, there has been some debate about the appropriateness of the assumptions of 'independence' and 'common priors' for a general theory of rational behaviour in game situations (see, e.g., Gul 1989). Aumann (1987) argues that a rational player need not conceive of the other players' actions as independent events, because a player may know that other players share a common background (e.g. they went to the same school) so that they probably take similar actions. Also, the arguments in favour of the common prior assumption do not seem to be fully compelling. Nau and McCardle (1990) argue that an outside observer can make a profit if and only if players do not share a common prior. In other words, the players can *jointly* increase their payoffs if they have distinct priors. In my opinion this reveals the weakness of the common prior assumption as an element of a *general* theory of rational behaviour, because it is not clear what decisions *individual* players should make *jointly* to increase their payoffs. These observations have led to such concepts as 'correlated rationalizability' and 'subjective correlated equilibria' which almost coincide with the concept of IUS. The notion of IUS is based on the weakest assumptions and seems to be closest to the idea of individual rationality in a strategic setting (see also the previous section). This is why I will use the notion of IUS in the rest of this study.[15]

In most games, however, the notion of IUS is not very powerful. In the first section, I argued that what constitutes rational behaviour depends on, among other things, the social or institutional context in which this behaviour takes place. Consequently, in particular cases the set of IUS can be further restricted by taking account of the social context of the behaviour under consideration. Common priors and independence may be two such elements of the social context. Above I have only argued that these two axioms should not be regarded as elements of a *general* theory of rational behaviour that applies to all situations. In some cases it may even be the case that a particular Nash equilibrium strategy is the only rational choice an agent can make even though it is not the unique IUS. An example of such a case is described in Schelling (1960) who considers two foreigners visiting New York city. If, before going to New York, they have talked a lot about the Empire State Building, this location seems to be a natural place to go in case they lose sight of each other and want to meet up as soon as possible. The reason for this is that even though all other places where they think they will meet each other are as good as the Empire State Building, the Empire State Building stands out precisely because they have talked so much about it: it is a 'focal point'. Intuitively, it is the only 'rational' expectation about where to find the fellow traveller. Hence, the only rational action seems to be for them to go to the Empire State Building. Of course, for other people there might be other focal points; for still others there might be none. If the social context is not specified in detail, however (as in most cases in game theory), we cannot restrict the set of strategies beyond the notion of IUS.

3

GENERAL EQUILIBRIUM ANALYSIS AND MACROECONOMICS: ALTERNATIVE PROGRAMMES

In the previous chapter the relation between 'micro' and 'macro' was discussed providing that these terms are interpreted as 'individual' and 'aggregate', respectively. In chapter 1 I also introduced another possible interpretation of the terms 'micro' and 'macro' in economics. I have employed the terms general equilibrium analysis (GEA) and macroeconomics to capture this alternative use of the terms 'micro' and 'macro'. In this view, GEA covers a particular conception of the economy in which the emphasis is on the determination of relative prices by the market and the allocation of a given quantity of resources over individuals. Yet, macroeconomics *in its traditional form* analyses the economy in terms of relations between some broad aggregates, focusing on the determination of the level of utilization of resources, especially output and employment. The present chapter provides the basis for a discussion of the way in which GEA and macroeconomics may be related.

A difficulty exists with the above delineation of GEA and macroeconomics: they are not confined to one single theory. On the contrary, GEA and macroeconomics are both *overall views* of the working of the economic system and in both subdisciplines there is a whole set of interrelated theories that is evolving over time. This renders a simple characterization of the two terms more difficult. Yet this picture corresponds with one of the most important changes in approach within the philosophy of science literature of the past decades, namely that scientific development should not be described in terms of sequences of single theories, but instead in terms of complexes of theories that are, in some way or another, related to each other. To describe these complexes of theories, Kuhn (1970) employs the terms 'paradigm' and

41

'interdisciplinary matrix', Lakatos (1978) the term 'research programme', and there are other terms in use. Although there are some philosophical differences between these terms, for the present purpose their similarities are more important. In what follows I will employ the term 'programme' in order to avoid any connotations with the terms just listed. It will be useful to distinguish two ideal types of programmes, descriptive and explanatory. A *descriptive programme* aims at providing an adequate overview of the empirical facts and regularities in a certain domain. An example might be the programme implicitly present in the search of Boyle, Gay-Lussac and others for the relation between the pressure, volume and temperature of a gas, which eventually resulted in the ideal gas law. In contrast, an explanatory programme aims at providing a theoretical account of empirical facts and relationships in a certain domain. We encountered examples of explanatory programmes earlier in the kinetic theory of gases and utility theory.[1] Frequently, explanatory programmes introduce theoretical terms.[2]

I will show how the notion of a programme can be used to characterize GEA and macroeconomics. The emphasis will be on the major developments within the programmes and on the broad relation between the programmes. As far as the relation between the programmes is concerned the discussion will give some hints with respect to the way the new classical and new Keynesian microfoundations literature employs methods commonly used in GEA to discuss traditional macroeconomic concerns as the business cycle and government policy. It is not the intention here to provide many details or to criticize the arguments that are provided by either side. Also, I do not want to discuss the issue of whether the programmes to be considered are research programmes in the sense of Lakatos (1978).[3] This chapter simply sketches the broad lines of the interaction between different lines of research. The issue of the relation between the programmes of GEA and macroeconomics will be taken up in chapter 9, where I will provide more details to support the claim that the microfoundations literature does not provide macroeconomics with foundations in the theory of individual behaviour.

GENERAL EQUILIBRIUM ANALYSIS

Before characterizing general equilibrium analysis in terms of a programme, I must say what I consider to be GEA. This will be done by stating what it is not. It is *not* neoclassical economics, although GEA is a part of neoclassical economics, and it is *not* only the Arrow–Debreu model (ADM), which is considered to be part of GEA. Among other things, neoclassical economics also consists of consumer theory, the theory of the firm, human capital theory and partial equilibrium analysis. General equilibrium analysis is founded on the idea that individual agents make optimal choices in interrelated markets and that these markets are in some sort of equilibrium. Contrary to GEA, consumer theory and other parts of neoclassical economics do not offer an overall view on the functioning of an economy.

On the other hand, ADM is only a part of the programme of GEA. ADM restricts itself to economies for which the following conditions hold: there is a large number of firms and households on every market, each of them taking prices as given, each agent has perfect foresight, there is a complete set of (future) markets and prices equate demand and supply on every market at any point in time. The first and second welfare theorems are important results of the assumptions of ADM: competitive (Walrasian) equilibria of ADM are Pareto efficient and any Pareto-efficient allocation can be sustained as a Walrasian equilibrium. Other parts of GEA study, for example, economies with incomplete markets or economies with a small number of firms. Usually, in economies in which *not* all the conditions of ADM are satisfied, the first and second welfare theorems do not hold.

The characterization of the programme of GEA below corresponds with the one given by Weintraub, who asserts that the programme is organized around the following hard-core propositions (see, e.g., Weintraub 1985: 26):[4,5]

HC1. there exist economic agents;
HC2. agents have preferences over outcomes;
HC3. agents independently optimize subject to constraints;
HC4. choices are made in interrelated markets;
HC5. agents have full relevant knowledge;
HC6. observable economic outcomes are coordinated, so they must be discussed with reference to equilibrium states.

Weintraub's formulation is subtle and different interpretations of the propositions are possible. If the propositions are interpreted in a narrow way, ADM results. Other interpretations of the propositions yield other theories that are part of GEA. The possibility of multiple interpretations also accounts for the fact that the programme can be applied to macroeconomic issues.

HC1–5 roughly cover the content of the definition of individual rational behaviour in chapter 2. HC1–3 are concerned with what I have called 'instrumental rationality.' HC4 is a particular interpretation of the idea that institutions as markets are allowed as primitive terms in an explanation of an individual agent's behaviour. HC5 hints at the discussion of what I have called 'cognitive rationality'. In what follows, HC5 will be interpreted in the following (broad) way: agents have knowledge of a well-defined set of relevant phenomena.[6] Yet proposition HC6 is *not* concerned with rational behaviour. The use of an equilibrium notion is a theoretical principle, which is regarded not to be verifiable by direct observation. In this study the term *equilibrium* is employed to describe a set of individual plans such that (*i*) each plan is the best an agent can achieve given the circumstances being faced and (*ii*) all plans are mutually consistent. Note that there are many different equilibrium concepts that fulfil the two requirements above; besides the Walrasian equilibrium notion of ADM there are several types of non-Walrasian equilibria (see, e.g., Hahn 1978 and Gale 1983).

As it stands, GEA employs two distinct theoretical principles: the notion of rational behaviour and the equilibrium notion. These notions can be interpreted as theoretical terms, because there is no clear empirical equivalent that corresponds with them. Both notions are employed in order to interpret empirical observations. Therefore, the programme of GEA has to be classified as an explanatory programme.

MAINSTREAM MACROECONOMICS

Keynes' *General Theory of Employment, Interest and Money* (1936) has frequently been regarded as the origin of modern macroeconomics. Unfortunately, there is no accepted account of the main insights of the book. One interpretation, that of Hicks (1937), is of particular importance for our characterization of 'mainstream macroeconomics'. Hicks summarized what he thought to be the essential ingredients of Keynes' theory by means of a simple mathematical system, the IS–LM model, containing only a few aggregate relationships. During the postwar period a standard interpretation of Keynes' *General Theory* gradually emerged. This interpretation, based on Hicks (1937) and known as the neoclassical synthesis, was laid down in many macroeconomic textbooks of which Samuelson (1948) is a good example. In the neoclassical synthesis the *General Theory* is transformed into a 'hydraulic'[7] conception of the entire economy based on some relations between homogeneous flows in a few markets.

The IS–LM model is part of the neoclassical synthesis. The term synthesis refers to the fact that Keynesian and pre-Keynesian (or 'classical') ideas were reconciled. The basic view expressed by the neoclassical synthesis was that Keynesian analysis is true in the short run, while the classical analysis holds in the long run (see, e.g., Patinkin 1956). In addition, Keynesian analysis was thought to be concerned with market imperfections that preclude the working of the price mechanism in the short run: when prices are rigid they cannot clear markets. Consequently, involuntary unemployment was regarded as a temporary phenomenon itself being a consequence of short-run rigidities in nominal (money) wages. In the long run, barriers to the functioning of the price mechanism were thought to be ineffective so that classical theory became operative: full employment would be attained in the long run.

The nature of macroeconomics as a *descriptive programme*, however, was not seriously affected by the above theoretical considerations. In particular, the existence of stable aggregate relationships and the descriptive adequacy of the programme of macroeconomics were *not* challenged. Together with a further development of the theory, the rise of empirical models that used available econometric methods and aggregate data occurred during the forties and fifties. The time period of the fifties and sixties can be regarded as the acme of this traditional macroeconomic approach. The empirically implemented models were regarded as capable of providing reliable empirical knowledge about the economy. Using the Keynesian approach, which was the most dominant at the time, economists believed that on the basis of these models government policies could be founded. Economists even believed that macroeconometrics eventually would yield sufficiently detailed knowledge to 'fine-tune' the economy as a whole.

The textbook varieties of both monetarism and Keynesianism shared the 'hydraulic' conception of the economy. Moreover, both schools of thought adhered to the neoclassical synthesis. Despite this theoretical agreement there were important differences of opinion between the two schools about the way the economy works in the short run. The basic idea in *Keynesian* models was that employment is related to aggregate output, which in term is determined by consumption and investment demand. Unemployment results when demand deficiencies exist. From time to time such deficiencies in aggregate demand exist, because the economic system is thought to be not self-stabilizing in the short run. In cases of such demand deficiencies, the government is in a position to stimulate aggregate demand, thereby increasing the level of employment. In addition, the long run is not considered to be very important for any practical purpose (it is only an analytical tool), because we will never live in the long run.

In constrast, the *monetarists'* view held that a short-run relationship between the level of aggregate output (and employment) and the money supply exists. In the short run, unemployment might result as a consequence of a fall in the money supply. In the monetarists' view this does not mean, however, that in case of unemployment, the monetary authorities should exploit this relation by increasing the quantity of money. On the contrary, the lag with which money affects output is difficult to foretell and an activist monetary policy could easily be procyclical rather than countercyclical. The best the monetary authorities can do is to fix the percentage increase of the money supply (see, e.g., Friedman 1968). This advice to abstain from an active policy is in line with the idea that the economy is self-regulating in the sense that a natural rate of unemployment will be attained in the long run. Active monetary policy easily leads to a situation in which the long-run Pareto-efficient equilibrium situation is never attained. As such monetarism is a particular species of the classical doctrine in economics, which in its crudest form states that in equilibrium the real part of the economy is independent of the monetary part. The monetarists believed that this classical dichotomy holds in the long run (see also Reder 1982). Accordingly, monetarism is more readily made compatible with ADM and its welfare theorems than Keynesian macrotheory.

From this sketch of the history of macroeconomics until the mid-sixties it is possible to distil some elements that are shared by the two mainstream macroeconomic approaches. The following propositions summarize the common elements of the Keynesian and the monetarist programmes.

> Ma1. The economy is described in terms of models consisting of a small number of aggregate relationships.
> Ma2. Many aggregate relationships are stable over an extended time interval.
> Ma3. The aggregate relationships can be quantified by means of statistical methods.

Besides these three common elements, the two programmes differ also on a number of issues. In order to characterize the *Keynesian* programme these common elements are supplemented by some typical Keynesian propositions.

> K4. A market economy does not automatically produce at an efficient level.
> K5. Unemployment is a consequence of deficiencies in aggregate demand.

K6. Government policies can push the economy towards more efficient levels of production.

The six propositions (Ma1–3 plus K4–6) together constitute the main characteristics of the Keynesian macroeconomic programme. The *monetarist* (classical) programme is characterized by the following three propositions. Ma1–3 and M4–6 constitute the important characteristics of the monetarist macroeconomic programme.

M4. In the short run, real output is capable of being altered by changes in the quantity of money.

M5. In the long run, the economy will produce at an efficient level and the classical dichotomy holds.

M6. There is no scope for discretionary policies.

This was the state of macroeconomics by the mid sixties, when the confidence in macroeconomics was at a maximum. There was agreement on the kind of theoretical (hydraulic) models that could fruitfully be employed in the discipline. There also was consensus on the need for and feasibility of econometric estimations of these models. Economists believed that these estimated models provide useful knowledge for the evaluation of alternative policy regimes. In the early seventies this idea lost power. The experience of world-wide stagflation made economists question the effectiveness of government intervention and the stability of aggregate relationships. As a result, the validity of the two programmes, especially the Keynesian, was challenged. In the terminology of Coddington (1976: 1266), the failure of public policy 'raises in a practical way the question of the scope of the hydraulic conception'.

Since the late sixties theoretical economists have shown a renewed interest in the underlying theoretical foundation of macroeconomics. Research in this direction has come to be known under the heading of 'microeconomic foundations of macroeconomics'. The character of macroeconomics has changed since then in such a way that only a limited number of papers in the field of theoretical macroeconomics do not have 'microfoundations'. It has even been argued that

> in recent years theoretical macroeconomics has become a somewhat eerie subject: although there are probably still quite a few economists who have a vague intuition that it should exist, it does not, in fact, seem to be with us anymore.
>
> (Peeters 1987: 456)

It is to this 'microfoundations' literature that I now turn.

'MICRO' FOUNDATIONS OF MACROECONOMICS: INTERACTING PROGRAMMES?

Theoretical curiosity with respect to the relation between the programme of GEA and the two macroeconomic programmes has existed from the beginning of modern macroeconomics. One of the main concerns was the issue whether macroeconomics and GEA would be consistent with each other. ADM, the main theory within the programme of GEA, studies a market economy in which prices equate aggregate demand and aggregate supply. This conception of the economy is in apparent conflict with the actual state of affairs, notably the underutilization of resources in general and unemployment in particular, with which macroeconomics was concerned. How were economists to conceptualize (involuntary) unemployment if prices (wages) equated, among other things, the demand for and the supply of labour? The neoclassical synthesis reconciled GEA and (Keynesian) macroeconomics by giving each of them their own domain of applicability: macroeconomics (with its assumption of sticky money wages) gives an accurate description of the economy in the short run, while the long-run developments of the economy were captured by ADM.

From a theoretical point of view this state of the discipline was unsatisfactory, however. One cannot simply attribute unemployment to sticky money wages while leaving the theoretical structure of ADM intact: the imposition of a fixed money wage (or, more generally, fixed prices) deeply affects the structure of the theory of supply and demand. This point was first put to the fore by Clower's seminal paper, *The Keynesian Counterrevolution* (1965). Clower was also one of the first economists who attempted to bring about a real synthesis between ADM and macroeconomic analysis. His emphasis on the *interdependence of markets* resulted in the view that demand and supply curves on all markets are affected if money wages are fixed. Older choice theoretic foundations of, for example, the macroeconomic consumption function and the demand for money function are partial and do not take this interdependence into account.

If prices are restrained from bringing about market clearing allocations, then, in order to stay within the programme of GEA, one has to look for variables that bring about other kinds of equilibria. Clower (1965) and Leijonhufvud (1968) set out a subprogramme in Keynesian economics, regarding two questions as important: (*i*) does an equilibrium between affected demand and supply curves exist and (*ii*) what kind of (Keynesian) characteristics do these equilibria reveal if they exist at all? Note that the first question is more related to the adoption of the method of GEA, while the second question is associated with the desire to establish Keynesian propositions. The subprogramme culminated in a variety of fixprice models. These models have microfoundations in the sense that they are based on decision-making individuals and a notion of equilibrium, the two cornerstones of GEA. Several types of so-called fixprice equilibria were proposed in which the allocation was brought about by quantity constraints. The existence of non-market clearing equilibria in such models was shown by, for example, Bénassy (1975) and Drèze (1975). Moreover, it turned out that the fixprice models capture quite a number of ideas associated with Keynesian economics. By means of these alternative equilibrium notions, involuntary unemployment could be regarded as an equilibrium phenomenon in which optimizing households face a quantity constraint on the amount of labour they can supply. Also, the Keynesian notions of effective demand and the multiplier were reformulated within the new models. Besides, the models provided arguments for demand policies by the government.

New classical macroeconomics

The new classical school had its own way of reconciling the empirical phenomenon of unemployment with the programme of GEA. According to this school of thought, the phenomenon of unemployment can be explained without abandoning the theoretical notion of Walrasian equilibrium. In this view

> involuntary unemployment is not a fact or a phenomenon which it is the task of the theorist to explain. It is, on the contrary, a theoretical construct which Keynes introduced in the hope that it would be helpful in discovering a correct explanation for a genuine phenomenon: large-scale fluctuations in measured, total unemployment.
>
> (Lucas 1978: 354)

Thus, the major challenge for the new classical school was to provide an explanation of (changes in) the level of employment that is consistent with the notion that markets clear at any point in time. The school criticized the Keynesian (fixprice) explanation of unemployment for the fact that the explanation is incomplete: no account is given of why prices are fixed. In particular, it is not clear why rational agents do not change prices once they know this is in their own benefit. In fact, new classical economists regard the competitive equilibrium notion as the only theoretically sound equilibrium notion (see, e.g., Lucas 1977).

New classical business cycle models provide an answer to the question of how to reconcile fluctuations in the level of employment with the notion of Walrasian equilibrium. The early models regard incomplete information about the aggregate money supply as the major cause of the cycle (see, e.g., Lucas and Rapping 1969 and Lucas 1972). Note that monetarists like Friedman also regarded fluctuation in the money supply as the main cause of the business cycle. In this sense, these new classical incomplete information models present a view on business cycles that is very close to the monetarist view. Lucas (1981: 1–2) acknowledges this inheritance by saying that new classical economics has 'reinforced many of the policy recommendations of Milton Friedman and other postwar monetarists but has contributed few, if any, original policy proposals'. The monetarist and new classical models that explain the link between the variability of the money supply and the business cycle differ considerably, however. We have seen that the monetarist model consists of some relations between homogeneous flows. On the other hand, the new classical models have 'microfoundations' in the sense that these models are based on decision-making individuals, incomplete information and market clearing. Thus, a new classical model is a particular instance of the programme of GEA. A simple way to summarize this state of affairs is that the early new classical models support the monetarist view while using a different method.

The situation is, of course, not as simple as it is stated above. Differences in methods between monetarists and new classical economists also have more substantial implications. A first example to illustrate this point is the following. Monetarists propose that the monetary authorities should increase the money supply by a fixed percentage per year. According to Friedman this percentage should be equal to the difference between the secular rate of growth of gross national product and the velocity of circulation of the money stock. In the short run, any other percentage would have real (but to a large extent unpredictable) effects. New classical economists adapt this idea by showing that a fixed rule is as good as any other: any fixed rule does not have real effect (see, e.g., Sargent and Wallace 1975). The modification of this policy prescription immediately follows from a difference in the models that are used. The new classical school adheres to general equilibrium models with rational expectations and agents with rational expectations will understand the rule and will not be fooled by monetary changes.

A second example of differences in implications between monetarist and new classical models concerns the conditions under which changes in the money supply have a short-run impact on real output. As we have seen, this short-run relationship holds unconditionally in the monetarists' view. This is because individual agents have adaptive expectations that are incorrect after each change in monetary policy. In the new classical monetary business cycle models, the short-run relationship between changes in the money stock and real output holds only for *un*anticipated changes in the money stock. Because of the assumption of rational expectations, anticipated changes in the money stock do not have any real impact in new classical models.

In the seventies the monetary incomplete information models of the business cycle became generally accepted by a large number of scholars. Then, in the eighties, new classical economists shifted their attention to real business cycle models. Real business cycle models regard the business cycle as the optimal response of the economy to exogenous shocks in real variables such as technology and utility factors. Nominal variables such as the money stock are assumed to have no role in explaining the business cycle. As such, real business cycle economists distance themselves from the monetarist and early new classical models. Instead, the business cycle is explained in terms of the 'pure form' of intertemporal general equilibrium analysis, the Arrow–Debreu theory. Another device that is frequently used in the real business cycle literature is Robinson Crusoe: the economy is represented as if it consists of only one individual.

Some authors have looked for empirical arguments that explain the transition from monetary to real models of the business cycle. However, the empirical arguments, apparently unfavourable to the monetary models (see, e.g., Sims 1980) can be interpreted in a variety of ways, so that the empirical studies are in fact undecisive (see, e.g., Hoover 1988). As a matter of fact, the first papers on real business cycles (Kydland and Prescott 1982, Long and Plosser 1983) do not mention any reason for dissatisfaction with the monetary models. The authors simply state that they provide an alternative account of the business cycle. Since empirical arguments are undecisive, one has to look for other reasons that explain the shift in analysis. One such argument is the following. From a strictly classical perspective, Lucas' monetary 'imperfect information' model is partly unsatisfactory because its argument apparently relies on some sort of failure in the market for information.[8] In this model the classical dichotomy between monetary and real sectors fails to hold in the short run. From a classical point of view it seems to be natural to enquire whether one can push the classical dichotomy farther than it has been pushed by Friedman and Lucas, among others. The question then is whether models of business cycles can be constructed in which the classical dichotomy holds even in the short run. Real business cycle economists provide such models.

New Keynesian macroeconomics

As the new classical critique on the fixprice assumption had been effective, Keynesian economists had to look for other sources that could explain the malfunctioning of markets. Authors like Hahn (1978) constructed models in which non-Walrasian equilibria result from firms misperceiving their demand curves. But also this approach could not withstand the new classical critique: rational agents will find out that their perceptions are incorrect and modify them accordingly. In the end, rational agents would know the objective demand curve and market clearing would be restored.

By the end of the seventies and the beginning of the eighties, Keynesian economics was in disarray. It was a widespread belief that irrational behaviour is at the heart of any Keynesian proposition. During that period new classical economics was regarded as the most important programme in mainstream macroeconomics, especially in the United States. The Keynesian approach has never been far from centre stage, however. The new Keynesian approach, as it has been called, accepts not only the programme of GEA, but also the new classical critique on earlier Keynesian models that a fixprice explanation of unemployment is incomplete as long as it is not explained why rational agents (with correct perceptions of the working of the economy) choose to fix prices at values that do not correspond to Walrasian equilibrium prices. As it is clear that at least one of the assumptions of ADM (but not which one) has to be discarded in order to account for Keynesian phenomena, it is not surprising to see that, during the eighties, different directions were explored in Keynesian economics. It is even not always clear what the 'Keynesian' element of new Keynesian economics is: in many of the models unemployment is *not* a consequence of deficiencies in demand and the desirability of monetary or fiscal policy is not universally subscribed to either (see, e.g., Mankiw and Romer 1991). New Keynesian models have a family relationship to each other. What keeps the family together is a belief that market imperfections (as asymmetric information, imperfect competition and sticky prices) are crucial for an understanding of the functioning of a market economy. Two branches will be distinguished here: (*i*) studies that supplement the fixprice models with an explanation why rational individuals might choose to set prices at non-Walrasian equilibrium values and (*ii*) studies that build models with relative prices determined 'by the market' and individuals having rational expectations. Papers in the second branch show that, even if these two assumptions hold, Keynesian results may apply.

Within the new Keynesian approach there are several attempts at providing an explanation for the idea that actual prices are relatively fixed even though they differ from Walrasian equilibrium prices. Yellen (1984) gives an overview of efficiency wage models of unemployment. In the basic efficiency wage model production depends not only on the number of workers employed, but also on the productivity per worker. If there is a positive relation between the wage rate and the productivity per worker, then profit-maximizing firms will choose to set the wage rate above the Walrasian equilibrium level. Unemployed workers would strictly prefer to work at the going wage rate or even at a lower wage rate, but firms do not lower wages because this would reduce the productivity of all workers. Azariadis and Stiglitz (1983) use the theory of implicit contracts with asymmetric information to demonstrate why unemployment might be an equilibrium phenomenon. Blanchard and Kiyotaki (1987) have a model of monopolistic competition in which there exist so-called small menu costs of changing prices. They show that *even if* menu costs are small, profit-maximizing firms may choose not to change prices, which in turn may cause large fluctuations in output.

The diversity of the second branch of studies distinguished above can be illustrated by going briefly into the arguments put forward by Hart (1982), Weitzman (1982) and Cooper and John (1988). Hart (1982) studies a general equilibrium model with oligopolistic competition. Unlike Hahn (1978), Hart's model employs objective demand curves. He shows that the model exhibits 'Keynesian' features such as the existence of underemployment equilibria and a multiplier that is larger than one. Moreover, a balanced budget fiscal policy is able to increase employment. In the Cournot–Nash equilibrium of the model, firms individually choose not to increase their production level, because the consequent fall in prices is such that the firm's revenue will decrease. It should be noted that in Hart's model prices are such that total production is sold and the amount of labour supplied is demanded. Accordingly, there is no involuntary unemployment in Hart's model. The concept of underemployment is used to indicate that the equilibrium level of employment is lower than in the corresponding Walrasian equilibrium. Weitzman (1982), on the other hand, argues that increasing returns to scale is a necessary condition for Keynesian economics in general and for involuntary unemployment in particular. His basic argument is that with non-increasing returns to scale the unemployed can produce goods at least as efficiently as the employed so that they can 'produce themselves out of unemployment'. Cooper and John (1988) point out a common element in many new Keynesian papers. Key concepts in their paper are strategic complementarity and coordination failure. They show that most of the new Keynesian literature departs from the perfect competition assumption underlying ADM. Under imperfect competition, an individual agent's optimal action depends on the actions undertaken by other agents. Strategic complementarity occurs when an individual's optimal strategy is increasing in another player's strategy.[9] When strategic complementarity exists, inefficient 'Keynesian' equilibria may arise as a consequence of the fact that individual agents are not able to improve upon their situation if all other agents stick to their actions. In some cases there may even be multiple equilibria that can be Pareto-ranked.[10] Agents might find themselves in a 'bad' equilibrium, but individually they have no means of changing their situation. They call this a 'coordination failure'.

Intermezzo
METHODOLOGY

4

ECONOMICS AND THE REAL WORLD

Many economists will agree that the ultimate goal of economic science is to understand the actual functioning of the economy and, if possible, to use this knowledge for prediction and policy advice. This means that we should have a good understanding of the empirical regularities that describe the behaviour of major economic variables. An important question then is what simple economic models (or theories) might add to empirical research in understanding the economy. The aim of this chapter is to try to clarify the role of (simple) models in economic research. In particular, I will focus on the question of what additional gain might be expected from models that have individualistic foundations.

Let me make it clear from the beginning that in my view economic models can fulfil a variety of roles. The function of a specific model depends to a large extent on the relation between the model and the real world. Here, three forms of possible relationships between a model and the real world are distinguished. First, some models can be regarded as attempts to approximate the real world in an accurate way. As it is clear that any model (by virtue of its being a *model*) abstracts from certain features of the world around us, an important question is what constitutes a good approximation. This is the subject of the next section. Second, some models are better regarded as providing a caricature (instead of an approximation) of the real world. According to Gibbard and Varian (1978: 676) a caricature is a 'deliberate distortion of reality' in such a way that it 'illuminates certain aspects of the world'. The second section develops this idea of economic models as caricatures further and it points at the difference between a model that attempts to approximate reality and a model that builds a caricature of reality. Finally, there are economic models that, in my view, do not directly bear on economic reality. This is the type of models that I have termed 'mathematical political philosophy' in the introduction to this study. The third section deals with this category of models. In the three sections I will give examples of models that fall into the category under consideration. This is not to say that all models can be easily classified. On the contrary, many models will contain elements of more than one of the categories distinguished below. Accordingly, the three sections of this chapter should merely be regarded as a way to structure the many facets of the possible relation between an economic model and the real world.

The fact that a model usually belongs to more than one of the categories is also true of the models that will be discussed in the remaining chapters. Although at some places in the book I will discuss the status of the model under consideration, I have decided to avoid the question in most of the cases. This is because the requirement of methodological individualism is more a requirement about the structure of an explanation (or a model) than about the empirical status of the explanation. Also, the empirical status of a model depends to a large extent on how the model is used, rather than on some inherent characteristics of the model itself.

ECONOMIC MODELS AS APPROXIMATIONS OF THE REAL WORLD

In order to be as clear as possible I will illustrate the discussion by means of an example. Suppose there exists some empirical macroeconomic research showing that there is a positive impact of the level of social security on the rate of unemployment. Suppose furthermore that at present there is a government that wants to reduce the rate of unemployment. The government in question proposes to lower the social security level by arguing that there exists research showing that this will have the desired effect. The difficulty with the government's position is that it simply *assumes* that the empirical relationship that has been found also applies to present circumstances. This assumption is unwarranted, because we know that most economic relationships do not hold unconditionally, i.e. most economic 'laws' are *ceteris paribus* laws and not 'general laws'. Before one is justified in applying *ceteris paribus* laws two requirements have to be fulfilled. First, one has to have an accurate idea of the conditions under which the *ceteris paribus* law holds and, second, one has to have reasons to believe that the conditions under which the law holds true also apply to the present circumstances.

If asked why there is a positive relation between the level of social security and the rate of unemployment, an explanation along the following lines might be given. The higher the level of social security, the less willing people are to take a job. (This is a kind of macro-to-micro transition.) Consequently, the competition among firms to attract potential employees will be more severe, pushing firms to raise their wages. Together with a rise in wages, individual firms will demand less labour. This increases the rate of unemployment. (This is a micro-to-macro transition.)

The above explanation provides a relatively detailed structure of the mechanism that lies behind the relation between the level of social security and the rate of unemployment. The implicit assumption of the explanation is that each part of the mechanism is more autonomous than the empirical relation itself, i.e. *in the absence of another* explanation of the observed relation, there is *no reason to expect* that the empirical relation remains an accurate description if one of the parts breaks down.[1] The concept of autonomy is, of course, a relative concept (cf. Haavelmo 1944: 29). The validity of each part of the explanation itself is conditional upon some other factors. For example, the macro-to-micro transition depends on the idea that an increase in the level of social security makes it more attractive to be unemployed. The increase in the level of social security might, however, also have an adverse effect, namely if it is taken as a signal that it is less likely to become employed once one is unemployed. The micro-to-macro transition depends, among other things, on the condition that the increase in the level of social security does not have a substantial positive impact on the demand for commodities.

The advantage of an individualistic explanation is then that it gives a systematic account of the mechanism that produces the observed empirical relation. Moreover, it delves into (some of) the conditions that have to be fulfilled in order for one to have reasons to believe that the empirical relation applies to the situation under consideration. Knowing these conditions serves three purposes. First, if the conditions are known one can do one's best to check whether they apply to the present circumstances. If there are no reasons to believe that the conditions do not apply, one can use the empirical relation for, for example, policy purposes. Of course, it is impossible to know for sure that the conditions do apply. Accordingly, it might be the case that *ex post* it turns out that the empirical relation does not hold despite careful *ex ante* investigations. The second purpose the conditions may serve then is to direct the search for an explanation of why the empirical relation did not hold after all if, in fact, it did not.[2] Third, when the conditions are known one can make a start with the investigation of what kind of relationships hold when the conditions do *not* apply.

Above, I have only provided an informal account of the mechanism that connects an increase in the level of social security and the rate of unemployment. In order to make the argument more precise, economists might like to construct a more formal model. In order to simplify the account, the formal model might employ, for example, the notion of a representative household which is supposed to behave rationally.

With respect to the model it is important to distinguish between a substantive and a non-substantive part. The substantive part of a good model coincides with the informal sketch of the explanation, the sole purpose of the model being to make this informal sketch more precise. The second part of the model consists of non-substantive hypotheses by which I mean hypotheses that are made for ease of exposition. It is obvious that these non-substantive hypotheses should be chosen in such a way that they do not modify the substantive part of the model. Above I have argued that the substantive part of the model should provide us with reasons why and when (under what conditions) an empirical relation is an accurate description of (some part of) the economy. For the substantive part of the model to fulfil this role it is necessary to believe that this part of the model accurately characterizes the actual economy. This is not the case for the non-substantive part of the model.

The question with respect to the non-substantive part of the model is whether it illegitimately abstracts from certain aspects. Let us focus the discussion by supposing that we have constructed a model in which individuals behave rationally and consider the question of whether the explanation that is given really assumes that individuals behave rationally and, if so, whether this hypothesis is unwarranted. The hypothesis of rational behaviour together with many other assumptions the model would have to make is *sufficient* to show that a higher level of social security leads to a higher level of unemployment. The important issue then is whether somebody who questions the given explanation, for example by arguing that apart from some rational individuals there are certainly also many individuals who do not seem to behave in a rational way, really makes a strong criticism. I doubt it. Surely, for some individuals, the assumption of rational behaviour seems to be contrary to fact, but the point is that this assumption is part of a sufficient condition for the explanation to hold and is itself far from being a necessary condition.[3] An economist who supports a model in which the hypothesis of rational behaviour is used might even grant that in the particular situation another hypothesis about individual behaviour is closer to 'the whole truth'. One of the following two cases then prevails. First, if the other hypothesis also yields the result that there is a (conditional) positive relation between the level of social security and the rate of unemployment, then one can argue that the 'fact' the individuals do not behave rationally is apparently not essential for the relation under consideration. Therefore, one has good reasons to work with the hypothesis that is most frequently used, namely the hypothesis that individuals behave rationally.[4] Second, if the other hypothesis does not yield the (conditional) empirical relation, then it clearly cannot be part of the model that explains the relation between the level of social security and the rate of unemployment.

Then, the question may arise of when one should be willing to look for alternative models (for example, models that are not based on the hypothesis of rational behaviour). The above discussion suggests two reasons to give up the model that uses the hypothesis of rational behaviour: (*i*) if the model would not have resulted in the (conditional) positive relation between the level of social security and the rate of unemployment; (*ii*) if the model on which the resulting relation is based relies heavily on contrary-to-fact assumptions. By the latter I mean that it should be possible to retain the same basic explanation if more realistic elements are brought into the model. In other words, if the hypothesis of rational behaviour really is contrary to fact, then it might not be part of the substantive hypotheses of the explanation.

The same conclusion holds true with respect to the notion of a representative agent. In many models in the microfoundations literature it is assumed that, for example, all individual households or all individual firms are identical. If agents behave non-strategically this assumption is mathematically equivalent to the assumption of a representative agent (household or firm). We know, however, that households and firms are not identical and that strategic considerations may be important. This means that the assumption of a representative agent cannot be considered part of the substantive hypotheses underlying the explanation that is formally described in the model. It is then important to know that the explanation itself (contrary to the model in which the explanation is moulded) does not depend on the assumption of a representative agent. In other words, it is important to know that the same explanation can be retained in models in which individual agents differ from each other or in which agents behave strategically. In chapter 8 I show with respect to the rational expectations hypothesis that the assumption of a representative agent yields completely different conclusions than the assumption that agents are identical if individual agents behave strategically.

Thus, in this context the representative agent model is not a good model from the above point of view.

One important qualification to the above discussion should be made, however. It might, for example, be argued that strategic considerations are negligible if the number of agents is large, i.e. the notion of a representative agent might be a good approximation even though each agent out of a large set thinks strategically. This argument is, I think, valid if a result like the following one exists. Consider two models, $\mathcal{M}_0$ and $\mathcal{M}_1$. The models are identical apart from the fact that the first model assumes a finite number n of agents who think strategically, while the second model assumes an infinite number of agents thinking non-strategically. Then, for the above qualification to hold true, there should be a result saying that the conclusions of $\mathcal{M}_0$ tend to the conclusions of $\mathcal{M}_1$ if n tends to infinity. If such a result exists and if in a particular application the number of agents is very large (although not infinitely large), then it is legitimate to simplify the exposition by making use of the notion of a representative agent. The qualification then consists in modifying condition (*ii*) above to the extent that it is only required that it should be possible to retain *approximately* the same explanation if contrary-to-fact assumptions are replaced by more realistic ones.[5]

At the end of this section, I will sum up the above discussion and give an example to clarify the issues involved. An individualistic explanation, like other types of explanations, attempts to provide conditions under which an empirical relation holds true. Typical of an individualistic explanation is that the important conditions are to be found in the macro-to-micro and the micro-to-macro transitions. The conditions are among the substantive part of the explanation and should therefore be realistic (or at least close to being realistic). This means that they should not depend on the context of the particular model in which they are embedded. Apart from the substantive part, a model also contains non-substantive assumptions. These latter may be contrary to fact only if it is clear that their falseness is not relevant for the overall explanation. (This might be interpreted as an *as if* element. Accordingly, regarding models as approximations of the real world does not mean that the model attempts to approximate the world in as many aspects as possible. It only implies that a model accounts for the *essential* aspects.) The purpose of the model is to provide at least one context in which the informal explanation can be made precise. Subsequent empirical research should make clear whether the conditions that appear in the theoretical explanation are also important in reality. (An individualistic explanation turns out to be fruitful if a careful examination of the macro-to-micro and the micro-to-macro transitions reveals conditions that turn out to be empirically important.) Accordingly, it is important then that these conditions have a clear meaning also outside the context of the model. We will see that this is not always the case. (In these cases a model might better be interpreted in line with what I have to say in the third section.)

An example from the previous chapter might help to clarify what I have in mind. Among other things, chapter 3 discussed the monetarist view that all changes in the money stock have a short-run impact on real output. We have also seen that in new classical monetary business cycle models this short-term relation holds only for *un*anticipated changes in the money stock. Thus, the new classical model provides a condition under which the short-run relation holds. This is the substantive part of the new classical monetary business cycle models. This substantive part is placed in a representative agent type of model. The assumption of a representative agent is considered to be an element of the non-substantive part of the model. The substantive part should also be valid outside the context of the specific model. Some empirical work has been done in order to check whether only unanticipated changes in the money stock have an impact on real output (see, e.g., Barro 1977). As this is not the place to dwell upon the example, we just note (without commenting) that Barro finds some support for the new classical condition.

ECONOMIC MODELS AS CARICATURES OF THE REAL WORLD

Above we have seen what kind of considerations are important when an economic model is considered as an approximation to the 'real world'. The substantive part of the model should yield conditions under which a certain empirical relationship holds, conditions that should also be relevant *outside* the context of the specific model. Besides this substantive part a model also consists of a non-substantive part, which might consist of contrary-to-fact assumptions. Many models in the microfoundations literature, however, do not claim to offer substantive hypotheses that also hold true outside the context of the specific model. Instead, they argue that the formalizations are only meant as *examples* (cf., e.g., Hart 1982 and Bryant 1983). Authors often acknowledge the fact that the results of their paper are (largely) due to specific assumptions that are made. The purpose of an example is to show what the economy *would be like* if it could fulfil certain assumptions. Unlike the type of models in the previous section there is not really a claim here that an example is robust to changes in the non-substantive part of the explanation. In fact, the whole distinction between a substantive and a non-substantive part collapses. Unlike the view expressed in the next section, examples do not claim that there is no connection whatsoever between the example and the real world. An example simply points at the possibility that a certain state of affairs would result *if* the example provides an accurate description of the economy.

The view that only examples are provided comes very close to the view that economic models should be considered as 'caricatures', a view expressed by Gibbard and Varian (1978). Caricatures usually have *some* relation with reality, although the precise connection is not spelled out. I want to develop this idea of 'economic models as caricatures' further in two directions. First, a caricature is related to a style. There are different styles of making caricatures and a style can be characterized by the use of some methods. For example, the style of macroeconomics since the early seventies is (loosely) characterized by the six propositions of the GEA as defined in chapter 3. Second, a caricature is not intended to be value free. Any caricature attempts to establish a certain opinion on the case that is depicted. The 'deliberate distortion of reality' is needed in order to highlight the point the author wants to make. In my view, the opinions that are highlighted in the microfoundations debate derive from the 'old' Keynesian and classical programmes in macro-economics. For example, the Keynesian opinion that Bryant (1983) wants to highlight is that the economy may get stuck in inefficient underemployment equilibria.[6]

I will briefly illustrate these observations with some examples. In chapter 3 it was argued that it is difficult to say that real business cycle models give a better approximation of reality than monetary models of the business cycle. Both types of models simply have different views on the principal causes of the business cycle. In order to establish a particular view, models are built 'that do the job', not to mimic the actual economy. Instead, they provide a caricature that employs the method of GEA. Lucas (1972) pictures the economy in terms of a large number of small islands. There is one resident per island and each individual is imperfectly informed about what happens on the other islands. The caricature employed by the real business cycle literature is even more simple. The economy is depicted as Robinson Crusoe's island. As the only inhabitant of the economy, Robinson Crusoe is consumer and producer at the same time. Accordingly, coordination problems of any kind are assumed to be non-existent. In new Keynesian caricatures, on the other hand, coordination problems are at the core of the analysis. Diamond (1982) employs the caricature of a coconut economy, where individuals are strolling along the beaches looking for coconuts to pick from the trees. Since, by assumption, the individuals have to exchange coconuts for coconuts before eating them, there is a situation in which hardly any coconuts are collected, because other individuals do not collect them either. I think it is accurate to say that all these models 'deliberately distort economic reality' in order to concentrate on a possible state of affairs.

It should be noted that the distinction between 'models as approximations' and 'models as caricatures' is not as sharp as I have indicated above. The sharpness of the distinction depends to what extent one can distinguish between the substantive and non-substantive hypotheses of a model. In some cases the distinction between the two kinds of hypotheses is transparent; in some other cases it is clear that no such distinction can be made. However, in the majority of the cases this distinction is not as clear cut as one wishes it to be. This will typically be the case when it is not known to what extent the contrary-to-fact assumptions are crucial for the result of the model. In those cases it is also difficult to say whether a model is meant to approximate the real world or whether it is only meant to provide a caricature of the real world.

ECONOMICS WITHOUT THE REAL WORLD

There is still another view on the relation between economic models and the real world, a view that is the easiest characterized by saying that there is no relation between the two. This view has forcefully been argued for by Sen (1976: 317–22). Sen traces the origins of 'many exercises in economic theory' (p. 321) back to an abstract question in political philosophy, namely the question 'to what extent egoistic behavior achieves the general good' (p. 321). This is the question that has been at the heart of much of the mathematical literature in general equilibrium theory. Sen argues that

> the primary concern here is not with the relation of postulated models to the real economic world, but with the accuracy of answers to well-defined questions posed with preselected assumptions which severely constrain the nature of the models that can be admitted into the analysis.

> (Sen 1976: 322)

According to this view, (a part of) economic theory deals with abstract questions in terms of abstract models. Economic theory is then a kind of political philosophy using mathematical tools. The relation between the mathematical objects thus created and the real world is irrelevant. The interest of such a mathematical object lies in its relation to other mathematical objects. Progress can take on several forms: showing that a conclusion also holds under more general assumptions, constructing counterexamples to conjectures previously considered to be true, illuminating some hidden assumptions of a conjecture and so on. In order to emphasize again that no relation with the real world is intended, one can say that some of the assumptions employed should be regarded as *even if* (instead of *as if*) assumptions.

Some examples might make the general discussion more appealing. Grandmont (1985) discusses a classical type overlapping generations (OLG) model. He shows that under *laissez-faire* a competitive monetary economy may display large endogenous fluctuations in output that continue indefinitely. This is contrary to the classical idea that a competitive economy (eventually) reaches a natural (and efficient) rate of output. In order to prove his point the agents' utility functions have to be of a particular form. Grandmont's contribution is interesting primarily because it provides a counterexample to the classical conjecture of the efficiency of *laissez-faire*, not because of the relation with the real world. Geanakoplos and Polemarchakis (1986) study a classical type OLG model and demonstrate that there is a continuum of equilibria because of the fact that there are not enough equations to determine all unknown variables. A unique equilibrium can be obtained if some variables are treated as exogenous variables. Classical propositions are obtained only if a particular variable is chosen to be exogenously determined. They show that for other choices of exogenous variables Keynesian propositions can be obtained. Finally, the question of whether a precise definition of the concept of involuntary unemployment can be given in a world in which agents are free to express their desires can be considered in a similar context.

Again, it should be emphasized that the distinction between the type of models considered in this section and the type of models considered in the other two sections is not as sharp as suggested above. For example, many models in economics prove that a result of a particular model also holds true (or does not hold true) under alternative assumptions. This activity can be regarded from two different points of view. First, it can be regarded either as an activity of mathematical interest only or as a contribution to a purely philosophical debate. This would fit into the type of models discussed in this section. Second, it can also be regarded as a way of finding out whether the result of a particular model crucially depends on a contrary-to-fact assumption. This is important to know from the point of view of 'models as approximations', because a contrary-to-fact assumption cannot be regarded as an element of the non-substantive part of an explanation if the explanation is not robust to a replacement of this assumption by a more realistic one. There is, nevertheless, another criterion that can sometimes be used to distinguish between the type of models of this section and those of the first section. It is whether or not the model results in a (conditional) explanation of an *empirical* relationship. Models that fall in the category of the present section usually have a theoretical proposition (like 'the allocation of goods in the economy is Pareto efficient'), i.e. not an explanation of an empirical relationship, as the main result. It is difficult to see what kind of empirical implications follow from such a theoretical proposition.

Part II
AGGREGATION ISSUES

5

AGGREGATION, ANALOGY AND THE REPRESENTATIVE AGENT

In chapter 2 we saw that methodological individualism (MI) does not deny the existence of aggregate relations. On the contrary, one of the key problems MI deals with is how aggregate relationships come about. It was argued that an aggregation step is one of the elements of an individualistic explanation of an aggregate relationship. This chapter concentrates on issues related to what economists have called the 'aggregation problem'. In particular, it will be assumed throughout this chapter that the individual level relationships that are postulated are based on a theory of rational decision making even though this step will not be made explicit.

It should be emphasized that aggregation over individuals is not the only form of aggregation that has been studied in economics; aggregation over goods and time have been studied as well. Although there are deep methodological problems on the modelling of causal processes related to aggregation over time, such issues fall outside the scope of the present enquiry into the relation between individual and aggregate relationships in economics. I do not discuss aggregation over goods either. In chapter 1 we saw that Malinvaud (1972), among others, poses that in microeconomic analysis the individuality of each good is respected, whereas in macroeconomic analysis usually only a few composite goods are considered. However, I have also argued there that in microeconomics often an arbitrary number of goods is studied. Thus, aggregation over goods does not need to be a central topic in an enquiry into the relations between individuals and aggregates in the way these terms are understood in this study.

Although the division of individual and aggregate relationships has a long history in economic theory, the actual analysis of the connection between the two types of relationships has not been undertaken until relatively recently; the first serious study devoted to the issue stems from

71

1946. Until that date, economists frequently assumed a straightforward analogy between individual and aggregate relationships. For example, Jevons (1879: 16) simply stated that 'the general forms of the laws of economics are the same in the case of individuals and the nations' and Hicks (1939: 245) wrote 'the transition [from individual to aggregate level] is made by using the simple principle ... that the behaviour of a group of individuals, or a group of firms, obeys the same laws as the behaviour of a single unit'.

This state of affairs changed mainly because of an article by Klein (1946a). Klein criticized models developed in the thirties to explain fluctuations in the level of economic activity by stating that

> the demand equations for the factors of production in the economy as a whole are derived from the assumption that entrepreneurs collectively attempt to maximize some aggregate profit; whereas the usually accepted assumption is that the individual firm attempts to maximize its own profit.
>
> (Klein 1946a: 93)

These demand functions are obtained from marginal productivity equations and Klein further observed that

> marginal-productivity equations are written, *without justification*, for the economy as a whole, in exactly the same form as the marginal-productivity equations for a single firm.
>
> (Klein 1946a: 93; my italics)

Klein's observations led to a subsequent discussion in *Econometrica*. The central topic of this discussion can be illustrated by means of the following simple example. Suppose that there are n households and m goods and that the consumption behaviour of individual households is described by a set of linear relationships:

$$c_{ij}^d = \alpha_{ij} + \beta_{ij} y_i, \qquad i = 1, \ldots, n \text{ and } j = 1, \ldots, m, \qquad (5.1)$$

where c_{ij}^d is the demand for good j by household i, y_i is household i's income level and α_{ij} and β_{ij} are parameters. Suppose further that the aggregate demand for good j, C_j^d, and aggregate income Y are defined by

$$C_j^d = \Sigma_{i=1}^n c_{ij}^d \text{ and } Y = \Sigma_{i=1}^n y_i. \qquad (5.2)$$

It is easy to see that a functional relation between aggregate demand for good j and aggregate income does not exist if the β_{ij}'s are not identical across households:

$$C_j^d = \sum_{i=1}^{n} (\alpha_{ij} + \beta_{ij} y_i) = \sum_{i=1}^{n} \alpha_{ij} + \sum_{i=1}^{n} \beta_{ij} y_i \qquad (5.3)$$

is not constant on $\{y_1, \ldots, y_n | \sum_{i=1}^{n} y_i = Y\}$ and so cannot equal $\alpha_j + \beta_j Y$. Observe that the main problem is that the households have 'non-identical reaction patterns' ($\beta_{ij} \neq \beta_{i'j}$ for some i and i'), so that the level of aggregate demand for good j depends on the way aggregate income is divided among the different individuals.

More generally, the aggregation problem can be presented in the following way. Suppose that we are interested in a certain aspect (variable) of the behaviour of individuals and that for each individual i there is some (unknown) relationship that specifies the determinants of this variable. The set of individual relationships (functions) can be written as:

$$y_i = f_i(x_{i1}, \ldots, x_{im}), \qquad i = 1, \ldots, n, \qquad (5.4)$$

where y_i is the independent variable of interest;

x_{ij} is the j'th explanatory variable for y_i.

Consider further some kind of aggregate relationship (function)

$$Y = F(X_1, \ldots, X_m) \qquad (5.5)$$

and some aggregating functions

$$Y = G(y_1, \ldots, y_n) \text{ and } X_j = g_j(x_{1j}, \ldots, x_{nj}), j = 1, \ldots, m. \qquad (5.6)$$

From (5.4)–(5.6) it follows that there are two ways to calculate Y on the basis of all x_{ij}, $i = 1, \ldots, n$ and $j = 1, \ldots, m$. First,

$$Y = G(f_1(x_{11}, \ldots, x_{1m}), \ldots, f_n(x_{n1}, \ldots, x_{nm})) \qquad (5.7)$$
$$= G'(x_{11}, \ldots, x_{1m}, \ldots, x_{n1}, \ldots, x_{nm})$$

and second,

$$Y = F(g_1(x_{11}, \ldots, x_{n1}), \ldots, g_m(x_{1m}, \ldots, x_{nm})) \qquad (5.8)$$
$$= F'(x_{11}, \ldots, x_{n1}, \ldots, x_{1m}, \ldots, x_{nm}).$$

The relations between the different variables and relationships are illustrated in figure 5.1.

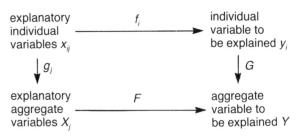

Figure 5.1 Relations between the diverse variables

The functions G' and F' are called *atomistic aggregate functions*. The question is under what conditions (5.7) and (5.8) yield identical results. Two types of approaches to this question were suggested in the *Econometrica* debate of the late forties. Klein (1946a), (1946b) and Nataf (1948) proposed to look for restrictions on the form of the functions f_i, G, g_j and F. May (1946), (1947) and Pu (1946), on the other hand, imposed certain restrictions on the values the variables x_{ij} may take. More recently, Van Daal and Merkies (1988) have advocated the Klein/Nataf approach, while Johansen (1972), Muysken (1979) and Schlicht (1985) favour the May/Pu approach. In the next two sections I go into the details of both approaches. The third section evaluates them in the light of the discussion in chapter 2.

Note that in the above formulation the households have non-identical 'stimuli', i.e. the level of a household's consumption demand is determined by its *own* income level. Yet it is sometimes assumed that a household's consumption demand is determined by variables that take the same values for all households. Suppose, for example, that instead of being determined by its own income level, a household's consumption demand is determined by the prices of the goods and that these prices are the same for all individual households. In this case, we have

$$c_{ij}^d = f_{ij}(p_1, \ldots, p_m), \qquad i = 1, \ldots, n \text{ and } j = 1, \ldots, m, \qquad (5.9)$$

where p_j is the price of good j. This equation can easily be aggregated by using (5.2):

$$C_j^d = \sum_{i=1}^{n} c_{ij}^d = \sum_{i=1}^{n} f_{ij}(p_1, \ldots, p_m), \qquad j = 1, \ldots, m. \qquad (5.10)$$

Therefore, in this case there is not really an aggregation problem:

aggregate relationships can easily be derived by aggregating individual relationships. There is, however, an empirical problem related to (5.10). Usually, in economic theory, equations like (5.1) and (5.9) are considered to result from utility-maximizing behaviour on the part of individual households. It is well known that a standard model in which individual agents maximize utility subject to a budget constraint imposes some restrictions on the form the system of equations (5.9) may take. The question of whether utility maximization also imposes some restrictions on the form of the aggregate equations (5.10) will be discussed in the fourth section.

In the first four sections we will examine some of the differences between individual and aggregate relationships. The following section gives a more complete account of the qualitative differences that may occur between the two types of relationships. The last section concludes with some general observations on the use of the notion of a representative agent as far as aggregation issues are concerned.

THE KLEIN/NATAF APPROACH

Above we mentioned that Klein (1946a) observed that some theorists in the thirties employed some relationships for the economy as a whole that were analogous to relationships usually supposed to hold only at the individual level. These theorists did not bother themselves with the conditions under which these aggregate relationships could be legitimately employed. It was Klein's intention to fill (partially) this gap. Thus, he studied the conditions that have to be satisfied in order to justify the use of this kind of reasoning by analogy.

In what follows it is assumed that all the functions involved are differentiable. If the variables x_{ij} are free to take any value, then a necessary condition for the individual relationships (5.4) to be aggregated to the aggregate relationship (5.5) is easily obtained by looking at equations (5.7) and (5.8). The impact on Y of a change in variable x_{ij} is, according to equation (5.7),

$$dY = \frac{\partial G}{\partial f_i} \frac{\partial f_i}{\partial x_{ij}} dx_{ij}.$$

According to equation (5.8) this impact is

$$dY = \frac{\partial F}{\partial g_j} \frac{\partial g_j}{\partial x_{ij}} dx_{ij}.$$

Since the variables x_{ij} are free to take any value, $(\partial G/\partial f_i)(\partial f_i/\partial x_{ij})$ must equal $(\partial F/\partial g_i)(\partial g_i/\partial x_{ij})$ for any $i = 1, \ldots, n$ and $j = 1, \ldots, m$.

Nataf (1948) proved the theorem that aggregation is feasible if and only if all functions are additively separable.[1] Proofs under different assumptions (continuous functions instead of differentiable ones, or monotonic functions) are provided by Gorman (1953) and Pokropp (1972).

Theorem 5.1 (Nataf 1948) Consider the functions (5.4)–(5.6) and assume that the first derivatives are non-zero. A necessary and sufficient condition for an aggregate relationship such as (5.5) to be derivable from some set of individual relationships as (5.4) and some aggregating functions as (5.6) is that the functions f_i, F, g_j, G and their composites F' and G' are additively separable.

Proof. A proof of this theorem can be found in, for example, Nataf (1948), Pokropp (1972) and van Daal and Merkies (1984).

The theorem states that aggregation is possible if and only if all the functions involved satisfy some severe restrictions. Note that additive separability of the functions f_i, G, g_j and F is not sufficient for aggregation to be feasible: the composites F' and G' have to be additively separable as well.

Equations (5.7) and (5.8) show that the aggregate variable Y can be calculated in two ways on the basis of all x_{ij}'s. This is also illustrated by figure 5.1. The function F' is based on g_j and F and the function G' is based on f_i and G. The theorem can then be reinterpreted as saying that aggregation is feasible if the functions G' and F' are also decomposable in 'the other way':[2]

$$
\begin{aligned}
G'(x_{11}, \ldots, x_{1m}, \ldots, x_{n1}, \ldots, x_{nm}) = \\
\mathscr{G}[\mathscr{g}_1(x_{11}, \ldots, x_{n1}), \ldots, \mathscr{g}_m(x_{1m}, \ldots, x_{nm})] \\
\\
F'(x_{11}, \ldots, x_{n1}, \ldots, x_{1m}, \ldots, x_{nm}) = \\
\mathscr{F}[\mathscr{f}_1(x_{11}, \ldots, x_{1m}), \ldots, \mathscr{f}_n(x_{n1}, \ldots, x_{nm})].
\end{aligned}
\tag{5.11}
$$

The theorem will be illustrated by means of the following two examples.

Example 5.1 **Linear Functions**

Suppose the individual relationships are given by $y_i = \alpha_{i0} + \Sigma_{j=1}^{m} \alpha_{ij} x_{ij}$ and the aggregating functions are given by $Y = \Sigma_{i=1}^{n} y_i$ and $X_j = \Sigma_{i=1}^{n} x_{ij}$. An example of this form has already been given in equations (5.1) and (5.2). Under these conditions does an aggregate functional relationship between Y and the X_j's exist? The answer is negative if $\alpha_{ij} \neq \alpha_{i'j}$ for some i and i' and $j \geq 1$, even though all the elementary functions are additively separable.

There are two conditions under which an aggregate functional relationship

76

can be obtained. First, $\alpha_{ij} = \alpha_j$ for all i and $j \geq 1$. This means that the impact of an individual explanatory variable x_{ij} on the individual variable of interest y_i is the same for all individuals. This is a severe restriction on the individual relationships. The aggregate functional relationship becomes $Y = \Sigma_{i=1}^{n} (\alpha_{i0} + \Sigma_{j=1}^{m} \alpha_j x_{ij}) = \alpha_0 + \Sigma_{j=1}^{m} \alpha_j \Sigma_{i=1}^{n} x_{ij} = \alpha_0 + \Sigma_{j=1}^{m} \alpha_j X_j$, where $\alpha_0 = \Sigma_{i=1}^{n} \alpha_{i0}$.

A second condition is obtained by adapting the aggregating formulae for all the X_j. For example, each of the aggregate explanatory variables X_j can be defined as a weighted average of the x_{ij}'s, where the weights are determined the α_{ij}'s: $X_j \equiv \Sigma_{i=1}^{n} (\alpha_{ij}/\alpha_j) x_{ij}$. In this case, the aggregate functional relationship is also $Y = \alpha_0 + \Sigma_{j=1}^{m} \alpha_j X_j$. Note that in this case it is difficult to give an interpretation to the α_j's. The value of the α_j's are simultaneously determined with the values of the aggregates X_j: for given x_{ij} and α_{ij}, the larger the value of X_j the smaller the value of α_j. This is different from the first case in which α_j measures the impact of x_{ij} on y_i for all i.

Example 5.2 Cobb–Douglas Functions

Suppose we have a set of individual functional relationships that is given by $y_i = \alpha_i \Pi_{j=1}^{m} (x_{ij})^{\alpha_j}$. By taking the logarithms of both sides one can see that this set of equations is additively separable. Note that if the aggregating functions are just summations, as in example 5.1, then an aggregate function does not exist. This fact reveals that the form of the aggregating functions cannot be independently chosen from the form of the individual relationships.

Instead, if the aggregating functions are some kind of products, e.g. $Y = \Pi_{i=1}^{n} y_i$ and $X_j = \Pi_{i=1}^{n} x_{ij}$, then an aggregate relationship exists and takes the form $Y = \Pi_{i=1}^{n} \alpha_i \Pi_{j=1}^{m} (x_{ij})^{\alpha_j} = \alpha \Pi_{j=1}^{m} (\Pi_{i=1}^{n} x_{ij})^{\alpha_j} = \alpha \Pi_{j=1}^{m} (X_j)^{\alpha_j}$, where $\alpha = \Pi_{i=1}^{n} \alpha_i$.

The second example demonstrates most pointedly that for aggregation to be feasible it may be necessary to employ aggregating functions that are void of any common sense if the individual explanatory variables x_{ij} are free to take any value. There are authors who have argued that the aggregating functions so obtained are 'monsters' that should not be used in economic analysis (see, e.g., Pu 1946). Some of these authors have proposed to restrict the values of the variables x_{ij} to a certain domain. It is to a discussion of these authors that I now turn.

THE MAY/PU APPROACH

I have noted that if the individual explanatory variables x_{ij} are free to take on any value, an aggregate relationship such as (5.5) can be regarded as the deductive consequence of some individual relationships and some aggregating functions *only if* the functions involved are of some specific form. From one point of view this may be no surprise. An aggregate functional relationship can only exist if the aggregate explanatory variables X_j contain all the information that is needed to explain the value of the aggregate variable of interest Y. This means that the way the individual explanatory variables x_{ij} are distributed may not affect the value of Y. It is clear that this can only be the case if some severe restrictions are satisfied.

As a reaction to Klein's (1946a) article, May (1946) and Pu (1946) argued that economic theory imposes restrictions on the values the x_{ij}'s may take. In other words, they argued that economic theory restricts the degree of freedom of the x_{ij}. May and Pu made their case by discussing the aggregation of individual production functions. Suppose that the individual production functions and aggregating functions are given by, respectively,

$$q_i = f_i(k_i, l_i), \qquad\qquad i = 1, \ldots, n, \qquad (5.12)$$

$$K \equiv \sum_{i=1}^{n} k_i \text{ and } L \equiv \sum_{i=1}^{n} l_i, \qquad\qquad (5.13)$$

where q_i, k_i and l_i are the output, the capital input and the labour input of firm i. In the theory of perfect competition all firms maximize profits subject to their individual production function. They take prices p, nominal wages w and nominal interest rates r as given. Individual profits π_i are given by $\pi_i = pq_i - rk_i - wl_i$. Assuming that the individual production functions are continuously differentiable and subject to decreasing returns to scale, the following necessary conditions for profit maximization can be obtained:

$$\frac{\partial q_i}{\partial l_i} = \frac{w}{p} \text{ and } \frac{\partial q_i}{\partial k_i} = \frac{r}{p}, \; i = 1, \ldots, n. \qquad (5.14)$$

The marginal productivity equations (5.14) determine the level of the individual production factors k_i and l_i for any level of q_i. There are $3n + 4$ variables, namely $(q_1, \ldots, q_n, k_1, \ldots, k_n, l_1, \ldots, l_n, K, L, w/p, r/p)$ and $3n + 2$ equations in (5.12)–(5.14). Under some regularity conditions the implicit function theorem can be applied so that q_i, k_i and l_i can be expressed in terms of K and L:

$$q_i = h_i^1(K, L), \; k_i = h_i^2(K, L) \text{ and } l_i = h_i^3(K, L), \qquad i = 1, \ldots, n. \quad (5.15)$$

Accordingly, an aggregate production function can be defined as $Q \equiv \sum_{i=1}^{n} q_i = \sum_{i=1}^{n} h_i^1(K, L) \equiv F(K, L)$.

If the degree of freedom is sufficiently restricted – as above by equation (5.14) – then it is always possible to define an aggregate function in the above way. The aggregate function thus defined depends on the model that determines the values of the individual components that make up the aggregate explanatory variables. In other words, the aggregate relationship is context dependent. If the values of the individual components change in a way that is inconsistent with the model that is supposed to determine them, then the aggregate function changes as well. In the production function case, the way the individual explanatory variables are distributed is determined by the marginal productivity equations (5.14). If these equations change, for example because the situation can no longer be described as one of perfect competition, then the aggregate production function changes as well.

THE TWO APPROACHES RECONSIDERED

In the previous two sections two approaches to the aggregation problem have been outlined: the first approach looks for conditions on *all* functional relationships involved, while the second approach looks for restrictions on the values of the individual explanatory variables. The latter approach employs functions of the form $x_{ij} = h_{ij}(X_j)$; see equations (5.15). In these equations values of the individual variables are expressed as functions of the values of the aggregate variables and the question is whether equations like (5.15) are allowed to play a role in an individualistic explanation of an aggregate relationship. A similar question has been discussed by Klein (1946b) and Nelson (1984).

Following the discussion on MI in chapter 2 I will argue here that a relation like (5.15) can be employed in an MI explanation. The definition of MI allows for the fact that decision making by individuals takes place in an institutional setting. We have assumed that this decision making results in an equation like (5.4) in which individual i takes the x_{ij}, $j = 1, \ldots, m$, as given. The question of why an aggregate relationship $Y = F(X_1, \ldots, X_m)$ exists (if indeed it does) can then be answered by saying that in an institutional environment in which the x_{ij}'s are determined according to $x_{ij} = h_{ij}(X_j)$ individuals decide to determine Y according to $Y = \Sigma y_i = \Sigma f_i(x_{i1}, \ldots, x_{im}) = \Sigma f_i(h_{i1}(X_1), \ldots, h_{im}(X_m)) = F(X_1, \ldots, X_m)$. The aggregate function is thus a combined result of the decision making of individuals and the institutional setting. Of course, one may wonder why an equation like $x_{ij} = h_{ij}(X_j)$ holds true, but this is a separate question that deserves a separate analysis. In the case of the aggregation of individual production functions treated in the previous section, a reductive explanation has been given of the functions $x_{ij} = h_{ij}(X_j)$; see equations (5.14) and (5.15). There, the functions took the form $k_i = h_i^2(K, L)$ and $l_i = h_i^3(K, L)$, and it was argued that these functions can be derived from the hypothesis that the individual firms maximize profits subject to their production function and given prices, wages and interest rates. Again, the explanation is a combined result of the decision making of individuals and the institutional setting of given prices, wages and interest rates.

The above remarks implicitly assume that the aggregate relationship is a behavioural relationship: it is the result of decisions made by individuals. However, the early literature on the aggregation problem primarily dealt with production functions. Individual production functions are often conceived of as purely technological functions that do not depend on the decisions made by the firms (see, e.g., Malinvaud 1972). If the May/Pu approach is adopted, then the *aggregate* production function is *not* a purely technological function. Instead, it also depends on the profit-maximizing behaviour of the firms. Klein holds this to be a major objection to the May/Pu approach. May (1947: 63) responds to this opinion by arguing that even the individual production functions depend upon both technological and non-technological facts. An example of a non-technological element of the production process is the organization of the production process. Whether the May/Pu approach is suited for the aggregation of production functions thus depends on how one interprets individual production functions. As this question falls outside the scope of the present enquiry, it will not be pursued any further.

A second point of difference between the two approaches concerns the way the aggregates should be constructed. We have seen that Pu rejects the 'distribution-free' approach, because the aggregating functions employed there are 'completely void of any economic significance' (Pu 1946: 299). In fact, Pu is of the opinion that 'natural' aggregating functions are usually sums. Klein (1946b) is not impressed by this criticism, stating

> It is true that the man in the street knows more about a sum than about many other types of aggregates, but in constructing scientific theory, we must look for useful results rather than things familiar to the layman. Any macroeconomic theory which will enable us to make people happier through an analysis of the interrelationships between aggregates of income, employment, output,

etc., is a good theory regardless of the specific form of the aggregates.

(Klein 1946b: 310)

Furthermore, Klein argues that 'in practice the correlation between these aggregates ... and the published ones will be so high that one set can be substituted for the other' (Klein 1946b: 311). In my opinion, Klein faces here an important difficulty with his own approach, for the collection of economic data is frequently not part of economic research. Applied economic research uses the data that are supplied by National Bureaux of Statistics. These Bureaux collect statistics in a way that generally is independent of the specific wishes of economists. As a result, applied work in economics employs these 'all-purpose' statistics and Klein hopes that the aggregates that are implied by his approach can be approximated by the published statistics. The problem I have with this view is that it is not clear why we should search for forms the aggregating functions have to satisfy if these complex aggregating functions are subsequently replaced by their published counterparts. In my opinion this replacement of one set of aggregating functions by another is only legitimate if there is knowledge that the size of the error one makes in doing so is not too large. This type of knowledge is not provided by the Klein/Nataf approach.[3] On this point, the May/Pu approach seems to approximate better the actual practice in applied work in which some 'naturally' defined aggregates are employed.

Finally, one issue frequently neglected (but see Nelson 1984) in the literature on aggregation should be emphasized. It is that the choice for one of the two approaches should primarily depend on the aim of the research and the kind of information one disposes of. Here, three possibilities are considered. First, Klein thought of his own research in the following terms: 'let us assume the theory of micro and macroeconomics and then construct aggregates which are consistent with the two theories'[4] (Klein 1946a: 94). This view is consistent with the idea that microeconomic theory is well established and that the aim of the research is to study the conditions that are implicitly made by macroeconomists who use models that are based on reasoning by analogy. Theorem 5.1 shows that reasoning by analogy is legitimate only if the relationships at the individual and the aggregate level are additively separable and if the aggregating functions are additively separable in a suitable way. Second, the Klein/Nataf approach is also the most suitable approach if an aggregate relationship has been observed and the aim of the research is to look for conditions under which this aggregate relationship can be regarded as resulting from some individual relationships and some aggregating functions. This line of reasoning would be very similar to the one discussed in chapter 2 in connection with the reduction of the IGL to the KTG and the reduction of Olson's hypothesis to expected utility theory. Here, the result of the explanation is predetermined. The fruitfulness of the exercise might then lie in suggesting conditions under which the aggregate relationship will hold true (see also chapter 4). Third, the May/Pu approach seems to be the most suitable of the two approaches if the aim of the research is to suggest a new (form of an) aggregate relationship. This approach is useful if one has some knowledge about the form of the individual relationships or if one wants to work out the aggregate implications of assuming certain individual relationships.

EMPIRICAL RESTRICTIONS ON AGGREGATE EXCESS DEMAND FUNCTIONS

In the previous sections I treated the case in which the variable to be explained *and* the explanatory variables have to be aggregated in order to arrive at an aggregate relationship. We have seen that in this case aggregation is only feasible under restrictive assumptions. The situation is totally reversed if the explanatory variables in the individual relationships are the same for every individual (see, e.g., equation (5.9)) so that only the variables to be explained have to be aggregated to arrive at an aggregate relationship. In this case, aggregation does not pose any mathematical problem (see, e.g., equation (5.10)), but some empirical problems arise. Especially, the question arises about what kind of restrictions on the aggregate relationships are imposed by economic theory in this case. This question has attracted attention in the context of aggregate excess demand functions in the Arrow–Debreu model (ADM) and it is to this literature that I will now turn briefly.

In the standard theory of consumer demand,[5] individual consumers are supposed to maximize utility subject to a budget constraint. Let there be m goods, indexed by $j = 1, \dots, m$, and n individual consumers, indexed by $i = 1, \dots, n$. Let us further assume that individual consumers possess a bundle of initial endowments, denoted by $\omega_i = (\omega_{i1}, \dots, \omega_{im})$ and that they derive utility from consuming goods: $U_i(x_i)$, where $x_i = (x_{i1}, \dots, x_{im})$ is the bundle of goods they consume and $U_i(\cdot)$ is the utility function of consumer i. The prices the individual consumers face are given by $p = (p_1, \dots, p_m)$. The consumers' problem can then be described as follows:

max $U_i(x_i)$

subject to $px_i \leq p\omega_i.$

The solution to this problem is the individual consumer's demand function, $x_i(p, y_i)$, where y_i denotes the value of i's initial endowments: $y_i = p\omega_i$. Individual excess demand functions are then given by $x_i(p, y_i) - \omega_i$. The aggregate excess demand functions are defined by $z(p) \equiv \sum_{i=1}^{n} x_i(p, y_i) - \omega_i$.[6] Under standard conditions, individual and aggregate excess demand functions are continuous and homogeneous of degree zero. Moreover, the sum of the values of individual excess demands is equal to zero. The same holds true for aggregate excess demand (this is known as Walras' law). The standard model of consumer demand imposes two additional restrictions on the form of the *individual* demand functions. These individual demand functions have to be such that the matrix of substitution effects is symmetric and negative semi-definite.[7] These two conditions can be used to test the applicability of the hypothesis of utility maximization subject to a budget constraint to a particular situation.

An important question is whether utility maximization subject to a budget constraint imposes similar restrictions on the shape of the *aggregate* excess demand functions. Among others, Sonnenschein (1972) and Debreu (1974) showed that the answer is negative: any set of continuous functions $z(p)$ that satisfies Walras' law and that is homogeneous of degree zero can be considered as a set of aggregate excess demand functions. The different proofs of this result employ some rather advanced topology on which I do not want to digress (for a good non-technical discussion, see Kirman 1989). The intuition may be grasped as follows. A utility function is a theoretical construct that is attributed to an individual agent by the economist. There is no empirical equivalent of this construct so that the theorist is not bound to a particular form of the utility function. Theoretical constructs are employed in all sciences and they are invoked in order to explain certain empirical regularities, in the hope that the context in which the theoretical constructs are employed is such that some useful restrictions on these empirical regularities are imposed. This is true, for example, for individual excess demand functions (see above). The difference between individual and aggregate excess demand functions is that in the individual case there is only 'one degree of freedom', while in the aggregate case the theorist is able to choose many different utility functions, one for each individual. Thus, the 'degree of freedom' is enlarged considerably and it is no surprise that economic theory imposes less restrictions on aggregate excess demand functions than on individual excess demand functions. In fact, the results by Sonnenschein and Debreu show that besides the three obvious restrictions mentioned above, utility maximization does not impose *any* restrictions on the shape of aggregate excess demand functions. Accordingly, the fruitfulness of the utility function as a theoretical construct for explaining aggregate excess demand functions can be doubted.

Recently, different authors have proposed some ways out of the dilemma. Grandmont (1987) proposes to restrict the distribution of preferences over individual agents. The idea is that although individual preferences are not identical they are not too dissimilar either. In the different proofs of the negative result referred to above, it may be necessary to assume that the distribution of preferences over individual agents is extremely unequal. If the distribution of preferences is restricted to a certain class, as Grandmont assumes, some further restrictions on the aggregate excess demand functions can be derived. The representative agent approach can be regarded as a rather extreme version of Grandmont's proposal: assuming that the preferences and the endowments of all individuals are identical is mathematically equivalent to the representative agent approach. In this case the 'aggregate' excess demand functions obey the same restrictions as individual excess demand functions. Hildenbrand (1983) proposes to restrict the distribution of income (endowments) to a certain class. Because Hildenbrand's approach results in a qualitative difference between the properties of individual and aggregate demand functions I will discuss his results in more detail in the next section.

ON THE DIFFERENCES BETWEEN INDIVIDUAL AND AGGREGATE RELATIONS: AGAINST REDUCTIONISM?

The 'reductionist' position of the present study holds that aggregate economic phenomena result from the interaction between individuals. Moreover, it is recommended that these phenomena are explained as such. In economics, this thesis is often held to imply another thesis, namely that individual and aggregate relationships are analogous. Schlicht (1985: 63), for example, attacks the reductionist view by arguing that analogies between individual and aggregate laws may be misleading. From the discussion in chapter 2 it will be clear that I agree with Schlicht to the extent that 'reasoning by analogy' may be unfounded (at least, the conditions under which it is legitimate should be carefully explored). Chapter 2 has discussed the reduction from the ideal gas law (IGL) to the kinetic theory of gases (KTG). Although IGL and KTG are quite dissimilar, the reduction of IGL to KTG turned out to be feasible under suitable conditions. The same holds true for the explanation of Olson's hypothesis in terms of individual maximization of subjective expected utility. The conditions used in the reduction can be interpreted as the 'hidden assumptions' under which the ideal aggregate relationships hold. So, there need not be any contradiction between the thesis that reasoning by analogy is misleading and the reductionist presumption.

In order to illustrate the above points, this section provides three examples in which there is a qualitative difference between individual and aggregate relationships. Moreover, I will demonstrate that the examples do not contradict the reductionist presumption that underlies this book by showing that the differences between individual and aggregate relationships are explained in the examples along the lines of the reduction scheme.

The impact of averaging: Hildenbrand on the 'law of demand'

The 'law of demand' poses that the demand (individual and aggregate) for a good decreases as its price increases. This 'law' holds true for many estimated demand curves. However, until recently there was no theoretical research explaining why this is so, for utility maximization under a budget constraint does not necessarily lead to decreasing individual demand curves. The standard textbook account decomposes the impact of a price change on individual demand into a substitution and an income effect using the Slutsky equation,

$$\frac{\partial x_{ij}(p, y_i)}{\partial p_j} = \frac{\partial g_{ij}(p, U_i)}{\partial p_j} - \frac{\partial x_{ij}(p, y_i)}{\partial y_i} x_{ij},$$

where the first term on the right hand side measures the substitution effect and the second term measures the income effect. It is well known that the income effect can be positive and large enough to dominate the negative substitution effect. In this case demand would be positively related to price. The sign of the 'aggregate' income effect can also be positive and large enough to assure that aggregate demand is positively related to price.

Hildenbrand (1983) provides a condition on the income distribution

85

such that the average income effect is negative. This, together with the negativity of the substitution effect, implies that aggregate demand curves are decreasing in their own price. Hildenbrand (1983) assumes that all the individuals in a group have identical preferences, but different income levels. In this case the income effect may be positive for some individuals (read: for some values of income), while for others it will be negative. In the example discussed below the incomes of individuals are assumed to be distributed uniformly over the interval [0, 1]. In the general case, Hildenbrand (1983) employs the assumption that the income distribution is independent of the price system and has a density function which is decreasing on [0, ∞). The income effect corresponding to a price change of commodity j of an individual with income y is

$$ - \frac{\partial x_j(p,y)}{\partial y} \, x_i(p,y). $$

Note that since all individuals are assumed to have identical preferences the subscript i is dropped. The average income effect is then given by

$$ - \int_0^1 \frac{\partial x_j(p,y)}{\partial y} x_j(p,y) dy = - \tfrac{1}{2} \int_0^1 \frac{\partial}{\partial y} x_j^2(p,y) dy $$

$$ = - \tfrac{1}{2}(x_j^2(p,1) - x_j^2(p,0)) $$

$$ = - \tfrac{1}{2} x_j^2(p,1) \le 0. $$

The aggregate (average) demand function for commodity $j, \mathscr{Z}_j$, is defined by

$$ \mathscr{Z}_j(p) \equiv \int_0^1 x_j(p,y) dy, \qquad j = 1, \ldots, m. $$

From the Slutsky equation and the fact that the substitution effect is negative it follows that

$$ \frac{\partial x_j(p,y)}{\partial p_j} < - \frac{\partial x_j(p,y)}{\partial y} x_j(p,y). $$

Hence,

$$ \frac{\partial}{\partial p_j} \mathscr{Z}_j(p) = \int_0^1 \frac{\partial}{\partial p_j} x_j(p,y) dy < - \int_0^1 \frac{\partial x_j(p,y)}{\partial y} x_j(p,y) dy, $$

$$ j = 1, \ldots, m. $$

From the above we know that the last term is not larger than zero. Accordingly, the aggregate demand functions are decreasing in their own price, if all individuals have identical preferences and the density of the income distribution is uniform on [0, 1], or more generally decreasing on [0, ∞). This holds true even if the individual demand functions are not decreasing in their own price. So, Hildenbrand's example shows that there may be a qualitative difference between individual and aggregate demand functions.

The analysis can be captured in terms of the reduction scheme. In the application step, the theory of utility maximization is applied to individual agents who have identical preferences, leading to individual demand functions of the form $x_j(p, y)$. Then, these individual demand functions are aggregated to arrive at aggregate demand functions of the form $\mathscr{Z}_j(p)$. The assumption (see H_2 in the reduction scheme) that is used in this aggregation step is that the density of the income distribution is decreasing.

Hildenbrand's analysis suggests that downward-sloping demand curves are more likely to be observed at the aggregate than at the individual level. There is, however, a severe limitation to his analysis. It is that individual preferences are not identical and also that the density function of the income distribution in most countries is not decreasing for all income levels (especially, at low income levels, estimated income distributions seem to be increasing; see also chapter 6). So, if asked why aggregate demand curves are downward sloping, one cannot point at Hildenbrand's analysis and say that it is because the income distribution is decreasing when it is known that it actually is *not* decreasing. Nevertheless, I think Hildenbrand's result is interesting, because it provides some conceptual clues on how to account for differences between individual and aggregate demand functions. It should be seen as a starting point for further research that should come up with a better explanation for the observation that aggregate demand curves usually are downward sloping. Such analyses might also provide hints of an explanation when demand curves are upward sloping (compare chapter 4).

The system effect: the paradox of thrift

A second source of differences between individual and aggregate relations lies in what might be called a system effect. By means of illustration this section discusses the paradox of thrift, a paradox that goes back to Keynes (1936) at least. The paradox is that although an individual agent may succeed in increasing his or her savings if he or she wants to do so, it cannot be the case that all individuals succeed in increasing their savings even if they want to do so. The exposition below crucially depends on the way the model is closed (see equation 5.16). The model should only be taken as an illustration of the general argument made in this section.

The paradox arises, for example, in the following simple model. Suppose there are n individuals, indexed by $i = 1, \ldots, n$, and there is just one good. The individuals' savings are proportionally related to their income levels, i.e.

$$S_i = s_i y_i$$

where S_i is total savings by individual i, s_i the proportion of savings to income for individual i and y_i individual i's income. Furthermore, there is an income distribution that functionally relates individual income to aggregate income, i.e. $y_i = h_i(Y)$, where Y denotes aggregate income. The functions $h_i(\cdot)$ are supposed to be increasing in Y. In the economic system, total savings have to be equal to investment so that

$$\Sigma_{i=1}^{n} s_i y_i = I \tag{5.16}$$

where I denotes investment. Investment is treated as an exogenous variable and this is the main reason why the paradox arises. It is easy to see that the individuals cannot simultaneously increase their total savings even if they want to do so. This is because the total savings equals investment equation (5.16) and the fact that investment is given exogenously.

The situation is qualitatively different if only one of the individuals wants to increase personal savings. Suppose individual 1's propensity to save increases, i.e. s_1 increases. The impact of this change in behaviour can be calculated as follows. First, equation (5.16) implicitly defines Y as a function of I and all the s_i's:

$$Y = \phi(I, s_1, \ldots, s_n).$$

It is easily seen that $\partial \phi / \partial I > 0$ and $\partial \phi / \partial s_i < 0$. Second, savings of individual i can be written as $s_i h_i(Y) = s_i h_i(\phi(I, s_1, \ldots, s_n))$. For all $i \neq 1$, this expression is decreasing in s_1. This means that an increase in the propensity to save by individual 1 leads to a decrease in savings of all other individuals. Finally, because of equation (5.16) and the observation just made, savings of individual 1 must be increasing due to the increase in s_1.

In words: an increase in the propensity to save has repercussions on aggregate and (thus) individual income. This is a property of the economic system described in (5.16). For an individual, these repercussion effects are not strong enough to offset the increased propensity to save: the amount saved (the product of the increased propensity to save and income) will increase in the case of an increased propensity to save. For the economy as a whole the repercussions on income are so strong that the total amount saved remains the same in the case of an increased propensity to save.

Clearly, this result does not contrast with the way I have interpreted the concept of reductionism, because the difference in impact between the increased propensity of one individual and the increased propensity of all the individuals is explained in terms of the interaction of the behaviour of individuals in a social setting. In this case the social setting is given by equation (5.16). As a matter of fact, the result can easily be captured in terms of the reduction scheme, because it has to be borne in mind that the application step of utility maximization is not presented in the exposition above (see also Bryant 1987 and Garretsen and Jenssen 1989).

Estimation effects: the relation between individual and aggregate parameters[8]

As a final example of the difference between individual and aggregate relationships, let us examine the relation between the estimators of the parameters of the two types of relationships. Consider a linear individual relationship in matrix taking the following form:

$$y_i = x_i \beta_i + \varepsilon_i, \qquad i = 1, \ldots, n, \qquad (5.17)$$

where $y_i = (y_{i1}, \ldots, y_{iT})'$ is a vector of values of the dependent variable;
   $x_i = $ a $T \times K$ matrix of K explanatory variables for y_i;
   $\beta_i = (\beta_{1i}, \ldots, \beta_{ki})'$ is a k-dimensional vector of parameters;
   ε_i is a vector of disturbance terms.

A column of the matrix x_i will be denoted by $x_{ik}, k = 1, \ldots, K$. The β_i's are estimated by means of econometric techniques, using the assumption that the disturbance term of equation (5.17) follows a distribution with zero mean: $E\varepsilon_i = 0$.

The corresponding aggregate relationship is

$$Y = X\alpha + \varepsilon, \tag{5.18}$$

where $Y = \Sigma_{i=1}^{n} y_i$;

X = a $T \times K$ matrix of K explanatory variables for Y;

$\alpha = (\alpha_1, \ldots, \alpha_k)$ is a vector of parameters;

ε is a disturbance term.

A column of the matrix X will be denoted by X_k. The columns X_k are defined by $X_k = \Sigma_{i=1}^{n} x_{ik}$ if $x_{ik} \neq x_{jk}$ for some i and j; and $X_k = (1/n)\Sigma_{i=1}^{n} x_{ik}$ if $x_{ik} = x_{jk}$ for all i and j. This definition is chosen in order to account for cases in which the x_i's have some columns in common. For example, the k'th explanatory variable may be the price level, which is the same for all individuals. In such cases, the variable entering the aggregate relationship is identical to (and not the sum of) the variables that enter the individual relationships.

Here, the relation between the parameters of the individual and aggregate relationships and their generalized least squares estimators will be considered. The generalized least squares estimator of the K-dimensional vector α is

$$a = (X'\Omega X)^{-1}X'\Omega Y, \tag{5.19}$$

for some positive definite matrix Ω. a is an unbiased estimator of α if and only if $\beta_i = \alpha$ for all $i = 1, \ldots, n$. This can be seen by noting that a is an unbiased estimator of α if and only if $E\varepsilon = 0$ and that $E\varepsilon = EY - EX\alpha = \Sigma_{i=1}^{n} Ey_i - (\Sigma_{i=1}^{n} x_i)\alpha = \Sigma_{i=1}^{n} x_i\beta_i - (\Sigma_{i=1}^{n} x_i)\alpha$.[9] As this last expression has to be equal to zero for all possible values of x_i, β_i has to be equal to α for all i. Thus, a is an unbiased estimator if and only if all the individual vectors of parameters are equal to each other and to the vector of aggregate parameters.

Let us denote the k'th column of a matrix $\mathcal{W}^i$ by $\mathcal{W}^i_k$ and let us define $\mathcal{W}^i_k \equiv (X'\Omega X)^{-1}X'\Omega x_{ik}$ if $x_{ik} \neq x_{jk}$ for some i and j and $\mathcal{W}^i_k \equiv 1/n (X'\Omega X)^{-1}X'\Omega x_{ik}$ if $x_{ik} = x_{jk}$ for all i and j. In the last case $\mathcal{W}^i_k = \mathcal{W}^j_k$ for all i and j and the k'th column of $\mathcal{W}^i$ consists of zeros, except for the k'th element which equals $1/n$. The definition of the $\mathcal{W}^i_k$'s is chosen such that $\Sigma_{i=1}^{n} \mathcal{W}^i$ is equal to the identity matrix. Consider a typical element of the vector a, a_h. Using the definition of Y, equation (5.19) and the assumption that $E\varepsilon_i = 0$ gives

$$Ea_h = \Sigma_{k=1}^{K} \Sigma_{i=1}^{n} \mathcal{W}^i_{hk}\beta_{ki}, \qquad j = 1, \ldots, K. \tag{5.20}$$

This shows that in general the expected value of the estimator of the j'th parameter of the aggregate relationship depends not only on the corresponding parameters of the individual relationships but also on all the other parameters. Thus, the interpretation of the estimator of a parameter of an aggregate relationship is different from the interpretation of the estimator of the corresponding parameters of the individual relationships.

This conclusion has an important corollary with respect to the issue of prediction. Suppose that for all individuals the k'th explanatory variable increases by one unit (say, everyone's income increases by a dollar) and we are interested in the impact on the aggregate dependent variable. Using equation (5.17) and the fact that $Y = \Sigma \, y_i$ the increase in Y can be calculated as $\Sigma_{i=1}^{n} \beta_{ki}$, which equals $\bar{\beta}_k n$, where $\bar{\beta}_k$ is the average of the β_{ki}'s over i. Yet the impact on the aggregate dependent variable can also be calculated by using equation (5.18) and the fact that the increase in the j'th aggregate explanatory variable equals n. With this way the estimated impact would be equal to $a_k n$. In general, as $Ea_k \neq \bar{\beta}_k$ the two predictions differ.

The above results on the relation between individual and aggregate parameters are obtained by using the definition of the aggregate variables. The results can thus be interpreted in terms of the reduction scheme so that (again) the qualitative difference between (the interpretation of parameters of the) individual and aggregate relationships does not raise significant objections to the individualistic presumption of this book. I will illustrate the main results of this subsection with an example.

Example 5.3 The Case of Money Illusion

One of the main tests to investigate whether economic agents behave rationally is to see whether they suffer from money illusion. Money illusion arises if individual demand curves are not homogeneous of degree zero in prices and nominal income. For example, an individual is said to suffer from money illusion if her or his consumption behaviour changes when both income and the prices of all goods are doubled. The point of this example is that the aggregate relationship need not be homogeneous of degree zero even if the individual relationships are. Thus, a test using aggregate data to investigate whether individuals suffer from money illusion may be misleading.

Suppose agent i's consumption behaviour is described by the following relation:

$$c_i/P = \beta_{0i}(y_i/P)^{\beta_{1i}}, \qquad\qquad i = 1, \ldots, n,$$

where c_i is individual i's nominal consumption expenditure;
P is the price level;
y_i is individual i's nominal income.

It is easy to see that these individuals do not suffer from money illusion. The equation can be rewritten as

$$\log c_i = \log \beta_{0i} + \beta_{1i}\log y_i - \beta_{2i}\log P, \qquad i = 1, \ldots, n,$$

with $\beta_{1i} = \beta_{2i}$ for all i. If data for individual i are available the parameters of this equation can be estimated and one can test whether or not β_{1i} indeed equals β_{2i}. If not, individual i suffers from money illusion.

A corresponding aggregate relationship is

$$\log C = \log \alpha_0 + \alpha_1\log Y - \alpha_2\log P.$$

The question arises here as to whether individual agents suffer from money illusion if $\alpha_1 \neq \alpha_2$. As α_1 and α_2 are unknown, the analysis is carried out in terms of their estimators, a_1 and a_2. The question then becomes: Does $Ea_1 \neq Ea_2$ imply $\beta_{1i} \neq \beta_{2i}$ for at least one i? From the discussion of the general case we know that $Ea_j = \Sigma_{k=0}^{2} \Sigma_{i=1}^{n} \mathscr{W}_{jk}^{i}\beta_{ki}$, $j = 0,1,2$. Because the first and the third explanatory variable are the same for all individuals, the matrix $\mathscr{W}^{i}$ is of the following form:

$$\mathscr{W}^{i} = \begin{bmatrix} 1/n & \mathscr{W}_{01}^{i} & 0 \\ 0 & \mathscr{W}_{11}^{i} & 0 \\ 0 & \mathscr{W}_{21}^{i} & 1/n \end{bmatrix}$$

This means that $E(a_1 - a_2) = \Sigma_{i=1}^{n} \mathscr{W}_{11}^{i}\beta_{1i} - \Sigma_{i=1}^{n} \mathscr{W}_{21}^{i}\beta_{1i} - 1/n \Sigma_{i=1}^{n} \beta_{2i}$.

Using the assumption that individuals do not suffer from money illusion, i.e. $\beta_{1i} = \beta_{2i}$, the right hand side of this expression equals $\Sigma_{i=1}^{n} (\mathscr{W}_{11}^{i} - \mathscr{W}_{21}^{i} - 1/n)$ β_{1i}. Although the sum of the weights, $\Sigma_{i=1}^{n} (\mathscr{W}_{11}^{i} - \mathscr{W}_{21}^{i} - 1/n)$, is equal to zero (note that $\Sigma_{i=1}^{n} \mathscr{W}^{i}$ is the identity matrix), the whole expression equals zero only if β_{1i} (hence, β_{2i}) is the same for all individuals. This means that $\beta_{1i} = \beta_{2i}$ does not imply that $Ea_1 = Ea_2$. Therefore, absence of money illusion at the individual level does not imply absence of money illusion at the aggregate level. One can conclude that testing the 'rationality' of individuals by investigating whether an aggregate demand equation is subject to money illusion may be quite misleading.

AGGREGATE RELATIONS AND THE REPRESENTATIVE AGENT

Above we have seen that the results of research on the aggregation problem are largely negative. Aggregation is considered to be feasible only if the functions involved are of a rather specific form (the first section) or if the values of the individual explanatory variables are such that they obey some particular distribution (the second section). In the light of these negative results, it is not surprising to see that many authors simply sidestep the aggregation problem by using representative agent models. In the previous section I have discussed results that show why representative agent models may be quite misleading: in general, aggregate relationships are qualitatively different from individual relationships. The fourth section on 'empirical restrictions' suggests that employing the notion of a representative agent gives more restrictions on aggregate excess demand functions than could be obtained by aggregating individual excess demand functions. These extra restrictions are not legitimately employed if demand behaviour differs significantly from one individual to another. So, representative agent models seem to get results at the expense of a proper individualistic foundation. If these results are corroborated in applications, one might argue that the idealizations made are justified in that particular case. One should, however, always carefully check whether the idealizations are good approximations in the case of prediction and policy advice.

Relatively recently, Schlicht (1985) has argued that any aggregate analysis is just one of the many examples in economic research in which a *ceteris paribus* clause is applied. He postulates that aggregate relationships can be isolated from the individual relationships by considering (in line with the May/Pu approach) a particular distribution of the aggregate explanatory variables as a sufficient condition for the analysis to apply. These conditions are subsumed in a *ceteris paribus* clause. He subsequently argues that the use of aggregate models in economic applications is questionable only in so far as any analysis that uses *ceteris paribus* clauses is questionable. I agree to a large extent with these remarks; nevertheless, I think this view is not incompatible with the view of MI put forward in chapter 2. In applying models that use *ceteris paribus* clauses, it is important to know exactly what is subsumed under the clause. This is no less different for aggregate relationships: one has to know under what conditions they can legitimately be used. In other words, aggregate relations (at least the ones that we know) do not hold unconditionally. Usually, they are idealized descriptions of the world around us. An attempt to reduce an aggregate relationship is one of the ways to uncover (some of) the hidden conditions (see also chapter 2). The two approaches to the aggregation problem provide two different kinds of conditions under which deterministic aggregate relations can be fruitfully employed. The fact that these conditions are very restrictive indicates that in general we cannot expect deterministic aggregate relations to be stable over time.

6

ON THE PROBABILITY
DISTRIBUTION OF
AGGREGATE DEMAND

In the previous chapter I discussed the aggregation problem at some length. The problem as discussed in the first two sections has been called one of 'consistent aggregation' by Green (1964), among others. He says that aggregation is consistent 'when the use of information more detailed than that contained in the aggregates would make no difference to the results of the analysis of the problem at hand' (Green 1964: 3). This terminology is not used above, because I think it is confusing. Aggregate variables contain less information than individual variables do. It is obvious that in general the use of more detailed information yields more determinate predictions than the use of less information. In other words, it is not surprising that aggregate variables contain enough information to yield determinate predictions only when some restrictive conditions hold true. This suggests another way of looking at the aggregation problem, a way that goes back to Nataf (1948).

Nataf (1948: 233–4) formulates the aggregation problem as the problem of investigating the conditions the individual relationships and the aggregating functions have to fulfil in order for a functional relationship between the aggregates to exist. For Nataf, it was clear that, in general, functional relationships between aggregates do *not* exist. The non-existence of an aggregate relationship can be easily illustrated by looking back at equations (5.1)–(5.3). On the basis of knowledge of the individual incomes, the individual relationships (5.1) and the aggregating functions (5.2) the value of the aggregate demand for good j can be determined. In general, the value of aggregate demand for good j can*not* be predicted on the basis of knowledge of *aggregate* income only. For any given level of aggregate income the distribution of individual income over the different agents is also an important determinant of aggregate demand as long as the propensities to consume are different across agents.

In the light of the discussion in chapters 2 and 4 we can argue that it is not surprising that restrictive assumptions have to be invoked in order to derive an aggregate relationship. There, we have argued that aggregate relationships like the ideal gas law and Olson's hypothesis only hold true under ideal circumstances. The same is true for functional aggregate relationships in economics like the relation between aggregate consumption demand and aggregate income. The restrictive assumptions that have to be fulfilled in order to solve the aggregation problem can be regarded as the conditions under which a functional aggregate relationship can be justified. In the present chapter I will investigate what kind of results can be obtained if those restrictive conditions do not hold. It will be shown that a probabilistic aggregate relationship can be derived from a set of functional (or, deterministic) individual relationships and some aggregating functions. I am of the opinion that this is also a form of consistent aggregation, although it is not the kind of consistent aggregation Green (1964) had in mind.

Another way to look at the results in the present chapter is the following. In the previous chapter I discussed three ways in which aggregate relationships may qualitatively differ from individual relationships. This present chapter points at another kind of qualitative difference between individual and aggregate demand functions. It is that aggregate relationships may be of a probabilistic variety even if the individual relationships are of a deterministic kind. In a subsection in chapter 5 we saw that Hildenbrand (1983) arrives at *deterministic* aggregate demand functions. There are two assumptions that are crucial in this respect. First, he assumes that all individuals have identical preferences, implying in this context that the way individual incomes are distributed does not affect the level of aggregate demand. Second, the income distribution is regarded as a continuous theoretical distribution with a continuum of individuals. In the present chapter, I show that aggregate demand can be described as a probability function conditional upon mean (or, aggregate) income in situations in which individual preferences differ from each other. Moreover, I discuss some properties of the conditional distribution of aggregate demand. Among other things, it is shown that the expected value of aggregate demand is increasing (decreasing) in mean income if individual demand is increasing (decreasing) in individual income for all individuals. In this respect the behaviour of the *expected value* of aggregate demand is qualitatively similar to individual demand behaviour.

The results of this part of the chapter can be expressed in terms of the reduction scheme. It is standard to show that individual demand functions can be derived from the hypothesis of utility maximization. This application step is suppressed (but implicitly assumed to be present) in the first section, where I discuss the properties the individual demand functions are assumed to satisfy. In the next section the individual demand functions are aggregated by means of the statistical auxiliary assumption that the incomes of individuals are distributed according to a distribution which is supposed to satisfy a certain condition. The assumption used in this aggregation step can be compared with the statistical assumption made in the reduction of the IGL (see chapter 2). The last section provides a discussion of the results obtained in this chapter. The proof of the main theorem is presented in the appendix.

INDIVIDUAL DEMAND

Consider an economy with m goods and n consumers and a system of individual demand functions of the form

$$x_{ij} = x_{ij}(p,y_i), \qquad i = 1, \ldots, n \text{ and } j = 1, \ldots, m,$$

where x_{ij} is the demand for good j by individual i, $p = (p_1, \ldots, p_m)$ is a price vector and y_i is total expenditure (income) of individual i. We focus on the impact of changes in aggregate (mean) income on the demand for *one* good. Therefore, the subscript j and the argument p in the demand functions will be suppressed in what follows.

In general, x_i may be an increasing (non-inferior good) as well as a decreasing (inferior good) function in income. To keep the subsequent analysis tractable the following assumption is introduced.

Assumption 6.1 For all individuals, $x_i(y_i)$ is either an increasing or a decreasing function on the whole domain of y_i.

The fact that individual preferences may differ is reflected in the subscript i in the demand function (compare Hildenbrand's analysis described in chapter 5).

THE DISTRIBUTION OF AGGREGATE DEMAND

In chapter 2, the notion of an aggregate relation was introduced as a relation between aggregate variables only. If individual demand functions differ and there is no functional relationship between individual incomes and mean income,[1] aggregate income does not contain sufficient information to determine aggregate demand exactly. In this case a deterministic relation between aggregate income and aggregate demand does not exist.

Here, I will use the fact that the incomes of individuals follow a known distribution. For simplicity only, I assume that the income distribution is continuous[2] and conditional on mean income μ and a vector of other parameters τ. This distribution will be written as $f_{y_1,\ldots,y_n}(y_1,\ldots,y_n \mid \mu,\tau)$. Since the analysis concentrates on the effect of changes in mean income, τ is suppressed throughout the chapter. The domain of the income distribution is $\mathbb{R}_+^n$.

It has been argued above that as individual demand functions generally differ from each other, one will not expect to find a *deterministic* function relating aggregate demand x and mean income μ. In general, x follows a conditional distribution function upon μ. If the good is non-inferior the conditional distribution of aggregate demand can be written as follows:

$$F_x(\bar{x} \mid \mu) = P\{\Sigma_{i=1}^n x_i \leq \bar{x} \mid \mu\} = P\{\Sigma_{i=1}^n x_i(y_i) \leq \bar{x} \mid \mu\} =$$

$$P\{x_n(y_n) \leq \bar{x}, \; x_{n-1}(y_{n-1}) \leq \bar{x} - x_n, \; \ldots , \; x_1(y_1) \leq$$

$$\bar{x} - \Sigma_{i=2}^n x_i \mid \mu\} =$$

$$P\{y_n \leq x_n^{-1}(\bar{x}), \; y_{n-1} \leq x_{n-1}^{-1}(\bar{x} - x_n), \; \ldots , \; y_1 \leq$$

$$x_1^{-1}(\bar{x} - \Sigma_{i=2}^n x_i) \mid \mu\} =$$

$$\int_0^{x_n^{-1}(\bar{x})} \int_0^{x_{n-1}^{-1}(\bar{x}-x_n(y_n))} \cdots \int_0^{x_1^{-1}(\bar{x} - \sum_{i=2}^n x_i(y_i))} f_{y_1,\ldots,y_n}(y_1, \cdots, y_n \mid \mu)$$

$$dy_1 \ldots dy_n.$$

In the case of an inferior good,

$$F_x(\bar{x} \mid \mu) =$$

$$\int_{x_n^{-1}(\bar{x})}^\infty \int_{x_{n-1}^{-1}(\bar{x}-x_n(y_n))}^\infty \cdots \int_{x_1^{-1}(\bar{x} - \sum_{i=2}^n x_i(y_i))}^\infty f_{y_1,\ldots,y_n}(y_1, \cdots, y_n \mid \mu)$$

$$dy_1 \ldots dy_n.$$

This result shows that aggregate demand follows a probability distribution that is conditional on mean income, even if individual demand is a deterministic function of individual income.[3]

Next, I will discuss some properties of the distribution of aggregate demand. Following Stoker (1984) I assume that the income of individuals is a random sample from the continuous income distribution. Accordingly, $f_{y_1,\ldots,y_n}(y_1,\ldots,y_n|\mu) = f(y_1|\mu) \cdot \ldots \cdot f(y_n|\mu)$.

The concept of a stochastical ordering will prove to be useful in the present context. A family of cumulative distribution functions is said to be *stochastically increasing* if

$$\theta < \theta' \Rightarrow F(x|\theta) \geq F(x|\theta').$$

If X (respectively X') has distribution $F(\cdot | \theta)$ (respectively $F(\cdot | \theta')$), X' tends to have larger values than X and is said to be *stochastically larger* than X: $X \leq^{st} X'$. The marginal income distribution $F(y|\mu)$ and its density $f(y|\mu)$ are required to fulfil the following condition.

Assumption 6.2 (*i*) The marginal income distributions $F(y|\mu)$ are stochastically increasing, i.e. $\mu < \mu' \Rightarrow F(y|\mu) \geq F(y|\mu')$;
(*ii*) for every pair μ and μ' ($\mu \neq \mu'$) there is only one income level $\tilde{y} > 0$ such that $f(\tilde{y}|\mu) = f(\tilde{y}|\mu')$.

The assumption can be illustrated by the following two figures. At the same time, figure 6.1 also illustrates the notion of stochastical ordering.

There are many distribution functions that satisfy this assumption. In empirical research on the income distribution, lognormal and Pareto

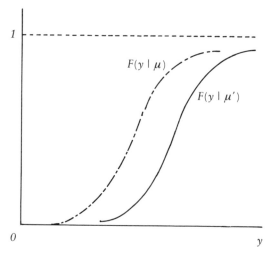

Figure 6.1 The marginal income distribution is stochastically increasing (assumption 6.2(*i*))

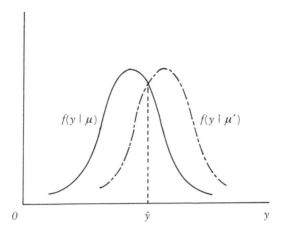

Figure 6.2 Densities of the marginal income distributions cut only once
(assumption 6.2(*ii*))

distributions (or a combination of them) are often used. The lognormal distribution gives a fairly accurate description of the income distribution at lower income levels, but it underscores the number of individuals with high incomes. The Pareto distribution, on the other hand, gives a good account of the income distribution at higher income levels, but cannot account for the positive slope of observed density functions at low income levels (see, also, Lydall 1968: 12–42). The Pareto and the lognormal distribution satisfy the two requirements of assumption 6.2. Hildenbrand's analysis, described in the previous chapter, holds true if the Pareto distribution is a good description of the actual income distribution, because the density function of the Pareto distribution is decreasing for all levels of income.

Theorem 6.1 If assumptions 6.1 and 6.2 hold and if the good is non-inferior for all individuals, then[4]
(*i*) $E(x|\mu)$ is increasing in μ, i.e. $\mu < \mu' \Rightarrow E(x|\mu) < E(x|\mu')$.
(*ii*) $F_x(\cdot|\mu)$ is stochastically increasing, i.e. $\mu < \mu' \Rightarrow F(x|\mu) \geq F(x|\mu')$.

The proof of the theorem appears in the appendix to this chapter. The intuition behind the theorem is the following. The second part says that if we compare, say, two countries which have the same shape of income distribution but different mean income, then aggregate demand for a non-inferior good tends to be larger in the country with the largest mean income. The first part then says that the expected value of the aggregate demand is larger in the country with the largest mean income.

DISCUSSION AND CONCLUSION

The results obtained in this chapter can be interpreted in the light of the discussion of chapter 2. There we saw that economics is not the only science in which certain phenomena can be described at different levels of aggregation. In his famous book *Gödel, Escher, Bach*, Hoffstadter (1979) discusses the trade-off in physiology/psychology between determinism and what he calls 'chunking', i.e. describing a system at a high level of aggregation. He argues that

> there is, however, perhaps one significant negative feature of a chunked model: it usually does not have exact predictive power. That is, we save ourselves of the impossible task of seeing people as collections of quarks (or whatever may be the lowest level) by using chunked models; but of course such models only give us probabilistic estimates of how other people feel, will react to what we say or do, and so on. In short, in using chunked high-level models, we sacrifice determinism for simplicity.
>
> Hoffstadter (1979: 306)

The attempt to make aggregation feasible by looking for probabilistic relations at the aggregate level is in line with the above observation by Hoffstadter.

An objection to the above analysis is possible, however: namely, that it is *not* the difference between individuals, but instead the assumption that individual incomes follow an income distribution that accounts for the probabilistic nature of aggregate demand. More precisely, the objection is that as the analysis is in terms of a *finite* sample from a continuous income distribution, aggregate demand is a probability function *by construction* and not because individual preferences differ. In the previous chapter we saw that Hildenbrand (1983) obtains a *deterministic* aggregate demand function by assuming the existence of a *continuum* of individuals with *identical* preferences. The argument put forward in this chapter would have been stronger if it had used a continuum of individuals with different preferences. To my knowledge this case has not been studied. It is clear, however, that if differences between individual preferences are taken seriously aggregate demand cannot be of a deterministic form.

Throughout this part of the chapter I assumed that income distributions are continuous only for ease of exposition. The same analysis can be applied to discrete income distributions provided that assumption 6.2(ii) is replaced by a discrete counterpart. In this case it is easily illustrated that the assumption that individual incomes are distributed according to some income distribution by itself is *not* sufficient for aggregate demand to be of a probabilistic form. Individual demand functions have to differ from each other as well. In my opinion, this means that the difference between individual preferences, and not the income distribution as such, accounts for the probabilistic nature of aggregate demand. The following hypothetical example illustrates this point.

Example 6.1 **Probabilistic and Deterministic Forms of Aggregate Demand: The Case of a Discrete Income Distribution**

Suppose the economy consists of only two individuals and that the income distribution takes on the following form:

$$P(y_1 = \alpha\mu;\ y_2 = \beta\mu) = 1 - P(y_1 = \beta\mu;\ y_2 = \alpha\mu) = \rho,$$

$$0 < \rho < 1,$$

where α, β and ρ are parameters with $(\alpha+\beta)/2=\mu$. First, consider a case where the demand curves of the two individuals are identical, i.e. $x_i = x(y_i)$, $i = 1,2$. Individual i demands either $x(\alpha\mu)$ or $x(\beta\mu)$, but if, say, individual 1 demands $x(\alpha\mu)$ units then individual 2 demands $x(\beta\mu)$ and vice versa. Thus, aggregate demand x is always equal to $x(\alpha\mu)+x(\beta\mu)$. This illustrates the point that if individual demand functions are identical, the aggregate demand function is of a deterministic form.

Second, consider the case in which the individual demand curves differ, i.e. $x_i = x_i(y_i)$, $i = 1,2$. In this case,

$$x = \begin{cases} x_1(\alpha\mu) + x_2(\beta\mu) & \text{with probability } \rho \\ x_1(\beta\mu) + x_2(\alpha\mu) & \text{with probability } 1-\rho. \end{cases}$$

This is an aggregate relationship of a probabilistic form. The probabilistic nature is due to the fact that the individual demand curves differ, because this is the only difference between the two cases considered.

The example can easily be generalized to n individuals.

In an interesting article, Henocq and Kempf (1984) also show that an aggregate relationship may be of a probabilistic type even if the corresponding individual relationship is of a deterministic type. The purpose of their analysis is, however, to show that the probabilistic component is not that important after all. Basically, they prove that the probabilistic term in the aggregate relationship between the average demand per consumer and average income vanishes if the number of individuals tends to infinity and if the sequence of functions $(1/n) \sum_{i=1}^{n} x_i(y_i)$ converges uniformly to a linear function. They prove their result by applying the law of large numbers. Their results can be interpreted as saying that one is justified in suppressing the probabilistic term of an aggregate relation if the number of individuals is large and provided that the conditions about linearity hold. Although this is not demonstrated formally, the analysis in this chapter can be interpreted as saying that the probabilistic term does *not* vanish if the average of the individual relationships does not converge to a linear function.

The present chapter might then also be considered as providing an alternative justification for the probabilistic approach to economics that is at the heart of econometrics. Most observed events in economics are outcomes of some kind of aggregation. In the previous chapter we saw that distribution effects can, in some very special cases only, be incorporated in deterministic relations between aggregate data. In this chapter, we have seen that if those conditions are not met aggregating deterministic individual demand functions yield probabilistic aggregate demand functions.

The results of this chapter are obtained by using the idea that the income distribution is relatively stable and satisfies assumption 6.2. This assumption seems to conform with much of the empirical research that has been done on income distributions (see, e.g., Lydall 1968). Assumption 6.2 has not been derived from a theory about the interaction of rational decision makers. As argued in chapter 2, assumptions that are not derived from individual decisions may be invoked in an MI explanation. Of course, it would be interesting to see whether the assumption on the income distribution itself could be explained by a theory of rationally behaving individuals.[5] This issue would, however, take us too far away from our present enquiry.

APPENDIX

In this appendix I will prove theorem 6.1. I only prove the second part of the theorem, because (i) is implied by (ii); see, for example, Marshall and Olkin (1979: 481).

The proof of the second part follows by induction. First, consider the case of two individuals. The distribution of the sum of the demands of the two individuals is, for arbitrary $\bar{x}$, given by

$$F_x(\bar{x}\,|\,\mu) = \int_0^{x_1^{-1}(\bar{x})}\int_0^{x_2^{-1}(\bar{x}-x_1(y_1))} f_{y_1,y_2}(y_1,y_2\,|\,\mu)\ dy_1 dy_2.$$

As individual incomes are assumed to be a random sample from the income distribution $f_{y_1,y_2}(y_1,y_2\,|\,\mu) = f(y_1\,|\,\mu)\cdot f(y_2\,|\,\mu)$, this implies

$$F_x(\bar{x}\,|\,\mu) = \int_0^{x_1^{-1}(\bar{x})} f(y_1\,|\,\mu)\cdot F(x_2^{-1}(\bar{x}-x_1(y_1))\,|\,\mu)\ dy_1.$$

By assumption 6.2(*i*), $F(x_2^{-1}(\bar{x}-x_1(y_1))\,|\,\mu)$ is decreasing in μ. Hence, for $\mu' > \mu$

$$F_x(\bar{x}\,|\,\mu) - F_x(\bar{x}\,|\,\mu') \geq$$
$$\int_0^{x_1^{-1}(\bar{x})} F(x_2^{-1}(\bar{x}-x_1(y_1))\,|\,\mu)\ \{f(y_1\,|\,\mu) - f(y_1\,|\,\mu')\}dy_1 >$$
$$F(x_2^{-1}(\bar{x}-x_1(\bar{y}))\,|\,\mu)\cdot\int_0^{\bar{y}} \{f(y_1\,|\,\mu) - f(y_1\,|\,\mu')\}dy_1 +$$
$$\int_{\bar{y}}^{x_1^{-1}(\bar{x})} F(x_2^{-1}(\bar{x}-x_1(y_1))\,|\,\mu)\{f(y_1\,|\,\mu) - f(y_1\,|\,\mu')\}dy_1,$$

for $x_1^{-1}(\bar{x}) > \bar{y}$. (For $x_1^{-1}(\bar{x}) < \bar{y}$ it is obviously true that $F_x(\bar{x}\,|\,\mu) > F_x(\bar{x}\,|\,\mu')$, because in this case $f(y_1\,|\,\mu) > f(y_1\,|\,\mu')$ for all $0 < y_1 < x_1^{-1}(\bar{x})$.) Note that the second inequality sign holds, because in the first term $x_1(y_1)$ is replaced by $x_1(\bar{y})$ and the good is supposed to be non-inferior. Again by assumption 6.2(*i*),

$$\int_0^{\bar{y}}f(y_1\,|\,\mu)dy_1 + \int_{\bar{y}}^{x_1^{-1}(\bar{x})}f(y_1\,|\,\mu)dy_1 \geq \int_0^{\bar{y}}f(y_1\,|\,\mu')dy_1$$
$$+ \int_{\bar{y}}^{x_1^{-1}(\bar{x})}f(y_1\,|\,\mu')dy_1.$$

So that

$$\int_0^{\bar{y}}\{f(y_1\,|\,\mu) - f(y_1\,|\,\mu')\}dy_1 \geq -\int_{\bar{y}}^{x_1^{-1}(\bar{x})}\{f(y_1\,|\,\mu) - f(y_1\,|\,\mu')\}dy_1.$$

Hence,

$$F_x(\bar{x}\,|\,\mu) - F_x(\bar{x}\,|\,\mu') > \int_{\bar{y}}^{x_1^{-1}(\bar{x})} \{F(x_2^{-1}(\bar{x}-x_1(y_1))\,|\,\mu)$$
$$- F(x_2^{-1}(\bar{x}-x_1(\bar{y}))\,|\,\mu)\}\cdot\{f(y_1\,|\,\mu) - f(y_1\,|\,\mu')\}dy_1.$$

The second term between the braces is negative because of assumption 6.2(*ii*). As the first term is also negative the integral is positive. This proves the case for two individuals.

In general, i.e. for *n* individuals,

$$F_x(\bar{x}\,|\,\mu) = \int_0^{x_n^{-1}(\bar{x})} f(y_n\,|\,\mu) \Big\{ \int_0^{x_{n-1}^{-1}(\bar{x}-x_n(y_n'))} \ldots$$

$$\int_0^{x_1^{-1}(\bar{x}-\sum_{i=2}^{n}x_i(y_i'))} f(y_1\,|\,\mu)\ldots f(y_{n-1}\,|\,\mu)dy_1\ldots dy_{n-1} \Big\}\, dy_n.$$

The induction assumption says that the part between the braces is decreasing in μ. Hence, the same argument as that used in the case of two individuals leads to the conclusion that $F_x(\bar{x}\,|\,\mu)$ is increasing in μ for arbitrary $\bar{x}$.

This proves the theorem. ∎

Part III

EQUILIBRIUM AND EXPECTATIONS

7

INDIVIDUALISTIC FOUNDATIONS FOR MARKET EQUILIBRIUM

Part II of the book has mainly been concerned with aggregation over individual consumers. In doing this, we have concentrated on one side of the market, namely the demand side, and aggregation took place over the demand for a certain good, *not* on the realized consumption of that good. Of course, one could assume that demand for and realized consumption of a good coincide.[1] In economic terms this would imply the assumption that the supply of the good is larger than or equal to the demand for that good. In a combined analysis of the aggregation of the supply of *and* the demand for goods such an identification of terms would imply the assumption that supply equals demand. This assumption of market clearing (or, more narrowly, of competitive equilibrium)[2] is often made in economic analysis. An interesting question then is whether this assumption can be derived from the interaction of rationally behaving individuals. This is the subject of the present chapter.

The notion of equilibrium, especially that of competitive equilibrium, is central to much of economic theory. It is an important element of the Arrow–Debreu model (ADM) and, more broadly, of the programme of general equilibrium analysis (GEA). Many authors (Bicchieri 1992 and Coleman 1990, among others) have regarded ADM and GEA as paradigmatic examples of the methodological individualistic character of mainstream economic theory. This view is also expressed by Rosenberg, who claims that

> it was Walras who first suggested that under conditions of constant or diminishing returns to scale, an economy composed of agents behaving in accordance with the classical theory will *attain* a 'general equilibrium'. That is, the maximizing behavior of consumers and producers *inevitably results* in an equilibrium

between amounts supplied and demanded in every market of the economy.

(Rosenberg 1976: 184–5; my italics)

In this chapter, I will scrutinize the view that is expressed by the above quote. It will turn out that the individualistic nature of the equilibrium notion in general and the notion of competitive equilibrium in particular is questionable. The first section shows in some detail that the use of the assumption of competitive equilibrium cannot be justified in individualistic terms in ADM.[3] Of course, there are others who have indicated some difficulties with respect to the individualistic nature of ADM and I will explore some game theoretic approaches that intend to resolve these difficulties. The next five sections discuss five game theoretic models that attempt to provide the notion of competitive equilibrium with individualistic foundations. It will turn out that the game theoretic approaches are only partially successful. I will discuss the relations between the game theoretic notions (as the core and the Nash equilibrium concept) and the assumption of competitive equilibrium and I will show that these relations can be captured in terms of the reduction scheme. The reduction scheme is used here as a way of showing where the difficulties with respect to the game theoretic approaches do *not* lie. The original question, of whether the competitive equilibrium notion is based on MI, brings us to the question of whether the notions of the core and the Nash equilibrium are founded on MI. For the Nash equilibrium a negative answer was formulated in chapter 2. This negative answer largely accounts for the fact that the game theoretic approaches are only partially successful. The fifth and sixth sections show, however, that some of the results obtained using the Nash equilibrium notion in the context of Bertrand and Cournot models remain true when this equilibrium notion is replaced by the notion of iteratively undominated strategies (IUS). This brings the results much closer to the tenets of MI. The conclusions are found in the final section.

Before proceeding to the main part of this chapter, I would like to make one more introductory remark on the notion of equilibrium in economics. The question of whether equilibrium notions are founded on MI may seem to be an odd question to non-economists. In other sciences the term 'equilibrium' is almost universally employed for the rest points of dynamic systems. In general, a dynamic system can be described in terms of a set of equations each of which determines the changes in one variable as a function of the values of all variables and parameters:

$$\dot{x}_i = f_i(x_1,\ldots,x_n;\ \kappa_1,\ldots,\kappa_m),\qquad\qquad(7.1)$$

where x_i = the value of variable i;

κ_j = the value of parameter j.

From such a dynamic system's point of view a balance of forces can be defined as a set of values $(x_1,\ldots,x_n)$ such that for a given set of parameter values $\dot{x}_i = 0$, $i = 1,\ldots,n$, and an *equilibrium* can be defined as a balance of forces that is (at least) locally stable. If the term 'equilibrium' is understood this way the question of whether the equilibrium notion has individualistic foundations reduces to the question of whether the system of differential equations has individualistic foundations and whether this system is locally stable. When the system of differentiable equations is shown to be based on individualistic foundations, the individualistic foundations for the equilibrium notion follow as a simple consequence.

Economists employ the term 'equilibrium' in many ways, one of which coincides with the one outlined above. Other ways economists have used the term include the following:

(i) A certain state of the economy is an equilibrium state if the rational actions of (groups of) individuals are consistent with each other, i.e. all individuals obtain their most preferred quantities out of the alternatives available to them (cf. Bénassy 1982 and Hicks 1965).

(ii) A certain state of the economy is an equilibrium state if demand equals supply on all markets. This is the notion of *market clearing*. It is, for example, a special case of the first definition if the economy is a perfectly competitive exchange economy in which the only restriction the (group of) individuals face(s) is the budget constraint.

(iii) A certain state of the economy is an equilibrium state if 'the relations that describe the system form a system sufficiently complete to determine the values of its variables' (Arrow 1968: 376).

(iv) A certain state of the economy is an equilibrium state if it is a 'balance of forces'; see the discussion above.[4]

From the above it is clear that in economics the term 'equilibrium' is also used without recourse to a dynamic system of which it is a stable rest point. So, the question of whether an equilibrium notion as the notion of competitive equilibrium is based on MI does *not* reduce to the question of whether the system of differential equations has individualistic foundations. It is thus a legitimate separate question to ask whether the notion of competitive equilibrium has to be adopted once one accepts the requirements of MI.

AN INDIVIDUALISTIC EXPLANATION OF COMPETITIVE EQUILIBRIUM PRICES?

In chapter 5 we discussed the differences between individual and aggregate excess demand functions. The aggregate excess demand function, relating prices and aggregate excess demand and (using the notation of chapter 5) denoted by $z(p)$, is one of the two aggregate relationships in ADM. It is easily seen that aggregate excess demand functions can be reduced to utility theory in two steps: an application and an aggregation step (see, e.g., the section on 'empirical restrictions' in chapter 5). In the application step individual agents maximize utility subject to a budget constraint. This yields individual demand functions. These individual demand functions are aggregated (and initial endowments are subtracted) to obtain aggregate excess demand functions. This explanation is also in line with the requirements of MI, because it can be represented as a micro-reduction and the agents can be regarded as decision makers.

Nothing has been said so far about how prices are explained. The second aggregate relationship of ADM says that prices are such that aggregate excess demand is less than or equal to zero, i.e. p is such that $z(p) \leq 0.$[5] With respect to this second aggregate relationship it is less clear whether an explanation in line with MI can be given. It is well known that *if* the individual utility functions and the initial endowments are known one can tell whether or not (and explain why) supply and demand are equal to each other *at a certain* price vector. Furthermore, it is known that at the equilibrium prices all individuals can obtain the most preferred commodity bundle of all bundles that satisfy the budget constraint. Finally, it is also known that this property is closely related to the competitive equilibrium notion of ADM: at non-market clearing prices there is at least one individual who *cannot* get his or her most preferred commodity bundle at the given prices and initial endowments. These are all characterizations of an equilibrium state. The question with respect to the individualistic nature of the second aggregate relationship is, however, whether the proposition that an economy finds itself in a state of (general) equilibrium can logically be derived from the proposition that individuals attempt to maximize their utility. Let me make the claim to be considered more precise by introducing the following 'AD-law'.

> AD-law.[6] For all economies in which a competitive equilibrium exists, all market prices at which trade takes place are competitive equilibrium prices and the allocation of commodities resulting from trade is a competitive equilibrium allocation.

As in ADM all individual agents are price takers it is not clear in individual terms why flexible prices should take on their competitive equilibrium values. What one would like to have is a theory specifying how the market outcome (prices) depends on the decisions taken by individual agents. ADM, however, only says what individual agents do at given prices; it is not about how prices result from individual actions. In Coleman's terminology, a micro-to-macro transition is missing. Merely saying that prices have to be such that *aggregate* demand equals *aggregate* supply begs the question from a methodological individualistic point of view.[7] Note that this conclusion radically differs from the commonly held opinion exemplified by the quote from Rosenberg (1976) in the introduction to this chapter.

Of course, there are also economists who have expressed opinions that are similar to the critique I have given above. Arrow (1959), in search for a rationale of the assumption of competitive equilibrium, remarks that this assumption is often regarded as the limit of a trial and error process known as the law of supply and demand. This law says that the price of a commodity goes up if the demand for the commodity is larger than its supply:

$$\partial p_i / \partial t = g_i(z_i(p_1,\ldots,p_m)), \tag{7.2}$$

where t denotes time and $g_i(\cdot) > 0$ if and only if $z_i(p_1,\ldots,p_m) > 0$. If this law were based on rational individual behaviour, then the assumption of competitive equilibrium would have individualistic foundations (cf. the discussion in the context of equation (7.1)). Among others, Arrow states, however, that this law is not on the same logical level as the hypotheses underlying the demand and supply schedules, because

> it is not explained whose decision it is to change prices. Each individual participant is supposed to take prices as given and determine his choices as to purchases and sales accordingly; there is no one left over whose job it is to make a decision on price.
>
> (Arrow 1959: 43)

111

Often, one of the following two interpretations of the law of supply and demand is given. First, this 'law' is sometimes interpreted as the result of Adam Smith's Invisible Hand. Giving the market mechanism a name such as the Invisible Hand cannot substitute, however, for the fact that a process description in terms of market institutions and individual behaviour is lacking, i.e. the Invisible Hand is a typical non-individualistic (holistic) concept. A second interpretation is obtained when the task of setting prices is conceived of as being performed by a sort of market manager (auctioneer). In markets in which such an auctioneer exists, equation (7.2) might be considered an (ideal) description of the auctioneer's behaviour. However, in most 'real' markets such an auctioneer does not exist. In these cases, the auctioneer is a fictitious entity, a fiction that describes the market process in terms of the behaviour of *one* individual. Accordingly, this interpretation is not in line with the notion of MI as it is used in this study.[8]

Some final observations about existence proofs have to be made here. It is well known that a competitive equilibrium exists if the aggregate excess demand functions are continuous, homogeneous of degree zero and satisfy Walras' law. Although these conditions all refer to the aggregate excess demand functions $z(p)$, it is fairly standard to show that they can be derived from (reduced to) more fundamental assumptions concerning maximizing individual behaviour. Thus, it can be proved that a competitive equilibrium in a pure exchange economy exists if some assumptions with respect to individual characteristics hold. It is sometimes said that this result provides individualistic foundations for the AD-law. I think that this is not the case. Existence proofs only show 'that a decentralized economy motivated by self-interest and guided by price signals would be compatible with a coherent disposition of economic resources' (Arrow and Hahn 1971: *vii*). In other words, existence proofs show that an economy populated with self-interested agents does *not necessarily* end up in a state of chaos. They do not show, however, that the general equilibrium allocation is the only allocation that may result in such an economy. They only point at the *possibility* of a coherent disposition of economic resources.[9,10] However, they neither show that this particular possibility will materialize, nor do they show how it results from the behaviour of individuals if it materializes at all.

112

AN AUCTIONEER WITH AN OBJECTIVE FUNCTION

In the previous section we saw that ADM does not give an individualistic explanation for the assumption of competitive equilibrium. In order to provide the competitive equilibrium with individualistic foundations, a number of authors have studied the relation between some game theoretic solution concepts and the competitive equilibrium notion. In this and the following sections I will consider five different game theoretic approaches to provide the AD-law with a (deeper) foundation in MI. The results are presented in terms of the reduction scheme presented in chapter 2.

In an influential paper, Arrow and Debreu (1954) offer a game theoretic approach that can be interpreted as an attempt to offer an individualistic explanation of prices. In their paper there are two kinds of agents, hereafter referred to as players. The first kind of players are similar to the agents populating the ADM economy: they take prices as given, their initial endowments are fixed and they maximize their utility functions subject to the budget constraint. In chapter 5 we saw that this behaviour results in a demand function $x_i(p,p\omega_i)$, $i = 1,\ldots,n$. In addition to these players there is one player of the second kind, player 0 (a kind of auctioneer), who chooses a price vector at which the other players transact. Player 0's goal is to minimize the extent to which the economy is out of equilibrium. Thus, the competitive equilibrium state is the best state for player 0. A sophisticated formulation of player 0's payoff function is given by $\min_p p \cdot \max\{-z(p),0\}$. To see that this payoff function does what it is required to do, note that the optimal value is equal to zero, which is obtained if and only if aggregate excess demand is smaller than or equal to zero. To complete the description of the game, it is emphasized that it consists of two stages. In the first stage player 0 announces a price vector. Transactions take place in the second stage of the game. Hence, this is a game of perfect information.

It can be shown that a Nash equilibrium of this game coincides with a competitive equilibrium state (see, e.g., Friedman 1991: 97–100). The argument essentially is as follows. Consider an arbitrary positive price vector p. If at this price vector there is an excess supply in one market (a positive $z(p)$), there has to be excess demand in another market (Walras' law). This means that at this price vector the value of player 0's payoff function is positive. In this case, player 0 can do better by choosing a higher price for the good in excess demand and a lower price for the good in excess supply. As the game consists of two stages, the

113

price-taking players know the prices quoted by player 0 (and this is known by player 0). Thus, player 0's rational choice is a competitive equilibrium price vector. In the second stage of the game, the individuals transact the same amount of goods as they would transact in a competitive equilibrium state.

The question we have to consider now is whether the above approach offers an explanation of the assumption of competitive equilibrium that is in line with the requirements of MI as set forth in chapter 2. Recall that an explanation is in line with MI if (*i*) it is possible to represent it as a micro-reduction and (*ii*) the theory that is applied is about rational decision makers. A close look reveals that the explanation along the above lines only requires an application step in which non-cooperative game theory is applied to the economy sketched above. The *sequential nature* of the game assures that all players are informed about the prices player 0 announces in the first stage and player 0 knows that all agents are informed. In other words, individual players can be regarded as decision makers. From the structure of the game it follows that player 0 does not have an incentive to announce a non-market clearing price. Therefore, the fact that the economy ends up in a competitive equilibrium is a logical consequence of the assumptions about individual decision making that are made (compare the argument in example 2.2).

However, the first requirement of MI is not fulfilled. Instead of treating prices as aggregate phenomena, Arrow and Debreu introduce an artificial player 0 as a kind of 'auctioneer'. By doing so, the distinction between the individual and the aggregate level disappears. In other words, Arrow and Debreu convert a decentralized process of price setting 'by the market' into a centralized process of price setting.[11] The above approach to ADM thus does not provide an explanation of *market* prices that fulfils both requirements of MI.

THE LIMIT POINTS OF THE CORE

Before going into the relation between the core and the competitive equilibrium notion some basic notions of cooperative game theory have to be introduced. Since cooperative game theory is concerned with situations in which agents are allowed to make legally binding contractual agreements with one another, its natural focus seems to be on what rationale agents ought to agree on. Three kinds of restrictions on contracts immediately come to mind. A contract has to assign to each agent a payoff that is at least as much as this agent is able to make alone. Second, a contract should be designed in such a way that the agents cannot jointly improve upon it. These requirements are called individual rationality and group rationality (or Pareto-optimality), respectively. A third requirement is that a contract should assign to any subgroup (coalition) of agents a payoff vector that is at least as large as this subgroup is able to guarantee its members irrespective of what other agents do. The basic solution concept of cooperative game theory, the *core of a game*, is a solution that satisfies the above three requirements.

A cooperative game has the following elements:

$N = \{1,\ldots,n\}$ is the *set of players*;
$C \subset N$ is a *coalition*;
$v: C \to \mathbb{R}^C$ is the (set-valued) characteristic function (one for each $C \subset N$).

For each coalition C, $v(C)$ is the set of all payoff vectors that the coalition C can achieve irrespective of the other agents. The characteristic function assigns to each possible coalition a set $v(C) \subseteq \mathbb{R}^C$. If the payoffs are transferable, the characteristic function is a scalar-valued function. In this case the core of a game consists of the solutions $(\jmath_1,\ldots,\jmath_n)$ that satisfy

(i) $\jmath_i \geq v(\{i\})$ (individual rationality);
(ii) $\sum_{i=1}^{n} \jmath_i = v(N)$ (group rationality or Pareto-efficiency);
(iii) $\sum_{i \in C} \jmath_i \geq v(C)$ for all C (coalition rationality).

Two examples will clarify the basic notions of cooperative game theory.

Example 7.1 The Gloves Game

Suppose there are three players. Players 1 and 2 have a left hand glove, while the third player has a right hand glove. The players who form a pair of gloves will be awarded one dollar. How will this dollar be divided among the three players if the particular solution $(\jmath_1,\jmath_2,\jmath_3)$ has to be in the core? It is clear that this is a game with transferable payoffs and that in order to be in the core $\jmath_1 + \jmath_2 + \jmath_3 = 1$. The characteristic function is as follows:

$v(\{1,3\}) = v(\{2,3\}) = v(\{1,2,3\}) = 1$ and $v(S) = 0$ for all other coalitions.

This means that $\jmath_1 \geq 0$, $\jmath_2 + \jmath_3 \geq 1$ and $\jmath_1 + \jmath_2 + \jmath_3 = 1$ so that $\jmath_1 = 0$. Similarly, $\jmath_2 \geq 0$, $\jmath_1 + \jmath_3 \geq 1$ and $\jmath_1 + \jmath_2 + \jmath_3 = 1$ so that $\jmath_2 = 0$. Thus, $(\jmath_1,\jmath_2,\jmath_3) = (0,0,1)$ is the only solution in the core and player 3 gets the dollar.

Example 7.2 **A Cooperative Market Game**

One of the best-known applications of the theory of the core is the Edgeworth box. Consider a 'market game' with two agents and two goods. Let the agents have identical utility functions of the form $U(x_{i1}, x_{i2}) = x_{i1}^{\alpha} x_{i2}^{1-\alpha}$, $i = 1,2$, and let the endowments of agent 1, $(\omega_{11}, \omega_{12})$, be equal to $(2,1)$ and of agent 2, $(\omega_{21}, \omega_{22})$, be equal to $(1,2)$. There is no centrally organized price mechanism: the agents directly exchange goods for other goods. To think of this example as a game, the agents are considered as players and their utility functions are identified with the player's payoff functions. How does the core of this economy look? The situation is depicted in the Edgeworth box of figure 7.1.

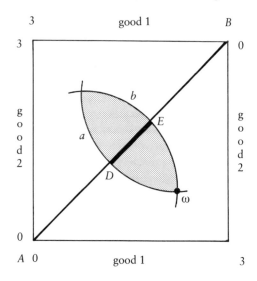

Figure 7.1 Edgeworth box of a market game

Good 1 is represented on the horizontal axis and good 2 on the vertical axis. The box is square because there is an equal and fixed number of units (namely three) of each good in the economy. Player 1's (2's) goods are measured from the origin at A (B). The point denoted by ω gives the distribution of initial endowments in the economy. The curve a gives the combinations of goods that provide agent 1 with the same utility level that person derives from consuming her or his initial endowments. The same holds true for curve b with respect to agent 2.

Individual rationality requires that only those exchanges are acceptable for individual 1 that provide a commodity bundle that lies above and to the right of the curve a. Individual 2 only accepts bundles that lie below and to the left of curve b. The shaded area gives the commodity bundles that are acceptable to both players. Trade results in a higher payoff (utility) for both players if a point in the interior of this area is agreed upon. Group rationality requires that the two players do not agree on a bundle that they can jointly improve upon. This means that the two players have to agree on a bundle in which their utility functions are tangent to each other. This is true for all points on the line segment between E and D. This line segment is the core of the economy.

The competitive equilibrium can easily be calculated. In equilibrium, individual 1 holds $1+\alpha$ of both goods. The remaining $2-\alpha$ is for individual 2. So, we can conclude that the competitive equilibrium is an element of the core.

The second game theoretic approach to an explanation of why a competitive equilibrium may result is related to example 7.2. This approach studies the properties of the core of an economy and its relation to the notion of competitive equilibrium. There are three important differences with the Arrow–Debreu interpretation of the previous section: (*i*) player 0 is absent, (*ii*) the other agents do not take prices (the terms of trade) as given and (*iii*) individuals are allowed to co-operate in order to arrive at a certain allocation.

It is well known that the competitive equilibrium allocations are in the core (see, e.g., Arrow and Hahn 1971: 187–8). This is also illustrated in example 7.2. In general, however, the core contains more allocations. (In example 7.2 the core is represented by the line segment *DE*, while there is only one competitive equilibrium state.) It is also known that if the number of individuals in the economy gets larger the core gets smaller (see, e.g., Varian 1984: 238–9). Eventually, i.e. if there is an infinite number of individuals, with a fixed number of types of individuals and the same number of individuals per type,[12] all core allocations coincide with the competitive equilibrium allocations (see, e.g., Arrow and Hahn 1971: 195–8). This suggests the following reduction scheme. In the *application step* the theory of the core is applied to an economy as described above. In a second step, the *approximation step*, the allocations in the core are said to coincide with the competitive equilibrium allocations, if the number of individuals in the economy becomes infinitely large.

So far, nothing has been said about prices. Is it possible to give an interpretation of prices if individuals only bargain about allocations? If the individual utility functions are continuously differentiable, price ratios between commodities can be defined as the ratio of the marginal utilities of these commodities:

$$\frac{p_j}{p_k} \equiv \frac{\partial U_i(x_{i1},\ldots,x_{im})/\partial x_{ij}}{\partial U_i(x_{i1},\ldots,x_{im})/\partial x_{ik}}, \tag{7.3}$$

evaluated at the core allocation. As a core allocation is Pareto-efficient, the right hand side of (7.3) is the same for all individuals. Since the core allocation coincides with the competitive equilibrium allocation, it will be clear that the prices thus defined are the competitive equilibrium prices, in the sense that a competitive equilibrium allocation would result if individual agents were to treat these price ratios as given.[13]

The above discussion can be represented by the following scheme. Most of the auxiliary hypotheses H_1-H_3 that are needed have been mentioned in the text above.

(1) application step   theory of the core $+ H_1$
(2) approximation step   core allocation $+ H_2$
(3) identification/correlation step   ADM allocation $+ H_3$
                              ADM price ratios

The theory of the core thus gives a reductive explanation of competitive equilibrium allocations and prices, because an approximation step is present. This result indicates that if there are reasons to believe that exchange takes place in such a way that the resultant allocation is in the core, economists may well assume that the allocation arises from the notion that individuals act *as if* they are price takers. The assumption of competitive equilibrium can then be seen as an idealization which is justified if the number of individual agents participating in the bargaining is large. (Compare the discussion on ideal gases in chapter 2.) The question remains, however, of whether this justification of the assumption of competitive equilibrium is in line with MI. I think one may have doubts about it, because the mechanism by which a core allocation is supposedly reached is left undiscussed. The theory of the core is a theory in which the notion of group rationality plays an important role. There is one requirement about individual behaviour, saying that an individual should not agree with an allocation in which his or her utility level is lower than the utility level obtained by consuming his or her initial endowments. But this requirement is not sufficient to justify the notion of the core. The whole group and any subgroup (coalition) has to be rational as well (see above). This introduces an element of group intentionality, the existence of which MI denies. Moreover, the theory of the core discusses neither the individual decisions that supposedly lead to a core allocation, nor the way the resulting allocation depends on these decisions. In Coleman's (1990) terminology: a micro-to-macro transition is missing.

Of course, I do not deny that the outcome of the interaction between decision-making individuals *may* belong to the core, but, in general, it is not made clear that rational individual behaviour *should* lead to a core allocation (see also Roberts and Postlewaite 1976). In this respect an observation by Varian (1984: 235) is revealing. He presents the core of the market game as a suggested answer to the following question. 'Suppose we were *given a suggested allocation* as the outcome of such a [market game] process; how could we tell if it was reasonable?' (my italics). In other words, once an outcome is given, the economist is in a position to tell whether it has certain (desirable) properties. The process that has to result in such an outcome is left undiscussed.

STRATEGIC MARKET GAMES

A symposium issue of the *Journal of Economic Theory* (1980) is devoted to non-cooperative approaches to the theory of perfect competition. In his introduction to this volume, Mas-Colell (1980: 211) argues that

> Modern Walrasian Economics ... provides an analysis of the decentralized economic coordination problem under the hypothesis that prices are publicly quoted and are viewed by economic agents as exogenously given. If we regard this as the Hypothesis of Perfect Competition, then modern Walrasian economics is a theory of perfect competition only in the sense of examining the consequences of the Hypothesis but not in that of giving a theoretical explanation of the Hypothesis itself.

The position I have argued for in the first section coincides to a large extent with Mas-Colell's position as exemplified by the above quote. The contributions to the volume subsequently attempt to provide a theoretical explanation for the assumption of competitive equilibrium. Several types of non-cooperative approaches have to be distinguished (see, e.g., Hart 1986). In this section I deal with strategic market games. The following two sections will be devoted to Bertrand competition and Cournot competition, respectively.

Strategic market games are developed by Shubik (1973), Dubey (1982) and Bénassy (1986), among others. In these approaches individual agents decide upon a strategy that consists of price and quantity offers for all goods. A strategy is a message by an agent that she or he is willing to buy (sell) up to a certain amount of a good at a price that does not exceed (fall short of) a specific level. More formally, let there be n agents and let r_i be the vector of agent i's price message, with components r_{ij}, $j=1,\ldots,m$, and t_i be the vector of agent i's quantity message, with components t_{ij}, $j=1,\ldots,m$. Moreover, define the set of all agents' price and quantity messages by

$$r \equiv \{r_{ij} | i = 1,\ldots,n \text{ and } j = 1,\ldots,m\},$$
$$t \equiv \{t_{ij} | i = 1,\ldots,n \text{ and } j = 1,\ldots,m\}.$$

A *market outcome function* determines the actual trade and the market price that will be realized as a function of the price and quantity offers that are expressed by the individual agents:

$$p_{ij} = \Gamma_{ij}(r,t), \qquad\qquad i = 1,\ldots,n \text{ and } j = 1,\ldots,m,$$
$$x_{ij} = \Lambda_{ij}(r,t), \qquad\qquad i = 1,\ldots,n \text{ and } j = 1,\ldots,m,$$

where p_{ij} is the price of good j at which agent i can transact and x_{ij} is the quantity of good j agent i can transact. The market outcome function is supposed to represent the functioning of the market (see also below). As individuals derive utility from consuming the goods and as the quantities they obtain depend on the price and quantity offers by all individuals, their utility (payoff) function depends on all individual strategies: $U_i(x_i) = U_i(\Lambda_{i1}(r,t), \ldots ,\Lambda_{im}(r,t)) = V_i(r,t)$. Accordingly, one can define a Nash equilibrium in the usual way. The main aim of the strategic market game literature is to study the properties the market outcome function has to satisfy for the Nash equilibria of the games to coincide with the competitive equilibria of the corresponding competitive economy. The reader is referred to the original papers for the kind of conditions that are studied.

The market outcome function performs two tasks at the same time. It *aggregates* the individual price and quantity offers and it *transforms* 'offers' into 'realizations'. This transformation can be regarded either as a correlation or as an identification of terms (see also below). This suggests the following reduction scheme:

(1) application step   'theory of Nash equilibrium' + H_1

(2) combined aggregation $\dfrac{\text{Nash price and quantity offers} + H_2}{\text{AD-law}}$

       and id./corr. step

In contrast to the approach of the previous section, strategic market games do not employ the idea of 'a large number of agents'. Accordingly, the above scheme does not contain an approximation step. An aggregation step is involved, because in the present case all individuals make offers to buy and sell a certain good at a certain price. These individual messages have to be aggregated in order to arrive at market prices and a market allocation. Thus, the strategic market games approach can be represented as a micro-reduction. Note that the behaviour of individuals in this game depends on the form of the market outcome function. This is in line with the observations made in connection with the guessing game example in chapter 2, where it was stated that if individual payoffs depend on how individual behaviour is aggregated, the action a rational individual chooses also depends on the aggregating function. There are two further issues we have to address before a conclusion concerning the individualistic nature of the above explanation can be reached.

The first issue is about how to interpret the market outcome function. Two interpretations are possible. First, it can be considered as part of the rules of the game. Before the game is actually played the players agree to play according to these rules. Rules can, for example, be inherited from history. This is in line with an 'identity interpretation'. Second, a 'correlation interpretation' would simply state that there is an empirical relation between price and quantity offers on the one hand and actual prices and trade on the other hand. If the market outcome function were a well-established empirical relationship, one could accept it for the purpose of explaining why a competitive equilibrium results. As independent data on price and quantity offers usually do not exist, however, the correlation interpretation is not very suitable. Also, even if such an empirical relationship were to exist one would like to know, in the second instance, the process underlying this relation: who or what transforms offers into realizations? In answering a question like this the correlation interpretation might easily introduce something like a fictitious auctioneer through the backdoor. Thus, the identification interpretation seems to be more appropriate. This interpretation, however, also requires some independent empirical evidence, because the rules of the game that play a role in the formalization should be (idealized) representations of the 'actual' rules used in the economy. Here, I think some doubts should be raised. The contributors to this approach do not discuss whether or not the properties the market outcome function has to satisfy for a competitive equilibrium outcome to obtain mimic the actual relation between price and quantity offers, on the one hand, and market prices and quantities, on the other hand.

The second issue is whether the present approach also fulfils the requirement that the individual agents are regarded as rational decision makers. The quest for individualistic foundations of the competitive equilibrium assumption thus raises the question of why rational players should 'play Nash'. This question has attracted much attention in the literature on the foundations of non-cooperative game theory, a literature which I have briefly discussed in chapter 2. There, I pointed out that in general, in simultaneous move games such as the present one, the Nash equilibrium is not a consequence of common knowledge of the rules of the game and the rationality of the players. We have encountered two conditions under which the Nash equilibrium is based on rational behaviour on the part of individuals. First, when the Nash equilibrium is the unique iteratively undominated strategy (IUS) and, second, when the description of the game is rich enough that individuals can arrive at 'focal points'. Unfortunately, there is no analysis showing that strategic market games have a unique IUS and also the background of the players is not described in sufficient detail that a focal point argument would be compelling. Therefore, I have to conclude that this approach is not in line with the requirements of MI.

COMPETITIVE EQUILIBRIA AND BERTRAND COMPETITION

A second non-cooperative approach to the individualistic foundations of the competitive equilibrium notion is *Bertrand competition*. In the Bertrand model, firms produce a homogeneous good on a single market. There are $n \geq 2$ firms (players) each of whom sets a price p_i. The strategy space for each firm is $P \equiv \mathbb{R}_+$. All firms have access to the same production technology, which exhibits constant marginal and average cost. Marginal cost is denoted by α. There are a large number of consumers who act non-strategically. They simply demand the good and because the good is homogeneous they buy from the firms that are charging the lowest price. Accordingly, the market price is the minimum of the prices that are charged by the firms, i.e. $p = \min p_i$. Total demand is denoted by $d(p)$. The following additional notion is introduced: p_{-i} is the vector of prices set by all firms except firm i; $\min p_{-i}$ is the minimum of the elements of this vector; n^* is the number of firms that charge the lowest price and π_i is the profit made by firm i. Individual profits are then given by

$$\pi_i(p_i, p_{-i}) = \begin{cases} 0 & \text{if } p_i > \min p_{-i} \\ (1/n^*)(p_i - \alpha)d(p_i) & \text{if } p_i = \min p_{-i} \\ (p_i - \alpha)d(p_i) & \text{if } p_i < \min p_{-i}. \end{cases}$$

It is thus assumed that demand is equally distributed over the n^* firms that charge the lowest price. Note also that a firm's profit function is discontinuous in its own price. A Nash equilibrium for this game is a set of prices such that no firm can raise its profits by changing its price. It is easily seen that the competitive equilibrium of this model is reached when $p = \alpha$. Under mild conditions on the demand function, the unique Nash equilibrium of this game is such that every firm sets p_i equal to α. Thus, the Nash equilibrium coincides with the competitive equilibrium. This suggests the following reduction scheme. (Note that the market price has been defined by the minimum of all individual prices.)[14]

(1) application step   'theory of Nash equilibrium' + H_1

(2) aggregation step   individual prices equal marginal costs

$$\overline{\phantom{\text{individual prices equal marginal costs}}}$$

AD-law

One of the points of critique of the previous section, that the notion of Nash equilibrium is not a consequence of the view that individuals are rational, is also relevant in the context of Bertrand competition. However, in the present context it can be shown that a similar result obtains if the notion of Nash equilibrium is replaced by the notion of IUS. Three qualifications should be made. First, it is necessary to discretize the strategy space. This is due to the discontinuity in the profit function. Second, the result in terms of IUS is that instead of setting the price equal to marginal cost, all firms set the smallest price above marginal cost. Third, the notion of dominance should be slightly modified: the concept of strongly dominated strategies will not bring us very far, because $\pi_i(p_i, p_{-i}) = \pi_i(q_i, p_{-i}) = 0$ for all p_{-i} such that min $p_{-i} <$ min (p_i, q_i). The definition of undominated strategies that is used here is presented in Börgers (1992). Let $\mathscr{P}$ denote the discretized strategy space and $\mathscr{D}_i(\mathscr{P})$ the set of player i's undominated strategies with respect to $\mathscr{P}$:

$p_i \in \mathscr{D}_i(\mathscr{P})$ if and only if $p_i \in \mathscr{P}_i$ and there is no $q_i \in \mathscr{P}_i$ such that
(i) $\pi_i(p_i, p_{-i}) \leq \pi_i(q_i, p_{-i})$ for all $p_{-i} \in \mathscr{P}_{-i}$;
(ii) $\pi_i(p_i, p_{-i}) < \pi_i(q_i, p_{-i})$ for some $p_{-i} \in \mathscr{P}_{-i}$;
(iii) $\pi_i(p_i, p_{-i}) < \pi_i(q_i, p_{-i})$ for all $p_{-i} \in \mathscr{P}_{-i}$ whenever $\pi_i(p_i, p_{-i}) > 0$.

This definition is in between the traditional concepts of weakly and strongly dominated strategies.[15] The result is formally described in Börgers (1992, theorem 3.1). Here, the result will be illustrated by means of an example.

123

Example 7.3 **IUS in a Bertrand Model**

Consider a case in which two firms set prices in order to maximize profits. Marginal costs α are assumed to be equal to zero. The demand function is $d(p) = 4 - p$ for $p \leq 4$ and $d(p) = 0$ for $p > 4$. The discretized strategy space will contain only natural numbers. The normal form of the game is as follows (I only consider prices between 0 and 4).

p_1 \ p_2	0	1	2	3	4
0	0 \ 0	0 \ 0	0 \ 0	0 \ 0	0 \ 0
1	0 \ 0	$3/2$ \ $3/2$	0 \ 3	0 \ 3	0 \ 3
2	0 \ 0	3 \ 0	2 \ 2	0 \ 4	0 \ 4
3	0 \ 0	3 \ 0	4 \ 0	$3/2$ \ $3/2$	0 \ 3
4	0 \ 0	3 \ 0	4 \ 0	3 \ 0	0 \ 0

The normal form demonstrates that the monopoly price dominates $p_i = 3$ and $p_i = 4$ and that $p_i = 1$ dominates $p_i = 0$. If the dominated strategies are eliminated from the game, one can see that $p_i = 1$ dominates p^m in the remaining game. Thus, in this game $p_i = 1$ is the unique IUS. As $\alpha = 0$, this is the smallest price above marginal cost.

A second point of the critique might be that the Bertrand model only considers a single market. Accordingly, it is only able to provide foundations for the assumption of competitive equilibrium in a partial equilibrium framework. In Janssen (1992) I have shown that the main idea of the result in terms of IUS remains valid in a multi-market version of the Bertrand model. The assumptions of constant marginal cost cannot easily be modified, however (see, e.g., Janssen 1991a). In this sense, the Bertrand model gives a foundation for the competitive equilibrium assumption only in a very limited number of cases.

THE LIMIT POINTS OF COURNOT COMPETITION

The final approach to a foundation for the assumption of competitive equilibrium I want to consider here is Cournot competition. In the

Cournot model there are n firms who decide on their quantities taking the impact of their quantity decision on prices into account. A well-known result is that, under some conditions on the inverse demand function and the cost functions, the Cournot–Nash equilibria of these models tend to the equilibria under perfect competition as the number of firms becomes very large (see, e.g., Ruffin 1971). A similar result holds true if the demand *and* the supply side are replicated (see, e.g., Novshek 1985).[16] Some of the details of this result will be illustrated by means of the following example.

Example 7.4 Nash Equilibria of the Cournot Game

Suppose that there are n firms producing identical products and having identical cost functions of the form $C_i = c_1 q_i + c_2 q_i^2$, where q_i is the production of firm i, C_i is the cost of production of firm i and c_1 and c_2 are positive parameters that are the same for all i. (The form of the cost function is chosen in such a way that the competitive supply function is linear in price.) Moreover, let inverse demand be given by $p = a - bQ$, where p is the market price of the product, Q is total production ($Q = \sum_{i=1}^{n} q_i$) and a and b are positive parameters, with $a > c_1$. In the competitive equilibrium of this economy (each firm acts as if it is a price taker), each firm produces $q_i = (a - c_1)/(nb + 2c_2)$. If, on the other hand, firms act strategically and take their impact on prices into account, their optimal production is $q_i = \max\{(a - c_1 - bQ_{-i})/(2b + 2c_2), 0\}$. In the Nash equilibrium each firm produces $q_i = (a - c_1)/[(n + 1)b + 2c_2]$. So, if n goes to infinity, the Nash equilibrium production level converges to the competitive supply.

The example illustrates the claims made in chapter 2 about the way the micro-to-macro transition is made in game theory. There we noticed that aggregate concepts are usually employed in order to relate individual decisions and individual payoffs. In the example above, market prices mediate between individual firms' production decisions and their individual profits. Moreover, a market price is defined for every combination of production levels, not just for equilibrium quantities.

More concretely what the example shows is that if the number of firms is very large, Cournot–Nash equilibria are very close to the competitive equilibria of the corresponding perfectly competitive economy. The result is depicted in the following scheme:

(1) application step   'theory of Nash equilibrium' + H_1

(2) approximation step   Cournot quantities + H_2

(3) correlation step   ADM quantities + H_3
    ADM prices

So, if there are reasons to believe that a Nash equilibrium results and if the number of firms is large, the economist is justified in using the assumption of competitive equilibrium. There are two issues that remain to be discussed. The first issue is whether the results remain valid if the notion of Nash equilibrium is replaced by the notion of IUS. I will come back to this later. A second issue is how the inverse demand function should be interpreted in the present context. In the context of strategic market games I have noted that in principle two interpretations of the market outcome function are possible, an *identity* and a *correlation* interpretation. In the Cournot approach of the present section a correlation interpretation of the inverse demand function is, I think, the most appropriate. A correlation interpretation simply says that there is an empirical relationship between prices and total production and that the firms take this relationship into account when making their decisions. The above approach then says that in an economy in which such an empirical relationship holds firms produce their Cournot–Nash equilibrium production levels. The approximation step postulates that in large markets Nash equilibrium production levels are close to competitive equilibrium production levels and the correlation between prices and production can then be used to account for the competitive equilibrium prices. Of course, one would also like to have an individualistic explanation for the correlation between prices and quantities, but such an explanation is not offered by the Cournot approach. In other words, the above account does *not* give an explanation of why prices close to ADM prices result when the *quantities* firms produce are taken as *given*. What the approach offers is an individualistic explanation of why production levels close to competitive equilibrium production levels might result. It also offers an individualistic explanation of ADM prices when the *correlation* between quantities and prices is taken *as given* (see also chapter 2).

The other issue that was raised above concerns the question of whether the above result also holds when the notion of Nash equilibrium is replaced by the notion of IUS. An example by Bernheim (1984: 1024–5) shows that this is *not* the case. His example is discussed below.

Example 7.4 (continued) IUS of the Cournot Game (Bernheim 1984)

Bernheim's example is a special case of example 7.4 discussed above. In his example $c_2 = 0$, Bernheim uses the notion of rationalizability. As the profit function is quasi-concave, the results under rationalizability and IUS coincide (see also chapter 2). If $c_2 = 0$, the best response mapping reduces to $q_i = \max \{(a - c_1 - bQ_{-i})/2b, 0\}$. It is easy to see that the best response is decreasing in Q_{-i}. If $Q_{-i} = 0$, the best response q_i reaches its maximum, which is $q_m = (a - c_1)/2b$, the production level of a hypothetical monopolist. So, the best response q_i is always an element of the set $[0, q_m]$; not producing is a best response to any $Q_{-i} \geq 2q_m$. Two cases have to be distinguished: (i) $n = 2$ and (ii) $n \geq 3$.

(i)   In this case, both firms know that the maximal optimal production level of the other firm is equal to q_m. But this means that an optimizing firm will never produce a production level that is an optimal response to a production level larger than q_m, i.e. it will never produce a number between 0 and $(a - c_1)/4b$, the optimal response to q_m. Thus, after one more stage of elimination, the interval $[(a - c_1)/4b, q_m]$ remains. But as both firms know that the other will produce a quantity that belongs to this interval, they both decide not to produce a quantity close to q_m. This is because q_m is an optimal response to the other's not producing, but both firms know that the other minimally produces $(a - c_1)/4b$. This means that the interval of production levels that can possibly be optimal shrinks further to $[(a - c_1)/4b, 3(a - c_1)/8b]$. If one continues this elimination process, one can show that the Cournot production level, $(a - c_1)/3b$, is the unique rationalizable strategy. The beginning of the iterative process is illustrated in figure 7.2.

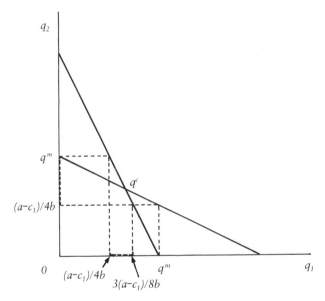

Figure 7.2

(ii) In this case, all firms know that the maximal optimal production level of the other firms is larger than or equal to $2q_m$. So, even though all firms know that the others individually will not produce more than q_m, they also know that the production levels of the others taken together might be equal to or larger than $2q_m$. Not producing is an optimal response to such a large total production level of the others. So, in contrast to the previous case, one cannot eliminate strategies of the interval $[0, q_m]$ if $n \geq 3$.

One can show that in the case $c_2 \neq 0$ the two cases to be distinguished are: (*i*) $n < 3 + 2c_2/b$ and (*ii*) $n \geq 3 + 2c_2/b$. The idea remains the same, however: if n is large enough a continuum of strategies is rationalizable (see also Basu 1991).

The example above seems to devastate the idea that if the number of firms is large, rational behaviour would force them to produce quantities that are close to the competitive equilibrium quantities. Recently, Börgers and Janssen (1991) have shown that Bernheim's example is sensitive to the way the economy is replicated. Bernheim replicates only the supply side of the market (the number of firms). If, however, the demand side is also replicated, one can show that for a large number of replications the Cournot–Nash equilibrium production level is the unique IUS if and only if the cobweb process of the corresponding competitive economy is globally stable. This is illustrated in the example below.

Example 7.4 (continued) **IUS of the Cournot Game[17]**

Replicating both the demand and the supply side of the original model of example 7.4 N times means that there are Nn firms and that the inverse demand function is given by $p = a - (Nb)Q$. The above analysis remains valid provided we replace n by Nn and b by Nb. This means that the two cases to be distinguished become: (*i*) $N(n - 2c_2/b) < 3$ and (*ii*) $N(n - 2c_2/b) \geq 3$. If the first (second) case holds, there is a unique (continuum of) IUS. Concentrating on a large number of replications N (the case in which the Nash equilibrium of the Cournot game is close to the competitive equilibrium), the first case holds when $n - 2c_2/b \leq 0$ and the second case holds when $n - 2c_2/b > 0$. The first inequality can be written as $n/2c_2 \leq 1/b$. The lefthand side $n/2c_2$ is nothing but the slope of the total supply function and the righthand side $1/b$ is nothing but the absolute value of the slope of the demand function of the original model. So, the first case prevails if supply is not steeper than demand; this is the condition for cobweb stability. In the same way, the second case coincides with the case of an unstable cobweb process.

From the above examples, we can conclude that the result that the outcomes of the Cournot games converge to the competitive equilibrium outcomes remains valid if the outcomes considered are those determined by IUS rather than the Nash equilibrium outcomes *provided that*:

(i) the notion of large markets is such that both the demand and the supply side are replicated; and (ii) the cobweb process is globally stable. A proof of this statement under fairly general conditions is found in Börgers and Janssen (1991). If these two conditions are not met, a continuum of IUS exists. In those cases the second requirement of MI is not fulfilled.

DISCUSSION AND CONCLUSION

This chapter has been concerned with a discussion of whether the notion of competitive equilibrium used throughout economics is based upon MI. In particular, I have addressed the question of whether 'the maximizing behaviour of consumers and producers inevitably results in a competitive equilibrium state', i.e. whether ADM is based on MI. First, I have shown that the textbook presentation of ADM is not in line with MI. Second, I have reviewed five game theoretic approaches that can be interpreted as attempts to base ADM on a version of MI. None of the game theoretic approaches that have been reviewed here can be regarded as providing the assumption of competitive equilibrium with an unconditional foundation in the theory of individual behaviour. I have treated the different approaches in some detail, because each of them illuminates some difficulties that may arise in providing a justification of an aggregate hypothesis that is in line with MI. Also, the treatment of the different approaches has allowed us to discuss the different elements of the reduction scheme in more detail.

The Arrow–Debreu approach, treated in the second section, suffers from the fact that a fictitious player (auctioneer) is introduced who sets prices. By doing so, this approach gives *one* individual the right to take a decision on a supposedly *aggregate* concept such as market price. Accordingly, one cannot say that the concept of price is an aggregate concept in this approach. The approximation step present in the third and sixth sections on the limit points of the core and of Cournot competition points at the possibility that if there is a large number of agents it might be justified to use the competitive equilibrium assumption as a simplifying device for real market processes provided that the theory used gives an adequate individualistic explanation of the real process (see also chapter 4). In the third section I have argued that the theory of the core does *not* give such an individualistic explanation, because of the fact that the notion of group rationality is used as a basic term.[18] The approach of the sixth section is more successful in this respect. However, the Cournot competition approach considered there shows that the competitive equilibrium assumption is a

129

good approximation only when some (non-trivial) conditions are satisfied. The same holds true for the results of the Bertrand model discussed in the fifth section. In this sense, both sections are in line with the general discussion on the merits of individualistic explanations in chapter 2: namely, that such an explanation often shows that an aggregate relationship only holds under certain circumstances. Finally, one of the weaknesses of the strategic market games treated in the fourth section is that they use the Nash equilibrium notion and it is not clear whether the results remain valid if this notion is replaced by the less demanding notion of IUS.

The above observations should not be interpreted as saying that the approaches considered in this chapter are void of any use. An important point is that the relation between different concepts has become more clear. Also, it has been suggested under what kind of conditions the competitive equilibrium condition can be legitimately used as a simplifying device. Some of those conditions are, of course, difficult to interpret in an empirical way and as such one might question whether these conditions can fruitfully be used when we apply simple models to problems of the real world (see also chapter 4).

8

THE INDIVIDUAL RATIONALITY OF RATIONAL EXPECTATIONS

Although the notion of rational expectations has been in the economics profession for more than thirty years now, there is still no consensus about the motivation for using the notion in macroeconomics. On the one hand, many economists see the notion of rational expectations as the 'natural' assumption to make about expectations, because it would extend the notion of purposeful behaviour to the domain of expectations:

> Each alternative expectational hypothesis ... explicitly or implicitly posits the existence of some particular pattern of *systematic* expectational error. This implication is unattractive, however, because expectational errors are costly. Thus purposeful agents have an incentive to weed out all systematic components.
>
> (McCallum 1979: 718)

Interpreted in this way, rational expectations seems to be a hypothesis about individual behaviour. Originally, however, the rational expectations hypothesis was advanced by Muth (1961) who postulated the hypothesis

> that expectations of firms (or, more generally, the subject probability distribution of outcomes) tend to be distributed about the prediction of the theory (or the 'objective' probability distribution of outcomes).
>
> (Muth 1961: 316)

Interpreting rational expectations in the way Muth defines the notion seems to lead us to a notion of behaviour in the aggregate: Muth's definition does not restrict expectations by individual firms. It only says that *on the average* firms' expectations are distributed in a certain way (see also Snippe 1986).

In this chapter I will go into the relation between the individual and the aggregate version of the rational expectations hypothesis. The aggregate version is usually employed in many economic models and when, in the rest of this chapter, I use the term rational expectations hypothesis (REH), I will have this aggregate version in mind. In the previous chapters it was argued that many aggregate relationships do not hold unconditionally. It was also argued that this is one of the main reasons for exploring the individualistic foundations of these aggregate relationships. From the perspective of this book, it is then natural to explore the conditions under which REH can be legitimately employed. In other words, if the 'true' motivation derives from the hypothesis that rational individuals do not make systematic errors and if REH is the hypothesis that is employed the most, then one should enquire whether the 'true' motivation can provide a justification for using REH.

The rational expectations hypothesis has been critically discussed many times (see, e.g., Frydman and Phelps 1983). Quite a number of critical discussions concentrate on the question of whether agents are able to learn the 'true' (parameters of the) model (see, e.g., Frydman 1982 and for a more recent overview, Mongin 1991). A special interesting case is the one in which agents initially have different views about the 'true' model of the world (see, e.g., Kirman 1983). The results of this learning literature basically are that there is a wide class of circumstances in which agents' expectations do *not* converge to rational expectations. Another fundamental point has been made by Bray (1983). She argues that for REH to make sense, the objective probability distribution of outcomes should be rather stationary. However, the very process of learning changes agents' expectations and this, in turn, introduces a non-stationarity in the process.

Without belittling these contributions in any way, I would like to make two observations. First, from a logical point of view, one could argue that REH assumes that agents know the true model of the economy (including the parameters) so that learning issues are not all that relevant. Second, in most models in this learning literature, no distinction is made between the subjective expectations of different agents. Chapter 2 has argued that in order to give individualistic foundations for an aggregate relationship (hypothesis) it does not suffice to assume the existence of *one* representative individual. Thus, in order to study individualistic foundations for REH the interaction between the expectations of at least two rational agents has to be analysed. More specifically, in this chapter I will discuss the question of whether the REH is a logical consequence of rational individual behaviour in models where at least two rational agents are distinguished and where the agents know the true model of the economy. Hence, I will assume that agents are cognitive rational in the strong sense (see also chapter 2). Surprisingly, the results show that in general REH cannot be seen as a consequence of the cognitive rationality of the agents even if these strong assumptions are made.

To illustrate the arguments I will use a version of the following simple partial equilibrium model:

$$Q_t^d = \alpha_1 - \beta_1 P_t + \gamma G_t + \varepsilon_t \qquad \alpha_1, \beta_1 > 0$$
$$\text{if } P_t \leq (\alpha_1 + \gamma G_t + \varepsilon_t)/\beta_1, \qquad (8.1)$$

$$Q^d = 0 \qquad \text{if } P_t > (\alpha_1 + \gamma G_t + \varepsilon_t)/\beta_1,$$

$$Q_t^s = \alpha_2 + \beta_2 P_t^e + \nu_t, \quad \alpha_2 < \alpha_1, \beta_2 > 0 \qquad (8.2)$$

$$Q_t^s = Q_t^d, \qquad (8.3)$$

where Q_t^d is the aggregate demand, P_t is the actual price, G_t is government expenditure, Q_t^s is aggregate supply, P_t^e is the subjective expectation of the price in period t and ε_t and ν_t are disturbance terms that have zero mean and are serially uncorrelated. The model is assumed to be common knowledge. Note that the above equations postulate the existence of aggregate relationships and of an equilibrium situation. In earlier chapters we analysed some of the difficulties of regarding these equations as a consequence of individual behaviour. In order to be able to focus our analysis on the individual rationality of REH, the above equations are used here *only as if* these difficulties did not exist.

The usual rational expectations solution is obtained in the following way. First, substituting (8.1) and (8.2) in the equilibrium condition and taking the expectation conditional on the information available at time $t-1$ yields

$$\alpha_1 - \beta_1 E(P_t | \Psi_{t-1}) + \gamma E(G_t | \Psi_{t-1}) = \alpha_2 + \beta_2 P_t^e,$$

where Ψ_{t-1} is the information set available to economic agents at period $t-1$. Second, REH requires that $E(P_t | \Psi_{t-1}) = P_t^e$. Using this equality in the above equation yields

$$P_t^e = \frac{\alpha_1 - \alpha_2}{\beta_1 + \beta_2} + \frac{\gamma E(G_t | \Psi_{t-1})}{\beta_1 + \beta_2}. \qquad (8.4)$$

How is equation (8.4) to be compared with the quotation from Muth (1961) above? Muth speaks about a distribution of expectations of individual firms, whereas there does not seem to be a role for individual expectations in (8.4). One way out of this dilemma is the following. Equation (8.4) shows that expected prices depend on the expected value of the exogenously determined G_t. One might argue that individuals have different views with respect to the way G_t is determined and that this creates differences in individual price expectations. The next section analyses a case in which the firms think that the government is a rational entity and that it decides on G_t accordingly. It is shown that this set-up leads to a fundamental conceptual difficulty concerning the question of which policy the government should take. As a consequence the firms do not know which policy to expect.

The next section still assumes that all firms have identical expectations. If we want to take seriously the *possibility* that firms have different expectations, equation (8.2) should be modified: having identical expectations is by no means a direct consequence of the firms being rational. The assumption behind equation (8.2) is that firms are price takers. It is well known, however, that the assumption of price-taking behaviour is valid only if the impact of each firm is small relative to the total supply of goods (see chapter 7). Accordingly, it is necessary to assume that a large number of firms exist who may have different expectations. The following two sections will work with the following adaptation of the supply function:

$$Q^s_t = \alpha_2 + (\beta_2/n)\Sigma^n_{j=1} P^e_t(j), \qquad \alpha_2 < \alpha_1, \beta_2 > 0, \quad (8.2')$$

where n is the number of firms and $P^e_t(j)$ is the subjective expectation of firm j about the price in period t. If multiple rational firms are distinguished, firms try to form correct price expectations knowing that the actual price depends on all (other) firms' expectations. In the second section it will be shown that correct expectations depend on expectations of other firms' expectations. In this case individual rationality and common knowledge of the true model are insufficient to rationalize REH; instead REH will be characterized as an equilibrium assumption. The third section investigates whether this equilibrium assumption can be justified in terms of (common knowledge of) the rationality of individual agents.

134

THE GOVERNMENT AND THE FIRMS AS TWO RATIONAL AGENTS[1]

In this section we take the model of equations (8.1)–(8.3) as our starting point. In order to facilitate the argument suppose that the government has only two policy options available: it can choose either a low level of expenditures ($G_{t,L}$) or a high level of expenditures ($G_{t,H}$). We have four possible outcomes corresponding to the cases that the government chooses a low or a high level of expenditures and that the firms expect a low or a high level of expenditures. Whether or not the firms correctly anticipate the government's expenditures, total production just depends on the expected value of G_t, i.e.

$$Q_t = \frac{\alpha_2\beta_1 + \alpha_1\beta_2 + \beta_2\gamma E(G_t|\Psi_{t-1})}{\beta_1 + \beta_2}.$$

Price is given by

$$P_t = \frac{\alpha_1 - \alpha_2}{\beta_1 + \beta_2} - \frac{\gamma\beta_2}{\beta_1(\beta_1 + \beta_2)}E(G_t|\Psi_{t-1}) + \frac{\gamma}{\beta_1}G_t.$$

Equations (8.2) and (8.4) reveal that in the case of correctly anticipated low expenditures $P_t = P_t^e$ and P_t and Q_t are lower than in the case of a correctly anticipated high level of expenditures. In the case when the firms do not correctly anticipate G_t, two cases might prevail. First, if a low level of expenditures is expected, while the government chooses a high level of expenditures P_t will be high; second, P_t will be low if a high level of expenditures is expected, while the government chooses a low level. The four cases are depicted in figure 8.1.

It is assumed that the government has a preference ordering over the four possible outcomes. The government prefers low above high prices and high above low quantities produced. This is described by the following matrix.

		Firms	
		Expect $G_{t,L}$	Expect $G_{t,H}$
	Choose $G_{t,L}$	$U(G_{t,L},G_{t,L})$	$U(G_{t,L},G_{t,H})$
Monetary authority			
	Choose $G_{t,H}$	$U(G_{t,H},G_{t,L})$	$U(G_{t,H},G_{t,H})$

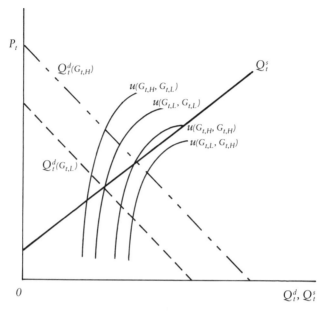

Figure 8.1

In this matrix $U(G_{t,H},G_{t,L})$, for example, is the von Neumann–Morgenstern utility of the government in the situation in which the government chooses $G_{t,H}$ and the firms expect $G_{t,L}$. It is assumed that $U(G_{t,L},G_{t,H}) > U(G_{t,H},G_{t,H}) > U(G_{t,L},G_{t,L}) > U(G_{t,H},G_{t,L})$, i.e. a situation with a large quantity produced and high prices is preferred to a situation with a relatively low quantity produced and low prices. The indifference curves in figure 8.1 depict the above preference ordering.

Let ω denote the government's (subjective) probability that the firms correctly anticipate G_t. The government's expected utility of choosing $G_{t,L}$, respectively $G_{t,H}$, can then be written as $\omega U(G_{t,L},G_{t,L}) + (1 - \omega)U(G_{t,L},G_{t,H})$, respectively $(1 - \omega)U(G_{t,H},G_{t,L}) + \omega U(G_{t,H},G_{t,H})$. If the firms are good predictors of the policy, i.e. if ω is close to 1, then $G_{t,H}$ maximizes the government's expected utility.[2] However, as $U(G_{t,L},G_{t,L}) > U(G_{t,H},G_{t,L})$ and $U(G_{t,L},G_{t,H}) > U(G_{t,H},G_{t,H})$, $G_{t,L}$ dominates $G_{t,H}$.

Rational expectations in the sense of REH clearly means that ω is close to or equal to 1. In this case the so-called Newcomb's paradox arises. The paradox says that in some cases two well-established theories of rational behaviour have conflicting implications. In the Bayesian view of rationality, agents maximize their subjective expected utility. In the above context, this suggests the choice of $G_{t,H}$. The other view on rationality is that rational agents do not choose a dominated strategy (see chapter 2). This suggests the choice of $G_{t,L}$. So, on the basis of considerations of rationality alone it is not clear what the government should do. If, in the deliberation process, the government assumes that the firms already know the outcome of the deliberation then the government should choose $G_{t,H}$. However, this assumption seems to be contrary to the sensible idea that the firms cannot know the policy decision by the government, if the government itself does not yet know what to do. If the government thinks that the firms have already decided upon their expectation, then the government should choose $G_{t,L}$. As the firms have no means of inferring which theory of rational behaviour is adopted by the government, they have no means of forming a rational expectation of government expenditure.

Of course, in specific cases the authority may use extra-rational processes (e.g. rules of thumb) which prescribe a unique action. The firms may know this and may use this knowledge to form their expectations. However, these expectations do not follow from the description of the theory. The REH is difficult to interpret in these cases, because relevant theories of rational behaviour contradict each other and processes which prescribe a definite choice are extra-rational.

The Newcomb paradox may arise in models in which the government's utility function depends on whether or not its policy decisions are anticipated. In repeated situations, the government might even have the incentive to behave in a non-systematic way, thereby destroying the possibility that its policy can be anticipated, i.e. destroying the very possibility of rational expectations.

'RATIONAL' EXPECTATIONS AS AN EQUILIBRIUM ASSUMPTION

In models in which government policy does not play a role, the problems discussed in the previous section do not arise. In this section we will study the interaction of expectations of different firms. As argued in the introduction to this chapter, perfectly competitive models assume that there is more than one firm and this opens the possibility for firms trying to outguess each other. Thus, the model that is used here is given by equations (δ.1), (δ.2') and (δ.3). For convenience, it is assumed that $G_t = 0$. Furthermore, the idea that firms try to have correct expectations is formalized by assuming that each firm i sets $P_t^e(i)$

such as to maximize its payoff function $-|P_t^e(i) - E(P_t | \Psi_{t-1})|$. Of course, the subjective expectations of the price in period t held by other firms is not part of the information set Ψ_{t-1}, i.e. subjective price expectations have to be formed simultaneously. Thus, firms have identical information sets.

The relation between the expected value of the actual price and subjective price expectations is now given by

$$\alpha_1 - \beta_1 E(P_t | \Psi_{t-1}) = \alpha_2 + (\beta_2/n) \Sigma_{j=1}^{n} P_t^e(j).$$

The subjective price expectation of firm i that turns out to be correct *ex post*, denoted by $P_t^{ce}(i)$, is then given by

$$P_t^{ce}(i) = \frac{n(\alpha_1 - \alpha_2)}{n\beta_1 + \beta_2} - \frac{\beta_2}{n\beta_1 + \beta_2} \Sigma_{j \neq i}^{n} P_t^e(j).$$

However, if all firms have to form their expectations simultaneously, they are not informed about the expectations of the others. An *individual rational price expectations for firm i*, denoted by $P_t^{re}(i)$, is defined as the expectation that maximizes firm i's payoff function given the available information:

$$P_t^{re}(i) = \frac{n(\alpha_1 - \alpha_2)}{n\beta_1 + \beta_2} - \frac{\beta_2}{n\beta_1 + \beta_2} \Sigma_{j \neq i}^{n} P_t^e(j(i)), \tag{8.5}$$

where $P_t^e(j(i))$ is firm i's expectation of firm j's price expectation.

The question of the individual rationality of REH can then be formulated in two slightly different ways. REH interpreted in a narrow way might lead to the question of whether $P_t^{re}(i)$ equals the rational expectations solution for all i, i.e. whether (8.4) equals (8.5) for the case $G_t = 0$. Interpreting REH in a broader way (compare the quotation by Muth) leads to the question of whether the average of $P_t^{re}(i)$ equals the REH solution, i.e.

$$\frac{1}{n} \Sigma_{i=1}^{n} P_t^{re}(i) = \frac{\alpha_1 - \alpha_2}{\beta_1 + \beta_2}.$$

Simple algebra shows that in general the answer to both questions is negative. For the first question to be answered positively an extra condition has to be fulfilled, namely

$$\frac{1}{n-1} \Sigma_{j \neq i}^{n} \ P_t^e(j(i)) = \frac{\alpha_1 - \alpha_2}{\beta_1 + \beta_2} \qquad \text{for all } i.$$

This means that all individual firms have to expect that the *average* price expectation of all other firms equals the rational expectations solution. For the second question to be answered in a positive way a similar condition has to hold, namely

$$\frac{1}{n(n-1)} \Sigma_{i=1}^{n} \ \Sigma_{j \neq i}^{n} \ P_t^e(j(i)) = \frac{\alpha_1 - \alpha_2}{\beta_1 + \beta_2} \qquad \text{for all } i.$$

This condition is slightly weaker. It says that *on the average* all firms have to expect that the average price expectation of all other firms equals the rational expectations solution. An important special case for both questions to be answered positively occurs when all firms expect that all other firms expect the rational expectations solution to prevail. In this case there is a Nash equilibrium in expectations. Accordingly, the REH can be regarded as an equilibrium assumption (see also Evans 1983). In chapter 2 I argued, however, that in general the Nash equilibrium concept is not a simple consequence of rational behaviour on the part of individuals. On the contrary, some coordinating device has to assure that individuals play Nash equilibrium strategies. The next section explores whether the assumption of Nash equilibrium can be replaced by the less demanding notion of IUS, or, more generally, whether the assumption on higher levels of expectations can be justified as a consequence of common knowledge of individual rationality.

The above result indicates that in a multi-individual economy individual rationality and knowledge of the true model are not sufficient to justify REH. In some way or the other, individuals have to expect the average expectation to be equal to REH. In other words, in order to justify REH we have to make a stringent assumption about expectations of expectations.[3] If the economy is supposed to consist of one individual, as is the case on Robinson Crusoe's island (but not in very many other cases), these difficulties do not arise, because the individual agent (Robinson Crusoe) is then in a position to derive a unique relation between his 'individual' expectation and 'aggregate' outcomes. (Of course, the distinction between individual and aggregate level disappears in this context.) In a multi-individual economy this is not possible, because aggregate outcomes are also determined by other agents' expectations.

RATIONALIZABLE EXPECTATIONS OF OTHER AGENTS' EXPECTATIONS

In the previous section we saw that individual rational price expectations coincide with the REH price expectation only if all individual agents expect the average price expectation to conform with the REH. A similar condition has to hold for the average of the individual rational price expectations to coincide with REH. In this section we will enquire whether this stringent condition on second-order expectations can be derived from the more fundamental notion that individual agents are rational and that this rationality is common knowledge. The result of this section is that the condition of cobweb stability is necessary and sufficient for there to be just one rationalizable expectation for all firms and for this expectation to coincide with the rational expectations solution.

The argument to derive REH from common knowledge of individual rationality runs as follows. For convenience, the expression for the best response of firm i to the subjective expectations held by the other firms is reproduced below (equation 8.5):

$$P_t^{re}(i) = \frac{n(\alpha_1 - \alpha_2)}{n\beta_1 + \beta_2} - \frac{\beta_2}{n\beta_1 + \beta_2} \, \Sigma_{j \neq i}^{n} \, P_t^e(j(i)).$$

This best response mapping is common knowledge; what firms do *not* know is the subjective price expectation of the other firms. In order to figure out what the other firms might expect, each firm can reason as follows. Price, and hence the subjective expected prices $P_t^e(j)$ and the expectation of others' price expectation $P_t^e(j(i))$, cannot fall below 0. Thus, all firms will not expect a price larger than $n(\alpha_1 - \alpha_2)/(n\beta_1 + \beta_2)$. But this fact is also common knowledge: a rational firm itself will never expect a price larger than $n(\alpha_1 - \alpha_2)/(n\beta_1 + \beta_2)$ and this firm knows that the other $n - 1$ firms will not expect a larger price as well. Using this knowledge and equation (8.5), the firm's expectation will satisfy the following requirement:

$$P_t^{re}(i) \geq \frac{n(\alpha_1 - \alpha_2)}{n\beta_1 + \beta_2} - \frac{\beta_2(n - 1)}{n\beta_1 + \beta_2} \cdot \frac{n(\alpha_1 - \alpha_2)}{n\beta_1 + \beta_2}.$$

Moreover, all firms also know that the other firms' expectations will satisfy this requirement (and they know that others know that, and so on). Applying the same argument as above, all suppliers also know that

$$P_t^{re}(i) \leq \frac{n(\alpha_1 - \alpha_2)}{n\beta_1 + \beta_2}\left[1 - \frac{\beta_2(n - 1)}{n\beta_1 + \beta_2} + \left(\frac{\beta_2(n - 1)}{n\beta_1 + \beta_2}\right)^2\right].$$

Eventually, i.e. if the argument is applied an infinite number of times, we find that all firms know that

$$P_t^{re}(i) \leq \frac{n(\alpha_1 - \alpha_2)}{n\beta_1 + \beta_2}\left[1 - \frac{\beta_2(n - 1)}{n\beta_1 + \beta_2} + \left(\frac{\beta_2(n - 1)}{n\beta_1 + \beta_2}\right)^2 - \left(\frac{\beta_2(n - 1)}{n\beta_1 + \beta_2}\right)^3 + \ldots\right].$$

Provided that $\beta_2(n - 1)/(n\beta_1 + \beta_2) < 1$, this expression equals $(\alpha_1 - \alpha_2)/(\beta_1 + \beta_2)$, the rational expectations solution (and equilibrium price). By the same token, $P_t^{re}(i) \geq (\alpha_1 - \alpha_2)/(\beta_1 + \beta_2)$ for all i. Thus, provided that $\beta_2(n - 1)/(n\beta_1 + \beta_2) < 1$, the only individual rational price expectation that is consistent with common knowledge is the rational expectations price. If the condition does not hold, $P_t^{re}(i)$ can take on any value in the interval $[0, n(\alpha_1 - \alpha_2)/(n\beta_1 + \beta_2)]$. In this case, all individual rational price expectations, $P_t^{re}(i)$, or the average of them, $(1/n)\sum_{i=1}^{n} P_t^{re}(i)$, can nevertheless be equal to the rational expectations solution. But this would be a matter of pure chance, instead of being a consequence of individual rationality.

The above condition can be rewritten as $\beta_2 - 2\beta_2/n < \beta_1$. For large n, this condition reduces to $\beta_2 < \beta_1$, which is the stability condition of the cobweb process. Thus, for large n the result is that the rational expectations solution is the only expectation consistent with common knowledge of rationality if and only if the cobweb process is stable.[4] Of course, the interpretation of the iterative process is different from the traditional cobweb process. The cobweb process is a dynamic process in real time with 'naive expectations', while the present argument hinges upon a dynamic process in artificial time with 'individual rational expectations'. Note that we encountered the cobweb stability condition also in chapter 7 while applying the notion of rationalizability in the context of large Cournot games. In fact, the model discussed in this section can be rewritten in terms of example 7.4.

The above discussion shows that an extra condition has to be fulfilled for the rational expectations solution to be regarded as being based on the assumptions of common knowledge of individual rationality. Although this result is obtained in a very special context (a partial equilibrium model), it has more general validity. So, we can conclude that in general REH is *not* a consequence of common knowledge of individual rationality.

DISCUSSION AND CONCLUSION

This chapter has analysed the question of whether REH can be derived from a theory of rational individual behaviour as required by MI. The first section considered a case in which the firms are represented as one decision maker and the government as another. The notion of rational behaviour turned out to be quite problematic in this case and it was unclear what the firms should expect the government to do. In the next two sections I considered a case in which many firms are distinguished. In this case the REH can be considered as a Nash equilibrium in expectations and only under rather special conditions can the Nash equilibrium strategies be considered the only strategies firms can rationally choose. The term 'rational expectations' is thus rather misleading. It *suggests* that the REH is an extension of the rationality principle to the domain of expectations. This chapter has argued that in general this is *not* what the REH does. Thus, REH is an aggregate hypothesis that cannot unconditionally be regarded as being based on MI.

Of course, one can argue that as an aggregate hypothesis, REH is the 'natural' hypothesis to make in macroeconomics. McCallum (1979), for example, has argued that the suggestion that

> expectations should be modeled as different for different agents, seems to amount to an objection to macroeconomics – i.e., analysis that abstracts from distributional and (most) relative price effects – rather than rational expectations. Of course, expectations will 'actually' differ across individuals. But ... these differences will be unimportant in the aggregate unless they are significantly correlated with other cross-sectional differences among agents.
>
> (McCallum 1979: 718)

Another perspective on the present chapter then would be that it analyses the claim that differences in individual expectations are unimportant in the aggregate so that REH might be a good hypothesis as far as macroeconomics is concerned. If individual expectations are independent of each other and if there is a large number of agents, then the law of large numbers might be invoked to support the claim that differences between individual expectations cancel out in the aggregate. However, if individuals are truly rational, they might figure out that what actually happens in the economy depends on the behaviour of all other individuals, which in turn depends on what they expect to happen. This is the point of view taken in this chapter. In this case, I have shown that there is no reason to believe that differences in individual expectations cancel out. On the contrary, considerations of higher-order expectations become important and this may make expectations by rational individuals indeterminate. If individual rationality leaves expectations indeterminate, individuals should have other means to determine what to expect. In general, economic theory has little to say about what individuals do if rational choice is indeterminate. It may be that in cases of indeterminacy individuals have, on the average, expectations in conformity with REH, but this would be a matter of chance and chance is a weak foundation for such an important concept as rational expectations.

Part IV

MICROFOUNDATIONS

9

WHAT IS THIS THING CALLED MICROFOUNDATIONS?

After having discussed aggregation problems in economics and individualistic foundations for equilibrium notions we come back to the question of whether the microfoundations literature provides macroeconomics with individualistic foundations that are in line with methodological individualism. Here, we will supplement the general discussion about microfoundations in chapter 3 by going into some details of new classical[1] and new Keynesian models. In the context of specific models it will be argued that 'microfoundations' does *not* mean 'foundations in the theory of individual behaviour'. The argument I will put forward essentially is that many models in the microfoundations literature employ the concepts of (competitive) equilibrium and rational expectations. In the previous part of the book we saw that only under special conditions can these concepts be considered as consequences of a theory of rational individual behaviour. In most of the new classical and new Keynesian models that will be considered in this chapter those conditions will not be fulfilled. Hence, the conclusion with which I started follows.

When this argument is taken for granted the natural question is how the microfoundations literature should be interpreted. It will be argued that the methods of general equilibrium analysis (GEA) – individual optimizing behaviour *and* equilibrium – are employed in the literature that provides macroeconomics with microfoundations. Accordingly, a characterization of the literature in terms of the programme of GEA may seem to be appropriate. The use of the methods of GEA covers, however, only part of the characterization, because it leaves unexplained what microfoundations has to do with macroeconomics. The second part of the characterization then contains the statement that the questions with which mainstream macroeconomics has been concerned since its origin are still raised in the microfoundations literature.[2] The interaction between the programmes of mainstream macroeconomics and GEA will be described by means of Zandvoort's (1986) model of cooperating and competing programmes.

NEW CLASSICAL MICROFOUNDATIONS

One of the most frequently used new classical models is the following simple model, which originally was developed in Lucas (1973):

$$y^s = y^n + \alpha(P - P^e), \quad \alpha > 0 \tag{9.1}$$

$$y^d = M - P + V \tag{9.2}$$

$$y^s = y^d = y, \tag{9.3}$$

where y^s, y^d are aggregate supply of and demand for the single commodity in the economy; y^n is the natural rate of output; y is actual output; P is the price level; P^e is the price level expected by the suppliers; M is the money stock and V is the velocity of money circulation. All variables refer to the same period in time and are measured in logarithms (logs). The demand equation is simply a restatement of the quantity theory of money.

The above system of equations is usually solved by assuming that P^e is formed in conformity with the rational expectations hypothesis (REH). The relation between prices and expected prices is

$$P = (M+V)/(1+\alpha) + \alpha P^e/(1+\alpha) - y^n/(1+\alpha). \tag{9.4}$$

Taking expectations of both sides of this equation, using REH and solving for P^e yields

$$P^e = M^e + V - y^n \tag{9.5}$$

where M^e is the level of the money supply expected by the suppliers. Using equations (9.1)–(9.5) we arrive at the following solution of the model:

$$y - y^n = \alpha(M - M^e)/(1 + \alpha). \tag{9.6}$$

This is the well-known result that, in new classical monetary models of the business cycle, only an unexpected monetary policy has an effect on aggregate output.[3]

On the basis of considerations in previous chapters the following observations can now be made. It is clear that the notions of a natural rate (of output), market clearing and rational expectations are used. In chapter 2 I criticized the notion of a natural rate for being an aggregate concept that is problematic from an individualistic point of view: the concept of a natural rate only makes sense at the aggregate level. In Lucas' model it remains unexplained how the interaction of rational agents produces such a natural level. The notion of market clearing was critically examined in chapter 7. There we reached the conclusion that the notion of market clearing is also problematic from the point of view of MI. Under some rather special conditions, market clearing can be regarded as being based on rational individual behaviour, but in general it cannot.

In the remainder of this section we concentrate on REH. The individualistic foundation of this hypothesis can be studied in the context of the above model without modifying the model in a drastic way.[4] In the previous chapter we considered two difficulties. The first one is related to the case in which the government (monetary authority) tries to make a rational decision and the suppliers attempt to forecast this decision. It was shown that under some additional restrictions, there is no unique way to make a rational decision about the policy variable. This precludes the possibility of forming expectations in a rational way. The same type of problem may arise in the context of the above model. This is shown in Frydman *et al.* (1982). The reader can easily check this by making the analogy between the model under consideration and the model presented in chapter 8.

The second difficulty arises when we allow for the possibility that different suppliers have different expectations. In order to concentrate on this case it will be assumed that all agents know the value of M so that $M^e = M$. Applying REH then yields $P^e = P$ and $y = y^n$. The assumption implicitly behind Lucas' model is that there is a large class of suppliers. Each supplier potentially has an expectation that differs from his or her competitors. Expectations by rational suppliers might be identical, but it should be shown why this is so (if it is so). In order to allow the suppliers to have different expectations, I rewrite equation (9.1) as

$$y^s = y^n + \frac{\alpha}{n} \Sigma_{i=1}^{n} \{P - P^e(i)\}, \quad \alpha > 0, \qquad (9.1')$$

where $P^e(i)$ is supplier i's price level expectation. An *individual rational price level expectation for supplier i*, $P^{re}(i)$, is the best expectation agent i is able to form *given the information available to the supplier*. Using equations (9.1'), (9.2) and (9.3) $P^{re}(i)$ can be calculated to be

$$P^{re}(i) = \frac{n}{n + \alpha n - \alpha} (M + V - y^n) +$$

$$\frac{\alpha}{n + \alpha n - \alpha} \Sigma^n_{j \neq i} P^e(j(i)), \quad (9.7)$$

where $P^e(j(i))$ is the price level expectation agent j is assumed to hold by supplier i.

The question of whether REH is a logical consequence of the basic hypothesis that agents have individual rational price expectations can be answered by comparing equations (9.5) and (9.7). The condition for the two equations to yield identical results is that

$$\frac{1}{n-1} \Sigma_{j \neq i} P^e(j(i)) = M + V - y^n \qquad \text{for all } i. \quad (9.8)$$

This means that all suppliers have to expect that the average price expectations of all other suppliers is equal to the expectation in conformity with REH.

In the previous chapter we encountered a similar (restrictive) condition in the context of a different model. We saw there that if the cobweb process is stable it is possible to derive this condition from the assumption of common knowledge of individual rationality. One may wonder whether a similar argument applies to the new classical model. At first sight such an application may seem to work. However, in Lucas' model there are no natural constraints on prices (as, say, $P \geq 0$) that trigger off the elimination process. This is because the variables are measured in logs and logs can take on all real values. The reason the model is written in logs is because the demand equation is just a version of the quantity theory of money. So, without changing the model, there is no way to justify the assumption on second-order expectations on the basis of common knowledge of individual rationality.

One way to trigger the elimination process is to allow for an independent authority, say the government, who announces credible price and/ or quantity restrictions. Let us imagine that the government announces a restriction that P has to be less than or equal to $M + V$. Applying the argument presented in chapter 8 yields the result that an individual rational price expectation has to satisfy the following requirement:

$$P^{re}(i) \le \frac{n}{n + an - a} (M + V - y'') +$$

$$\frac{a(n - 1)}{n + an - a} (M + V) = M + V - \frac{n}{n + an - a} y''.$$

A subsequent application of the above argument gives

$$P^{re}(i) \le M + V - \frac{n}{n + an - a} \left[1 + \frac{a(n - 1)}{n + an - a} \right.$$

$$+ \left(\frac{a(n - 1)}{n + an - a} \right)^2 + \dots \left. \right] y'' = M + V - y''.$$

The restriction $P \le M + V$, however, does not eliminate prices below $M + V - y''$. In order to eliminate prices below the equilibrium price, another restriction must be added. It is easy to check that, for example, the restriction $P \ge 0$ suffices for this purpose. Of course, the introduction of a government in the above model is at odds with the new classical emphasis on the efficiency of *laissez-faire*. However, without a central authority, a decentralized process of expectations formation does not converge in this model to expectations that are equal to the REH.

The difficulties alluded to above do not occur in economies with only one decision maker. In such economies there is no need for an assumption of market clearing (because the individual is producer and consumer at the same time) and the rational expectations hypothesis can be regarded as a logical consequence of cognitive rationality (if the true model that governs the situation is completely known), because there is no endogenous uncertainty in such an economy. Thus, a way to circumvent the difficulties that are posed by the quest for individualistic foundations is to build Robinson Crusoe models of the economy. Robinson Crusoe may produce and consume goods, he may save goods for future consumption and so on. These are also activities individuals may undertake in an economy consisting of two or more individuals. However, in the latter type of economy individuals are also able to exchange goods in which case prices (or, better, exchange ratios) emerge. Exchange and exchange ratios have no meaning in a Robinson Crusoe economy.

Among others, Kydland and Prescott (1982) and Long and Plosser (1983) construct real business cycle models in which there is just one inhabitant of the economy. Their models *may* be able to account for the actual pattern of consumption and production, but they cannot account for the level of exchange and exchange ratios in an economy, because – before Friday arrived – there is no other person Robinson Crusoë can exchange goods with.[5] Exchange ratios are typically phenomena that arise from the interaction between different individuals. But, even if real business cycle models can give a fairly accurate account of observed fluctuations in consumption and production levels, the models do not give explanations that are in line with MI. This is because the models assume a form of intentionality at the aggregate level, an intentionality MI denies to exist.

NEW KEYNESIAN MICROFOUNDATIONS

In chapter 3 we distinguished two different branches in new Keynesian economics: the first branch supplemented the fixprice models with an explanation why rational individuals might choose to set prices different from the Walrasian equilibrium levels; and the second branch showed that Keynesian results might apply even if prices are flexible (i.e. equate demand and supply) and agents have rational expectations. It is now time to discuss in more detail the structure of a typical model of each of these branches.

Efficiency wage models

The efficiency wage model is one of the models that is used to explain why prices might differ from their Walrasian equilibrium values. The following presentation is based on Lindbeck and Snower (1987). In its simplest form, the efficiency wage model posits that a firm's production Q_i depends not only on the number of employees L_i, but also on the average labour productivity per employee e_i: $Q_i = f(e_i \cdot L_i)$. In addition, e_i is assumed to depend positively on the firm's wage offer w_i: $e_i = e_i(w_i)$, $e'_i > 0$. There are n firms and each of them chooses its wage offer and its labour demand so as to maximize profits. Profits π_i are given by

$$\pi_i = p \cdot f(e_i \cdot L_i) - w_i L_i,$$

where p is the exogenously given price of the product. The optimal solution to this problem in terms of the wage offer and labour demand will be denoted by w^*_i and L^*_i, respectively. A simple case occurs when all optimal solutions are identical to each other, i.e. $w^*_i = w^*$ and $L^*_i = L^*$. In order to induce a high average labour productivity, it may be optimal for firms to choose a w^* that is higher than the competitive equilibrium wage. In this case total labour demand, nL^*, will be smaller than the labour supply at that wage and unemployment results. This unemployment is of an involuntary nature, because at w^* the unemployed workers would strictly prefer to work than to be unemployed. Nevertheless, the firms do not lower their wage offers, because of the negative impact this would have on the average labour productivity.[6]

Unlike other approaches in the microfoundations literature considered in this chapter, the efficiency wage model seems to give an explanation of (involuntary) unemployment that is in line with the requirements of MI. This can be seen as follows. Firms are considered to be rational decision makers. Their environment is such that there is a positive relation between the average labour productivity and the wage offered. An overview of the variety of explanations that have been offered for this relationship can be found in, for example, Yellen (1984). The simple point that concerns us here is that in such an environment firms set a wage above the competitive equilibrium level and demand less labour than the corresponding competitive labour demand. This is the application step of the reduction scheme. The aggregation step involves adding up individual labour demand. Unemployment is then simply defined (by the economist) as the difference between aggregate labour demand and aggregate labour supply.

The efficiency wage model does not assume any intentionality at the aggregate level, nor does it assume a form of coordination by the market that is itself not explained in terms of individual behaviour. Does (a part of the) microfoundations literature then establish individualistic foundations for macroeconomics? The answer I would like to give is 'yes, but the individualistic foundations are obtained as an unintended consequence'. Let me explain. Not one economist in the microfoundations literature questions the individualistic foundations of the notions of competitive (Walrasian) equilibrium and rational expectations. Although it is clear that these notions sustain the (classical) idea of the perfect functioning of markets more easily than a Keynesian idea of market imperfections, even new Keynesian economists do not question the foundations of these two notions. New Keynesians depart from the ADM, not because of the lack of individualistic foundations for the market clearing hypothesis, but in order to establish 'Keynesian' phenomena as involuntary unemployment. The fact that (some of) the models so obtained are in line with MI is an unimportant by-product that has been unnoticed thus far. The conformity with MI is never used as an argument in favour of the efficiency wage model (against, say, the coordination failures literature or the new classical models). So, as long as many other models in the microfoundations literature are not in line with MI, I do not see a reason to withdraw the claim that this literature does not provide macroeconomics with individualistic foundations.

Coordination failures

Bryant's (1983) paper 'A Rational Expectations Keynes Type Model' considers an economy with n individual agents. The production technology of the economy as a whole is characterized by a production function of the form $Y = \min(L_1, \ldots, L_n)$, where L_i is the labour input by individual i and Y is total output. Each individual has $\bar{L}$ units of time to be devoted to leisure and labour. The agents simultaneously have to decide upon their labour input L_i. When the output is produced it is divided equally over the agents so that each agent consumes $1/n$ of the total output level. Individuals are assumed to have identical utility functions with leisure and consumption as arguments: $U(\bar{L} - L_i, Y/n)$. Let us call $L(max)$ the labour input at which the marginal utility of an extra unit of consumption equals the marginal disutility of an extra unit of labour input, i.e. $U_1(\bar{L} - L(max), L(max)/n) = U_2(\bar{L} - L(max), L(max)/n)$. Thus, $L(max)$ is defined in such a way that even if the other individuals were to decide on a very high level of labour input, the individual in question will not choose a labour input that is larger than $L(max)$. It is easy to see that all individual agents prefer to have their labour input L_i equal to the lowest labour input of all the other individual agents as long as this does not exceed $L(max)$. Accordingly, there is a continuum of Nash equilibria, each of which involves an equal labour input of all individuals. The lower and upper boundaries of the continuum are, respectively, 0 and $L(max)$. In figure 9.1 the situation is depicted for $n = 2$. The best response functions for individual i are represented by $L_i = BR(L_{-i})$.

Bryant's paper is a typical example of a recent paper written within the new Keynesian coordination failures literature. This literature argues that an economy can get stuck in a low output (employment) situation in such a way that agents individually do not find it profitable to modify their behaviour. This is the 'Keynesian' message that this literature delivers. The model accounts for situations of underemployment, not of involuntary unemployment (see also chapter 3). On the other hand, there are also a number of non-'Keynesian' aspects to the coordination failures literature and to Bryant's model in particular. First, it is clear that deficiencies in demand are *not* the principal source of an

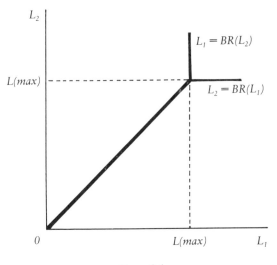

Figure 9.1

underemployment situation, but imperfections on the supply side. Second, it is not very clear how government policy should be analysed. It is very easy to say 'that there may be a role for government intervention to "coordinate" a movement to a superior equilibrium' (Mankiw and Romer 1991: 8), but it is more difficult to conceive the question of what exactly the government should do in order to achieve such a Pareto-superior move.

From the perspective of MI it should be noted that Bryant regards the Nash equilibrium as an unproblematic concept. In his paper, he does not give any argument, however, about why a Nash equilibrium should be expected to result. If individual agents face a situation as described in the model, then it is very unlikely that a Nash equilibrium results. Some sort of coordinating device has to assure that the players will end up in a Nash equilibrium.[7,8] A coordinating device can take on two forms. First, it can be an existing institution or norm which players take into account when making their decision. This form would be in line with the requirements of MI, but institutions and norms are typically not discussed in this literature (as in much of economic theory). Second, the coordinating device can be thought of as similar to the Invisible Hand. This form would be inconsistent with MI. On both accounts, the co-ordination failures literature does not provide individualistic foundations.[9]

Bryant (1983) himself makes it very clear that he wants to provide

155

the same kind of 'microfoundations' for Keynesian economics as the new classical economics provides for monetarism. He starts his paper by arguing that

> The rational expectations school of macroeconomics . . . provide a microfoundation for a version of monetarism. It is tempting to conclude from this that the tools of rational expectations, and more generally of microfoundations, themselves 'argue' against Keynes. . . . This conclusion is wrong.
>
> (Bryant 1983: 525)

In the previous section we argued extensively that the microfoundations of the new classical school is not equivalent to individualistic foundations according to MI. This conclusion is easily transposed on to much of the new Keynesian literature.

COOPERATING AND COMPETING PROGRAMMES

Now it is clear that the microfoundations literature does not provide macroeconomics with a foundation in MI,[10] it is appropriate to spend some time on characterizing the microfoundations literature in a more positive way. This will be done by using some ideas that are developed by Zandvoort (1986). Zandvoort discusses relatively recent developments in the physical sciences in terms of interacting programmes. In what follows I will concentrate on the elements of his model that are relevant to understand the developments in macroeconomics. Other elements of his model are less suited for our purposes and will not be discussed. According to Zandvoort one can understand quite a number of recent scientific developments only in terms of asymmetric cooperation between different programmes. He distinguishes a *guide programme* that determines the issues that are important enough to be discussed and a *supply programme* that provides the language and methods by means of which the issues can be tackled. The nature of the two programmes differs considerably, hence the asymmetric cooperation. Roughly speaking, the guide programme has a well-defined domain of issues with which it is concerned, but it does not have a method of its own. The reverse holds true for the supply programme, which is characterized by a clear-cut method and a rather vague domain of intended applications. These methods can often be applied to many different fields of enquiry. The confrontation of a supply programme with a guide programme leads to the establishment of specific research questions and is thus potentially fruitful.

This model of scientific development provides our basis for a description of the developments in modern macroeconomics in terms of interactive programmes. In chapter 3 I indicated the central propositions of the programme of GEA and of a monetarist (or classical) and a Keynesian macroeconomic programme. I propose to regard the two macroeconomic programmes as two guide programmes and to regard the programme of GEA as the supply programme. Macroeconomics guides the programme of GEA by providing the issues at stake, while the programme of GEA supplies the macroeconomic programmes with methods to discuss the issues with which they are concerned. The differences of opinion between the two macroeconomic programmes of the fifties and sixties largely carry over to the modern literature. In chapter 3 we briefly mentioned that new classical economists try to establish the monetarist (classical) position from within the programme of GEA. The same holds true for the new Keynesian programme with respect to the Keynesian position. In fact, the microfoundations debate is actually the continuation of an old debate in a new language. The microfoundations literature can thus be understood in terms of two competing macroeconomic guide programmes that cooperate with the same supply programme.

This suggested interpretation of the modern history of macroeconomics differs in an important way from a Lakatosian view on research programmes. Lakatos' model discusses developments in science in terms of developments *within one* programme. I have tried to argue that the principal developments took place on the border of different programmes. The two macroeconomic programmes present particular views on the functioning of the economy and the programme of GEA is a toolbox waiting to be used in a creative way. *One of the ways* the programme of GEA can be used is to deal with specific macroeconomic issues. For example, the real business cycle literature makes use of the ADM to explain the business cycle (a macroeconomic phenomenon).

It should be kept in mind that the guide and supply model does not imply that the programme of GEA plays a passive role only. The toolbox metaphor suggests that the programme of GEA is more suited to deal with one kind of problem than another. Some kinds of problems simply cannot be discussed in terms of the programme of GEA (see also Shubik 1975). Thus, in the *General Theory* Keynes paid considerable attention to the consequences of 'fundamental uncertainty'. In his view, there are no objective data upon which to base long-run expectations that are important for investment decisions. These long-run expec-

tations, and hence the level of investment (and output), are highly vola-
tile. Unfortunately, this reasoning cannot be represented in the language
of the programme of GEA, because there is no place for fundamental
uncertainty in this programme. Accordingly, Keynesians who want to
employ the methods of GEA cannot rely on this argument, and for this
reason other Keynesians criticize the programme of GEA.[11] The
example shows that the supply programme of GEA cannot satisfy all
potential demands of the guide programmes. This does not mean,
however, that the *asymmetric* nature of the cooperation is at stake.

One may wonder why macroeconomists have used the programme of
GEA as a supply programme, or in other words, what kind of problems
did the two macroeconomic programmes encounter and how did the
programme of GEA solve these problems? Clearly, the new classical use
of the programme of GEA is not (primarily) based on empirical grounds,
because (early) new classical models have more or less the same empirical implications as models in the monetarist tradition. We have seen
that the same holds (more or less) true for the transition in Keynesian
economics. There are, however, theoretical arguments in favour of the
adoption of the GEA method.

The first reason for adopting the programme of GEA is that the
macroeconomic method of the fifties and sixties (Ma1–3 in chapter 3)
does not impose a certain modelling discipline. This makes the
approach rather informal and subject to basic (logical) flaws. At the end
of the sixties it became apparent, for example, that quite a number of
existing macroeconomic models had neglected the fact that government
authorities are bound by a budget constraint (see, e.g., Christ 1968).
These internal inconsistencies in macroeconomic models made the
profession suspicious towards macroeconomic modelling in general.
Two examples will clarify this point. First, Lucas' main intention was to
provide a rigorously formulated model in which some monetarist
propositions were shown to be valid (see, e.g., Lucas 1972: 109). The
programme of GEA provides a way of modelling economic features in a
rigorous way. Second, one of Clower's (1965) main contributions to
economics was the observation that the assumption of sticky money
wages deeply affects the theory of demand and supply. Accordingly,
macroeconomists cannot simply impose the assumption of a fixed
money wage on a model that is otherwise akin to (a simplified) ADM:
all the consequences of the assumption have to be modelled in a
rigorous way.

A second reason for adopting the programme of GEA is that it
attempts to go beyond the appearances of empirical relationships. In

chapter 3 it has been argued that the two traditional macroeconomic programmes primarily focus upon empirical relationships like the Phillips curve and the macroeconomic consumption function. Within the context of a macroeconomic model these relationships have not been provided with any (theoretical) explanation whatsoever. Lucas' early monetary business cycle model attempts to provide an explanation of one of these relations, namely the Phillips curve. The major advantage of the new classical approach is that 'the Phillips curve emerges not as an unexplained empirical fact but as a central feature of the solution to a general equilibrium system' (Lucas 1981: 89).

A final question upon which the use of the guide/supply model may shed some light is the proliferation of papers in the Keynesian approach. This is not surprising. It is often argued that the paradigm of general equilibrium modelling, ADM, supports classical propositions with respect to macroeconomic policy issues. It is clear that Keynesian propositions are incompatible with ADM. Recent papers within (new) Keynesian economics can be characterized by a search for satisfactory alternative models that share the essential elements of the programme of GEA, but support Keynesian propositions. Consequently, Keynesian economists have to depart *in some way or another* from ADM. As of yet there is no convergence of opinion with respect to the question of how Keynesian features are best represented in the language of the programme of GEA.

10

RATIONALIZABLE ANIMAL SPIRITS

After having criticized the microfoundations literature for not providing macroeconomics with individualistic foundations, it is time to see in what way we can bring this literature closer to the tenets of MI.[1] It will be clear that once the requirements of (Nash) equilibrium or rational expectations are relaxed many outcomes are possible. The view that MI itself does not impose severe restrictions on the possible state of affairs at the aggregate level is very close to one of the possible readings of Keynes' *General Theory*. In Keynes' view, investment, and hence equilibrium output, largely depends on entrepreneurial expectations. According to Keynes, hardly any restriction can be imposed on these expectations, so that almost any level of output can be justified as an equilibrium level. Two arguments are used to sustain this view. The first is that there is no scientific basis to make (probabilistic) predictions about the magnitude of economic variables in the distant future: long-run expectations are determined by 'animal spirits'. It is this fundamental uncertainty that the economic theories considered in this study have problems dealing with.[2] The second argument is that economic agents might realize that the (future) state of the economy depends on the behaviour of all (other) agents. In forming expectations about this (future) state, they will realize that other agents' behaviour also depends on their expectations. (This is the problem of endogenous uncertainty, referred to in chapter 2.) Thus, an iterative process of expectations of other agents' expectations is set in motion. Both arguments can be found in Keynes (1936), but the second one is more pertinent to the present study. In a discussion of the famous beauty contest Keynes argues

> It is not the case of choosing those which, to the best of one's judgment, are really the prettiest, nor even those which average

opinion genuinely thinks the prettiest. We have reached the third degree where we devote our intelligences to anticipating what average opinion expects average opinion to be. And there are some, I believe, who practise the fourth, fifth and higher degrees.

(Keynes 1936: 156)

The present chapter shows that the concept of rationalizability can be fruitfully used to capture this idea of higher-order expectations. The (only) restriction rationalizability imposes is that agents' expectations must be internally information consistent, i.e. they have to be consistent with common knowledge of rationality. In general, there are many such rationalizable expectations. Some of these rationalizable expectations may turn out to be incorrect. The notion of (cognitive) rationality requires that expectations may *not* be *correctibly in*correct. This is precisely what it means to have rationalizable expectations: they are consistent with everything agents know at the moment they have to decide what action to choose.

The point of this chapter can also be approached from a different angle. In the previous chapter we saw that part of the new Keynesian economics explains low employment levels by pointing to a coordination problem. Formally, the coordination problem is represented by the existence of (multiple) Pareto-ranked Nash equilibria. It is the intention of this chapter to contribute to an understanding of the extent to which individual agents are able to coordinate their activities. From the critique on the Nash equilibrium given earlier in this study it may be no surprise that in my opinion the Nash equilibrium solution concept is not well suited for this purpose, because it already *assumes* a form of coordination among individuals. Playing Nash strategies is only optimal *if* all the other agents are expected to play the same Nash equilibrium strategy. In other words, if all players *share the expectation* that a particular Nash equilibrium results (maybe this is the case if all players share the same cultural background as neoclassical economists do) then this equilibrium will definitely result. However, this is only true if there is some underlying (aggregate) process that coordinates the expectations individuals form. The coordination failures literature, however, typically does not specify such a process. In the absence of such a process there is also no reason to believe that a Nash equilibrium results. Accordingly, for the analysis to be in line with MI either such a process has to be specified or the Nash equilibrium assumption has to be abandoned. Here, I have chosen to follow the latter route.

Thus, there are two (related) sources of the coordination problem.

One arises from the existence of multiple Nash equilibria; the other stems from the fact that expectations may be mismatched. This chapter analyses, in the context of a specific model, the implications of both sources of the coordination problem. It is shown that the application of the concept of rationalizability imposes upper and lower bounds on the set of expectations and, hence, on the rationalizable output levels.[3] The natural question from a 'Keynesian point of view' then is whether there exist policies a government can use to remedy the coordination problem. It turns out that such a policy exists: the government is able to change the firms' environment in such a way that there is a unique rationalizable output. This unique rationalizable output is Pareto superior to all the output levels that are rationalizable without government intervention.

A MODEL

The model presented below is based on Heller (1986). The economy consists of two goods: a consumption good and labour. There are two types of agents: households and firms. Households demand the consumption good and supply labour, firms supply the consumption good and demand labour. (The government's role is not considered until the fourth section.) The wage rate is used as numéraire and the price of the consumption good p is expressed in terms of the numéraire.

Identical households derive utility from consuming leisure l and the consumption good y. The behaviour of the household sector is described using the notion of a representative agent. This reflects the idea that the differences between households are considered to be unimportant for present purposes. Also, households are assumed to behave non-strategically. The representative household is endowed with one unit of time and zero consumption goods. It receives income from profits π, and from supplying labour. Hence, the budget constraint for the household can be written as $py = (1 - l) + \pi$. The utility function of the representative household is, apart from a monotonic transformation, of the following form:

$$U(y,l) = (y - 1)^{\gamma} l^{1-\gamma}, \qquad 0 < \gamma < 1. \tag{10.1}$$

The constant 1 can be interpreted as a kind of subsistence level.[4] Households take the price ratio as given. Maximizing utility leads to a demand function of the form

$$y^d(p,\pi) = \frac{\gamma(1 + \pi)}{p} + (1 - \gamma).$$

The inverse demand function $p_c(y,\pi)$ is then given by

$$p_c(y,\pi) = \frac{\gamma(1 + \pi)}{y - 1 + \gamma}. \qquad (10.2)$$

There are n firms who are assumed to be oligopolists in the consumption good market. All firms have exactly the same technology, in which labour L is the only input factor. Production of firm i is denoted by y_i. It is assumed that the marginal product of labour is constant and that there are no fixed costs:[5]

$$y_i = \alpha L_i, \qquad i = 1,\dots,n, \ \alpha > 1. \qquad (10.3)$$

In order to guarantee that firms produce more than the subsistence level, the set of admissible strategies Y_i is restricted to $[1/(n - 1), \infty)$.

Firms are supposed to be profit maximizers. They have common knowledge about the inverse demand function[6] $p_c(y,\pi)$ and each others' objective and production functions, but are ignorant of the actual output levels chosen by other firms. Thus, the problem faced by the individual firm is to maximize

$$\pi_i = p_c(y_i + y^e_{-i},\pi)y_i - \frac{y_i}{\alpha},$$

where y^e_{-i} denotes the expectation held by firm i of the total sum of output of all other firms. Firm i takes y^e_{-i} to be independent of its own choice y_i.

Note that the problem as formulated above has a simultaneous character, because the inverse demand function depends on total profits π (and thus on π_i). Here, it will be assumed that firms are aware of this feedback from profits to demand (see also d'Aspremont et al. 1990).[7] So, firms take account of the effect of total expected profits on consumer prices by solving the equation

$$\pi = \Sigma \pi_i = \left(p_c(y_i + y^e_{-i},\pi) - \frac{1}{\alpha}\right)(y_i + y^e_{-i})$$

for π. This gives

$$\pi = \frac{\gamma y}{(1 - \gamma)(y - 1)} - \frac{y - 1 + \gamma}{(1 - \gamma)(y - 1)} \frac{y}{\alpha}, \tag{10.4}$$

where y is used as a shorthand notation for $y_i + y^e_{-i}$. Firm i's maximization problem becomes

$$\max_{y_i} \pi_i = \left(p_c(y_i + y^e_{-i}, \pi(y_i + y^e_{-i})) - \frac{1}{\alpha} \right) y_i$$

$$= \left(p(y_i + y^e_{-i}) - \frac{1}{\alpha} \right) y_i, \tag{10.5}$$

where, using (10.2) and (10.4),

$$p(y) = \frac{\gamma}{y - 1 + \gamma} \left(1 + \frac{\gamma y}{(1 - \gamma)(y - 1)} \right)$$

$$- \frac{\gamma y}{(1 - \gamma)(y - 1)} = \frac{\gamma(\alpha - y)}{\alpha(1 - \gamma)(y - 1)}. \tag{10.6}[8]$$

Profit maximization implies that firms set their output levels such that

$$\frac{\partial \pi_i}{\partial y_i} = p'(y_i + y^e_{-i})y_i + p(y_i + y^e_{-i}) - \frac{1}{\alpha} = 0, \tag{10.7}$$

where

$$p'(y) = \frac{\gamma(1 - \alpha)}{\alpha(1 - \gamma)(y - 1)^2}.[9]$$

Profit maximization yields 'reaction curves' $y_i = BR(y^e_{-i})$. In this static model reaction curves have to be interpreted as the optimal output response of firm i to an *expected* output level of the other firms. It can be shown[10] that the reaction curves are of the following form:

$$y_i = \begin{cases} 1 - y^e_{-i} + \sqrt{\gamma(\alpha - 1)(y^e_{-i} - 1)} & \text{for all } y^e_{-i} \\ & \text{such that } y_i > 1/(n - 1) \\ 1/(n - 1) & \text{for all other values of } y^e_{-i}. \end{cases} \tag{10.8}$$

This finishes the description of the model.

NASH EQUILIBRIA AND RATIONALIZABLE STRATEGIES

Before solving the model in terms of the set of rationalizable strategies, it turns out to be fruitful to analyse the properties of the set of Nash equilibria. The model can have one, two or three Nash equilibria. First, observe that there is always a trivial equilibrium, namely $y_i = 1/(n-1)$ for all i. Second, note that there are no non-symmetric Nash equilibria. This is because in a Nash equilibrium $y_i = 1 - y_{-i} + \sqrt{\gamma(\alpha - 1)(y_{-i} - 1)}$ holds for all i, which in turn implies that $y - 1 = \sqrt{\gamma(\alpha - 1)(y_{-i} - 1)}$ holds for all i. Thus, in a Nash equilibrium $y_{-i} = \ldots = y_{-n}$ has to hold for all i, or $y_1 = \ldots = y_n$. Third, symmetric Nash equilibria can be computed by solving $(ny_i - 1)^2 = \gamma(\alpha - 1)((n-1)y_i - 1)$ for y_i. Two non-trivial Nash equilibria arise if

$$
\begin{aligned}
D &= 4n^2 + 4n(n - 1)\gamma(\alpha - 1) + (n - 1)^2\gamma^2(\alpha - 1)^2 \\
&\quad - 4n^2 - 4n^2\gamma(\alpha - 1) = (n - 1)^2\gamma^2(\alpha - 1)^2 \\
&\quad - 4n\gamma(\alpha - 1) > 0.
\end{aligned}
$$

So, there are two symmetric (non-trivial) Nash equilibria if $\alpha > 1 + 4n/(n - 1)^2\gamma$. There is one non-trivial equilibrium if the expression holds with equality and there is no non-trivial equilibrium if the reverse inequality holds. Note that as n gets larger, the constraint becomes less severe so that multiple equilibria are more likely to occur. For $n = 2$ the condition amounts to requiring that $\alpha > 1 + 8/\gamma$. Figure 10.1 shows the reaction curves for $n = 2$, $\gamma = 0.5$ and $\alpha = 19$. It can be shown that there are three Nash equilibria for this case: $y_1 = y_2 = 1$, $y_1 = y_2 = 5/4$ and $y_1 = y_2 = 2$.

Having explored the properties of the set of Nash equilibria, it is interesting to look for the relation between this set and the set of rationalizable strategies. It is clear that all Nash equilibria are rationalizable. However, the set of rationalizable strategies is, in general, larger than the set of Nash equilibria. Among other things, Milgrom and Roberts (1990) show that in games with strategic complementarities (positively sloping reaction curves) all strategies $y_i \in [\underline{y}, \bar{y}]$ are rationalizable, where $\underline{y}$ ($\bar{y}$) is the lowest (largest) Nash equilibrium output for agent i. (Observe that, because of the symmetry of the model, $\underline{y}$ and $\bar{y}$ are the same for all firms.) The output levels of the firms in the above model are strategic complements when output is low. With some modifications, Milgrom and Roberts' result can be used in the present context. Thus,

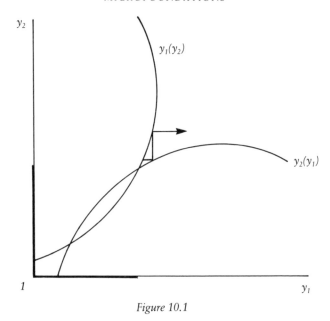

Figure 10.1

whenever the model has only one Nash equilibrium, there is also one rationalizable strategy. If the model has two or three Nash equilibria, then there is a continuum of rationalizable strategies that includes the interval bounded by the lowest and the highest Nash equilibria output levels.

The following calculations serve as a way to illustrate the above result. Concentrating on the parameter values $\gamma = 0.5$ and $\alpha = 19$, it will be shown that for $n = 2$ the set of rationalizable strategies is $[1, 2]$, while for $n \geq 3$ all strategies $y_i \in [1, 9/4]$ are rationalizable.

First, consider the case where $n = 2$. The set of best responses to a $y_{-i} \in Y_{-i}$ is $[1, 9/4]$, where 9/4 is a best response to $y_{-i} = 13/4$. Now, the set of best responses to a $y_{-i} \in [1, 9/4]$ is $[1, 2.11]$. In the third round only those y_i in $[1, 2.05]$ remain, and so on. If the process is repeated an infinite number of times only the interval $[1, 2]$ remains. To see this, note that if firm i plays a best response it never sets y_i larger than 9/4. The firm sets y_i equal to 9/4 if $-i$ is expected to choose 13/4. In the next round the firm 'knows' that $-i$ chooses 13/4, but 9/4 at a maximum. The best response to 9/4 is 2.11 and so on. The set of rationalizable strategies is depicted in figure 10.1 as the bold line segment on the axes. The arrow in the figure shows that any output level $y_i > 2$ is not rationalizable, because such an output level would only be

166

consistent with an expectation a rational opponent would never realize.

Next, consider $n \geq 3$. Also in this case the set of best responses in the first round is $[1, 9/4]$, but now the firms cannot further eliminate strategies. To see this, note that firm i sets y_i equal to $9/4$ if all the other firms are expected to set their total output equal to $13/4$. For $n \geq 3$ it is perfectly rationalizable for firm i to expect each of the others to play $13/4 \ (n-1)$, because this is less than $9/4$. So, for $n \geq 3$ the set of rationalizable strategies is $[1, 9/4]$.

The above results make the distinction between a countable number of Nash equilibria and a continuum of Nash equilibria less important (see, e.g., Drazen 1987 and Cooper and John 1988). If multiple Nash equilibria exist a continuum of equilibria is rationalizable. Which of the rationalizable output (employment) levels actually obtains depends on the particular expectations held by individual firms. Thus, there is a crucial role played by expectations or 'animal spirits'. In this respect the model reflects the 'Keynesian' view on the economy outlined in the beginning of this chapter.

Some readers might want to argue that the above result is not very promising, because the model does not yield a unique prediction. As a reply to this possible objection, I want to make two observations. First, the urge to obtain unique outcomes goes easily against the idea of methodological individualism. This is because the additional restrictions that have to be imposed in order to obtain a unique solution are often hard to justify in terms of the rational behaviour of the individuals that populate the model economy (cf. the restriction imposed by the Nash equilibrium concept). Second, it is not the case that 'anything may happen' in the above model. Contrary to the Keynesian notion of 'animal spirits', about which nothing can be said on economic grounds, not all strategies (expectations) are rationalizable. In particular, (very) high output levels are not rationalizable in the above model.

WELFARE IMPLICATIONS

In the previous section we saw that a continuum of rationalizable strategies exists for certain parameter values. Here, the welfare implications of this result will be explored. First, however, I will introduce two relevant concepts. Two consumption leisure combinations (y,l) and (y',l') are said to be *Pareto-ranked* if (i) both pairs are feasible (i.e. $y \leq \alpha(1-l)$ and $y' \leq \alpha(1-l')$) and (ii) they are such that $U(y,l) < U(y',l')$. The locus of points (y,l) that satisfy $y = \alpha(1-l)$ is referred to as the social feasibility frontier (SFF).

The welfare implications of the continuum of rationalizable strategies can be stated as follows: all pairs (y,l) and (y',l') with $y < y' < y^w$ on the SFF are Pareto-ranked with $U(y,l) < U(y',l')$. This is a consequence of the subsequent observations. At every pair (y,l) on the SFF the household's utility function can be written as $U = (y - 1)^\gamma(1 - y/\alpha)^{1-\gamma}$. Utility is increasing in y if $\partial U/\partial y > 0$. This is the case if $\gamma/y - 1 > (1 - \gamma)/(\alpha - y)$, or $y < \gamma(\alpha - 1) + 1 = y^w$. For the case of the numerical example presented in the previous section ($n = 2$, $\alpha = 19$ and $\gamma = 0.5$) the reader may verify that the utility level in the Nash equilibrium with a low and high output level equals $\sqrt{3}/2 \times 66/76$ and $\sqrt{3} \times 60/76$, respectively.

In the previous section it has been established that a continuum of rationalizable strategies exists if there are multiple Nash equilibria. Here we have seen that these strategies are Pareto-ranked: a combination of strategies that results in a low level of output is Pareto inferior to a combination of strategies that results in a high output level. In any case, if the number of firms is not too large, the largest rationalizable output is again Pareto inferior to the Walrasian situation. The latter inefficiency may be interpreted as a classical market failure due to imperfect competition, while the former inefficiency is what one may call a coordination failure.

GOVERNMENT POLICY

A natural question then is whether the government can be of any assistance in solving the coordination problem faced by the firms. First, note that any form of balanced budget taxes and subsidies does not have an impact in the present context. This is because of the fact that firms are aware of the feedback from profits to demand. Taxes and subsidies may have an impact on the behaviour of households, but firms simply take this affected behaviour into account.

A second policy one might want to consider is to stimulate more firms to enter the industry. A classical diagnosis of oligopolistic situations is that there are barriers to entry. If the government can remove these barriers, new firms will push the economy towards the competitive (Walrasian) equilibrium. It is easy to see that this solution does not work in the present circumstances either. Let (y^w, l^w) be the Walrasian equilibrium amounts of consumption and leisure in a corresponding perfectly competitive economy. In a Walrasian equilibrium $p = 1/\alpha$ and $y^w = 1 + \gamma(\alpha - 1)$. However, as n approaches infinity the total output levels of the two (non-trivial) Nash equilibria approach 1, the subsistence level, and $1 + \gamma(\alpha - 1)$, the Walrasian output level. In combination with the result that there is a continuum of rationalizable strategies if there are two or more Nash equilibria, this means that the introduction of new firms makes the problem even harder to coordinate, because the larger n is, the larger the set of rationalizable strategies.

Suppose then, as a third option, that the government itself considers the possibility of producing a 'public' good g. The good is produced according to a production function of the form $g = \alpha_g L_g$, where $\alpha_g \leq \alpha$ and L_g is the labour demand of the government. It is thus assumed that the government is *not more* productive than firms are. The government raises lump sum taxes T in order to pay its workers, i.e. $T = L_g$. The government has to announce its policy g before households and firms make their decisions. The policy is thus common knowledge.

The introduction of this type of policy modifies the representative household's budget constraint in the following way: $py + l = (1 - L_g) + \pi$. It is assumed that the household does not prefer consuming g to y: $U(y,l;g) = (y + \beta g - 1)^\gamma l^{1-\gamma}$, where $0 < \beta \leq 1$. Utility maximization yields the following demand for consumption goods:

$$y^d(p,\pi,g) = \frac{\gamma(1 + \pi - L_g)}{p} - (1 - \gamma)(\beta g - 1).$$

Following the same procedure as the one in the first section and taking the production function for the 'public' good into account yields the following inverse demand equation:

$$p(y;g) = \frac{\gamma[\alpha - (\alpha/\alpha_g)\beta g - y]}{\alpha(1 - \gamma)(y + \beta g - 1)}. \tag{10.9}$$

Somewhat tedious calculations (not fundamentally different from the case without government policy) show that the reaction curves take the following form:

$$y_i = \begin{cases} 1 - \beta g - \sum_{j \neq i} y_j^e + \\ \\ \sqrt{\gamma[\alpha - 1 - (\alpha/\alpha_g - 1)\beta g](\sum_{j \neq i} y_j^e + \beta g - 1)}, \\ \quad \text{for all } (\sum_{j \neq i} y_j^e, g) \text{ such that } y_i > 1/(n - 1) \\ \\ 1/(n-1) \text{ for all other } (\sum_{j \neq i} y_j^e, g). \end{cases} \tag{10.10}$$

169

What is the impact of government policy? In figure 10.2 the case is depicted where $\alpha = 3\alpha_g = 19$, $\beta = 1$, $\gamma = 0.5$, $n = 2$ and $g = 0$, respectively $g = \delta$, where δ is a small positive number. It is thus assumed that the government is three times less productive than firms are and that the representative household is indifferent between consuming the 'public' and the private good. The figure points to the fact that the optimal response to an output level of the other firms is increasing in g for small values of y_i. The reason can easily be checked by looking at equation (10.10) for the case $\alpha = \alpha_g$: g and $\sum_{j \neq i} y_j^e$ enter the equation symmetrically and the optimal response of firm i is increasing in g as long as the quantities are strategic complements, i.e. as long as the reaction curves are upward sloping. A similar argument holds true for the case $\alpha_g < \alpha$. One can see that the output of the lowest (largest) non-trivial Nash equilibrium decreases (increases) if the government announces a small production level of δ. Thus, a small production level results in a larger set of rationalizable strategies. In this sense the coordination problem deteriorates.

The situation is totally different for larger values of g. As the output level of the low Nash equilibrium decreases in the case of the introduction of a 'public' good, one may wonder whether this equilibrium disap-

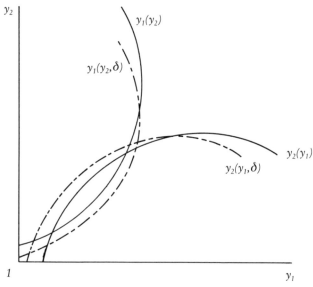

Figure 10.2

pears for a large enough value of g. For $n = 2$ this phenomenon occurs for[11]

$$\left| \beta g - \frac{\gamma(\alpha - 1) - 2}{2 + 2\gamma(\alpha/\alpha_g - 1)} \right| <$$

$$\frac{\sqrt{\gamma^2(\alpha - 1)^2 - 4\gamma(\alpha + \alpha/\alpha_g - 1)}}{2 + 2\gamma(\alpha/\alpha_g - 1)}. \quad (10.11)$$

This is illustrated in figure 10.3 for $g_0 = 1$, $\alpha = 3\alpha_g = 19$, $\beta = 1$ and $\gamma = 0.5$.

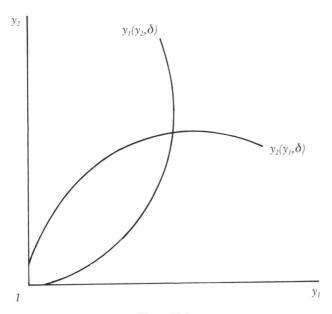

Figure 10.3

The figure shows that in this case the large output Nash equilibrium is the unique Nash equilibrium.[12] It is easy to verify that this is also the unique rationalizable strategy. Thus, by choosing an appropriate production level of the 'public' good, the government is able to solve the coordination problem.

So far we have seen that the government is able to solve the coordination problem by producing a 'public' good. What about the welfare consequences of this type of policy? Clearly, the government should pursue such a policy only if it is welfare improving. In the rest of this section I focus on the case where $\beta = 1$, i.e. the case in which the representative household is indifferent between the 'public' and the private good. Two cases can be distinguished.

If $\alpha_g = \alpha$, the optimal provision of the 'public' good is $1 + \gamma(a - 1)$, i.e. the Pareto-optimal output level for the correspondingly perfectly competitive economy. In this case firms choose not to produce (see equation (10.10)).

Of course, the more interesting case is where $\alpha_g < \alpha$: the production technology of the government is less efficient than the technology of the private firms. Although production by the government is less efficient, the representative household might prefer some government intervention, because it prefers to consume (and work) more than the largest rationalizable output level without government intervention. The optimal level of intervention is where the marginal value of an extra consumption unit equals the marginal disutility of the labour that is necessary to produce this extra unit, i.e.

$$p(y,g)\left(1 + \frac{\partial y}{\partial g}\right) = \frac{1}{\alpha_g} + \frac{1}{\alpha}\frac{\partial y}{\partial g}.$$

Unfortunately, it is impossible to determine the welfare-optimizing production level of the 'public' good. However, some qualitative statements can be made. It is intuitively clear that there is an upper bound on the optimal level of g, because it costs too much labour. This is illustrated by means of the following numerical example. For $n = 2$, $\alpha = 3\alpha_g = 19$ and $\gamma = 0.5$ there is a unique iteratively undominated strategy for all values of

$$\frac{7 - \sqrt{39}}{4} < g < \frac{7 + \sqrt{39}}{4}.$$

The utility level of the representative household is respectively 1.58, 1.60 and 1.48 for g values of $1/4$, $3/4$ and 2. Values of g larger than 2 yield a utility level that is below 1.48. Note that the utility level associated with the largest iteratively undominated output level without government is $\sqrt{3 \times 60/76}$ (≈ 1.54). So, even though the government produces with a less efficient technology, it is able to improve upon the welfare of the representative household. Note too that the government is not able to re-establish the Pareto-optimal Walrasian equilibrium, because the production of the 'public' good takes more labour than production by firms.

172

DISCUSSION AND CONCLUSION

The analysis of the previous sections illustrates the fact that some Keynesian features can be analysed by taking seriously the idea that endogenous uncertainty is a fundamental aspect of a world with more than one individual (firm). It has been shown that the firms face a severe coordination problem once one acknowledges that they are not in a position to know what the other firms will produce. In many situations, purely economic information is not sufficient to determine what other firms will produce. In those cases, norms and/or conventions might be important means of reducing the amount of endogenous uncertainty, but economists have traditionally been unwilling to take this kind of non-economic information into account. In the absence of norms and/ or conventions, however, rationality considerations are often insufficient to pin down the level of expectations. When expectations are undetermined, coordination failures are likely to result.

Individual firms and households are not able to solve the coordination problem. It has been shown that the government is in a position to remedy the coordination problem. The policy that has been considered for this purpose is the production of a 'public' good. The production of a 'public' good not only enables the government to solve the coordination problem, but also improves upon the welfare of the representative household.

CONCLUSION

This book has analysed the rationale for the concern of mainstream macroeconomists to build their theories on so-called microeconomic foundations. Most economists do not provide arguments for the search for microfoundations. It is clear, however, that the reasons that often implicitly lie behind the search for microfoundations derive from the premise that individual subjects are the only actors in society. The decisions individual subjects take depend among other things on existing rules and institutions and on the way individuals interact with each other. This premise is frequently transformed in the methodological rule that says that in order to account for aggregate phenomena one has to understand the individual decisions from which these phenomena originate. This methodological rule has been termed *methodological individualism* (MI).

The question this book has addressed is whether studies in the microfoundations literature are in line with the requirements of MI. The shortest answer to this question is a simple 'no'. The answer is a logical consequence of the following observations. First, MI says that individual subjects are the only agents that take actions; collective entities and social rules exist, but do not act themselves. In economics individual actions are usually interpreted as resulting from deliberate acts of choice: an action is the observable consequence of the (unobservable) presumption that individuals engage in making rational choices. Here, I have followed general practice among studies in the microfoundations literature, i.e. I have assumed throughout the book that individual agents decide on their actions in a rational way. Second, I have assumed that the individuals know the economic model (rules of the game), including the fact that the other agents in the economy make rational choices. Moreover, the individual rationality of the agents and the economic model are common knowledge. This assumption is not made because of its truthfulness, but instead because uncertainty about the true model is not an issue that is specific to the questions treated in this study. This second assumption is also often made in the microfoundations literature. Third, the solution concept that is a logical consequence of the two observations above is what is known in the game theoretic literature as *iteratively undominated strategies* (IUS). This solution concept is, in general, less restrictive than other solution concepts such as the Nash equilibrium or (in models for which this solution is well defined) the competitive equilibrium. Fourth, studies in the microfoundations literature typically use some sort of an equilibrium notion to arrive at a (unique) solution of the model. However, without an argument on why rational agents should choose equilibrium strategies, it is not clear why an equilibrium should be expected to result. An equilibrium notion assumes the existence of a *coordinating device* at the aggregate level that coordinates individual actions. If such a coordination device really exists in a given situation, individual agents can take it into account while making their decisions. In these (hypothetical) cases the use of the Nash equilibrium notion is in line with MI. However, many models are too abstract to be able to give an adequate description of the type of aggregate entity that might perform the role of coordinating device. Fifth, as in almost all studies in the microfoundations literature the notion of IUS does not coincide with the Nash equilibrium notion and as another justification in terms of the existence of a coordinating device is lacking, I conclude that the microfoundations literature does not provide macroeconomics with foundations that are in line with MI.

There are two issues that remain to be discussed. First, I have argued that hypotheses that cannot be derived from rational individual decisions may be invoked in an individualistic explanation. The question then is whether the use of an equilibrium notion can be made compatible with MI by regarding it as one of the extra-rational hypotheses of an explanation. Second, it is sometimes argued that a desirable property of a solution concept is that it determines a unique outcome (or at least a limited number of outcomes) whenever the concept is applied. As the notion of IUS does not have this property, one might argue that it is not an appropriate solution concept. I will address each of these issues in turn.

In chapter 2 I argued in favour of a form of MI in which institutions are allowed as primitive terms in an explanation of social phenomena. Assumptions about the properties of institutions (to be considered as rules of the game) are elements of that part of the explanation that is not based on individual decisions. The Nash equilibrium notion has, however, a different status than the rules of the game: it interferes with the decisions individual agents take. Whenever the properties of the relevant institutions (rules of the game) are specified, individual agents still have a choice as to what action to take. This is different for the Nash equilibrium notion: a Nash equilibrium determines for each individual agent which action to take. If a game has a unique IUS for each agent and there is common knowledge of the agents' rationality, each agent will choose his or her IUS. In the absence of a coordinating device this is the only case in which the choices individual agents make necessarily form a Nash equilibrium.

MI is based on the idea that only individuals take actions. Accordingly, a theory of individual action should be part of an individualistic explanation. More importantly, the theory should give reasons why an individual agent decides to take a specific action. The Nash equilibrium concept does not specify these reasons: it is more a 'social' theory of individual action, because it specifies a property of a combination of actions (strategy combination) and not a property of an individual action (strategy).

The second issue that has to be addressed is that, in the many cases it is applied, the notion of IUS predicts a wide class of possible outcomes. This surely is not a very desirable state of affairs. However, it can also be taken to reflect the fact that our knowledge of the economy is too imprecise to be able to make more definite, trustworthy, predictions. Also, it indicates that the notion of rational behaviour by itself is not very powerful, unless it is used in a context in which there is little endogenous uncertainty. The amount of uncertainty due to imperfect knowledge of the behaviour of others is reduced in our everyday life by the existence of social conventions, norms, rules and institutions. It is when we take these elements of our social context more explicitly into account in our models that we can hope to go beyond the wide class of outcomes that are predicted by the application of the notion of IUS to our presently existing models.

NOTES

INTRODUCTION

1 The phrase 'mathematical political philosophy' is not meant to belittle in any way the contributions of these branches of economics. I am of the opinion that political philosophy is an important subject (for example, it is quite likely that it has an important, albeit indirect, impact on public policy), especially when it is done in a rigorous way. The term is chosen here in order to emphasize that empirical arguments do not play a (significant) role in these branches of economics.

2 The question, so prominent in general equilibrium theory, of whether, to quote Arrow and Hahn (1971: vi), 'a decentralized economy motivated by self-interest and guided by price signals would be compatible with a coherent disposition of economic resources that could be regarded in a well-defined sense, as superior to a large class of possible alternative dispositions' is very close to the question of (nineteenth-century) political philosophy as to what extent egoistic behaviour achieves general good. For answering this question it is of no importance whether individual behaviour is egoistic or not (see also Sen 1976).

2 INDIVIDUAL BEHAVIOUR AND AGGREGATE RELATIONS

1 An individualist might even grant that utility factors are influenced by social factors.

2 Note, here, that an economy (and not an individual) is in a state of equilibrium.

3 In chapter 4 (on the relation between economic models and the real world) I will have more to say about this idealization.

4 Of course, this is not to deny that representative agent models of this second type may have some heuristic value.

5 For some individuals the size of the group beyond which they decide not to participate may be infinitely large.

6 There are quite a number of different notions of reduction in circulation, one of which poses that the method used in the physical sciences is also

NOTES

applicable to the social sciences. This is not the way I employ the notion, because as argued in the first section, individuals in the social sciences are regarded as decision makers, whereas physical 'individuals' are generally not regarded as decision makers. The notion of reduction employed here is defined below.

7 The reader is, again, referred to chapter 4 for a discussion of the importance of the above argument for economics.

8 The reader is reminded of the fact that the notion of an individual is treated here in a relative way.

9 Recently, Jackson and Pettit (1992) have argued in favour of a form of methodological pluralism as far as explanation is concerned. They give some nice examples to show that in some cases a macro-explanation gives more relevant information than a micro-explanation. Here is one example. Consider a closed flask filled with water. An explanation for the cracking of the flask is that the water in the flask boils. This is a macro-explanation and they argue that it is irrelevant to know which particular molecule caused the breaking of the flask. I fully agree with this position. Nevertheless, I think it is not inconsistent with the above account of MI. The reason is that the explanation can be divided into two parts. The first part (corresponding to the macro-to-micro transition) is that whenever water boils there are at least some molecules that reach a high level of motion. The second part (corresponding to the micro-to-macro transition) consists in positing a relation between a high level of motion of some molecules and the cracking of the flask. The macro-explanation is valid, because both parts of the explanation are highly stable. What Jackson and Pettit consider to be the corresponding micro-explanation is only a (narrow) version of the second part distinguished above. It is then not surprising to see that the micro-explanation is less informative. Moreover, the macro-explanation offered by Jackson and Pettit presupposes that stable aggregate relationships exist. I have argued that in economics aggregate relationships usually are not (very) stable. This fact questions the applicability of Jackson and Pettit's account to economics.

10 Readers who are familiar with game theory might skip this section.

11 The third section of chapter 7 will deal briefly with cooperative game theory.

12 This study only deals with games of complete information, i.e. every player knows who are the players, the strategy set of each player and the individual payoffs for every strategy combination. Again, this is done in order to concentrate on endogenous uncertainty (see also the first section). Players choose pure strategies only and the rules of the game and the rationality of the players are common knowledge. A fact f is common knowledge if each player knows f, each player knows that all the other players know f and so on.

13 This discussion should be seen in the light of the discussion on rational behaviour in the first section. There I have argued that the concept of rational behaviour is relative to the information an individual possesses.

14 As this study primarily deals with one-shot games, problems associated with common knowledge and rationality in the backward induction argument are not discussed. The reader is referred to Bicchieri (1988), Binmore

178

(1988) and Sugden (1991) among others.

15 In many cases discussed in this study, the notions of rationalizability and IUS coincide. As the notion of rationalizability is usually more easy to work with, I have introduced this concept in the previous section.

3 GENERAL EQUILIBRIUM ANALYSIS AND MACROECONOMICS: ALTERNATIVE PROGRAMMES

1 The term 'theory' is misleading in this context. In fact, the kinetic theory of gases and utility theory are complexes of theories (or programmes).

2 A theoretical term is a term that does not have a clear empirical equivalent outside the theory in question. For example, 'utility' is a theoretical term.

3 In Janssen (1991b), I claim that the programmes are *not* Lakatosian research programmes.

4 Weintraub uses the term 'neo-Walrasian program' for the propositions below. In a note he declares the term 'general equilibrium' 'to be too vague'. I have chosen to use 'programme of GEA' in order to avoid the introduction of yet another term.

5 The delineation of research programmes in economics has proved to be very difficult (see, e.g., de Marchi and Blaug 1991). Papers within a programme can be considered as having some kind of Wittgensteinian family relation with each other (see Hoover 1991). The idea of a programme should be interpreted in a flexible way. Accordingly, I do not regard Weintraub's definition as the only sound definition. It is, however, a reasonable and relatively simple attempt at giving some content to the family idea.

6 It has been argued (see, e.g., Backhouse 1991) that HC5 should be replaced by a less restrictive proposition that is very much in line with the way I will interpret HC5. I have chosen to reinterpret 'relevant knowledge' in such a way that it does not exclude very much. I have chosen this option in order not to suggest that the formulation of the other propositions is the only fully adequate formulation (compare the previous note).

7 This term is borrowed from Coddington (1983).

8 King and Plosser (1984) argue, for example, that information about monetary statistics is cheap and readily available.

9 This corresponds to the case of positively sloping best response functions.

10 Equilibria are said to be Pareto-ranked if all individual agents prefer one equilibrium above another one.

4 ECONOMICS AND THE REAL WORLD

1 Note that this is not to say that the empirical relationship necessarily breaks down if one of the parts does not hold anymore. The parts only give a set of *sufficient* conditions under which the empirical relation holds true.

2 This is what Hausman (1981) has called the condition of excusability.

3 Note that the distinction between necessary and sufficient conditions is

also crucial to Boland's defence of Milton Friedman's *as if* methodology (see Boland 1979).

4 Of course, the fact that the hypothesis of rational behaviour is often (successfully?) used is the major reason why one might want to use it also in the particular case under discussion here. In principle, economists could adopt several modes of explanation. However, when economic behaviour is under discussion there is, in quite a few cases, a strong impression that the agent in question has thought about what action to perform. An entrepreneur starting a new investment project; a farmer cultivating a plot of land or a speculator buying and selling bonds and equities: in all these and in many other cases agents make decisions that are deliberate acts of choice. If it is granted that economic behaviour involves making a choice, then this behaviour is almost by definition rational.

5 This is also one of the ideas behind the approximation step of the reduction scheme presented in chapter 2. A similar idea has been developed by Simon (1963).

6 See the second section of chapter 9 for a fairly detailed description of Bryant's example.

5 AGGREGATION, ANALOGY AND THE REPRESENTATIVE AGENT

1 A function $f(x_1, \ldots, x_n)$ is said to be additively separable if it can be written as a function of the sum of functions of individual arguments: $\phi(\zeta_1(x_1) + \ldots + \zeta_n(x_n))$.

2 I do not provide arguments for this statement here. See Pokropp (1972: 39–41) for a rigorous proof of this proposition.

3 There exists some econometric work on aggregation bias (for an early study, see Theil 1954), but this literature is unrelated to the type of problem discussed here. In the literature on the aggregation bias, one usually adopts simple summations to relate individual and aggregate variables.

4 It is clear that Klein uses the terms micro- and macroeconomics in the way the terms individual and aggregate are used in the present study.

5 Some readers might like to consult a microeconomic textbook such as Deaton and Muellbauer (1980) and Varian (1992) for more details.

6 Note that the aggregation problem discussed in the first three sections of this chapter does not arise here, because individual initial endowments are held constant and are (therefore) neglected as an argument of the aggregate excess demand functions.

7 An $m \times m$ matrix A with typical element a_{hk} is symmetric if, for all $h, k = 1, \ldots, m$, $a_{hk} = a_{kh}$. A matrix is negative semi-definite if $\Sigma_{h=1}^{m} \Sigma_{k=1}^{m} \zeta_h \zeta_k a_{hk} \leq 0$ for any vector $(\zeta_1, \ldots, \zeta_m)$.

8 This part is based on Theil (1954), Van Daal (1980) and Lewbell (1987). De Wolff (1941) wrote on the differences in interpretation between individual and aggregate elasticities.

9 Here, it is assumed that the x_i's do not have columns in common. A similar expression holds in case the x_i's do have columns in common.

6 ON THE PROBABILITY DISTRIBUTION OF AGGREGATE DEMAND

1 The May/Pu approach, discussed in the previous chapter, can be employed if all individual incomes are functionally related to mean income.

2 The same results can be obtained by assuming that the income distribution is discrete. In this case the integrals should be replaced by sums.

3 One may object that the income distribution and not the difference between individuals accounts for the probabilistic nature of aggregate demand. In the next section I show that the assumption that individual incomes are distributed according to a particular distribution is not a sufficient condition, by itself, for aggregate demand to be of a probabilistic form.

4 If the good is inferior for all individuals, the reverse of (i) and (ii) holds true.

5 After having discovered 'his' empirical income distribution, Pareto wrote that he was very surprised to see that the distribution was very constant and 'It is absolutely impossible to admit that they [these results] are only due to chance. There is most certainly a *cause*, which produces the tendency of incomes to arrange themselves according to a certain curve' (Pareto 1896, vol ii: 312; translated into English in Lydall 1968). So, in his time Pareto was already interested in explaining the shape of the income distribution.

7 INDIVIDUALISTIC FOUNDATIONS FOR MARKET EQUILIBRIUM

1 In terms of the reduction scheme this amounts to an identification step: consumption demand and realized consumption are identified with each other.

2 The difference between market clearing and competitive equilibrium is that the first notion applies to all cases in which supply equals demand, whereas the second notion assumes in addition that the market is perfectly competitive. For example, an equilibrium of a Cournot oligopoly model is not a competitive equilibrium, but it is a market clearing equilibrium.

3 Although the discussion will focus on the general equilibrium specification, all the points raised equally apply to a partial equilibrium specification.

4 Boland (1982: 52–3) observes that economists interchange the terms 'equilibrium' and 'balance of forces'.

5 One might like to argue that the inequality only holds for equilibrium prices and not for actual prices. But if one holds this view, ADM does not say anything about actual prices. This is why I have interpreted ADM in such a way that actual prices coincide with equilibrium prices.

6 This law has the following structure: $\forall x \in E \{(Px \to CEPx) \wedge (Ax \to CEAx)\}$, in which Px ($CEPx$) means 'x is a (competitive equilibrium) price', Ax ($CEAx$) means 'x is a (competitive equilibrium) allocation'; the domain of x is 'prices and allocations' and E is the set of prices and allocation in economies for which a competitive equilibrium exists. E

is the set of intended applications of ADM (see Janssen and Kuipers 1989).

7   A related view is that ADM *assumes* the existence of *aggregate* markets that coordinate individual activities quite well or to quote Weintraub (1979: 144–5): ADM 'hides the difficulties of ... coordination behind the construction of pre-existing markets'.

8   Fisher (1983) has attempted to give a foundation for equilibrium economics that is not based on the notion of an auctioneer. He builds a dynamic theory of price behaviour in which prices are set by firms. He shows that under some conditions prices converge to a rest point of the dynamic system, but this rest point need not coincide with the market clearing equilibrium of the economy.

9   Existence theorems only state that under the above assumptions the set of intended applications of the AD-law is not empty (see also note 6 above). They do not provide useful insight to the question of whether a general equilibrium state will be attained.

10   Another way to express this view is to say that '(A) general equilibrium would "exist" in the same sense that [in playing chess] a way exists for Black to mate White in three moves; it would not exist in the sense the table in this room or the city of Paris may be said to exist' (Roy 1989: 158).

11   De Vroey (1990) has made a similar observation. He has argued that ADM presents a paradox, because it is supposed to deal with decentralized economies, but in fact it needs a central authority to clear the markets.

12   Individuals are said to be of the same type if they have the same utility function and the same amounts of initial endowments.

13   One may wonder whether the relation between price ratios and ratios of marginal utilities should be understood as an identity or a correlation. The interested reader is referred to Janssen (1989).

14   It is important to note that the firms have to *know* this aggregation rule. If firms do not know that only those firms charging the lowest price will have customers, then the notion of rational behaviour is empty in this game (see also example 2.1). Aggregation is thus also an essential ingredient of rational behaviour apart from being a separate element of the reduction scheme.

15   The concept of weakly dominated strategies is not used, because of some problems with the justification of iterative elimination of weakly dominated strategies.

16   The reader is referred to the original papers for the exact form the conditions take.

17   This example is based on some notes by Tilman Börgers. I thank him for his kind permission to use them here.

18   It might be that future research will show why individual behaviour results in a core allocation. (For an attempt to base cooperative game theoretic concepts on non-cooperative ones, see, e.g., Rubinstein 1982).

8   THE INDIVIDUAL RATIONALITY OF RATIONAL EXPECTATIONS

1   The ideas presented in this section are based on Frydman *et al.* (1982).

2 M_L maximizes the authority's expected utility if ω is such that $\omega/(1 - \omega)$ $> [U(M_H, M_L) - U(M_L, M_H)]/[U(M_L, M_L) - U(M_H, M_H)]$.

3 It is interesting to note that Keynes (1936) wrote about higher-order expectations when discussing the famous beauty contest; see also chapter 10.

4 For a more general discussion of the above argument in the case of a continuum of firms, see Guesnerie (1989).

9 WHAT IS THIS THING CALLED MICROFOUNDATIONS?

1 The new classical school is sometimes called the rational-expectations school. I will use the term new classical school throughout this chapter.

2 In this way I avoid the conclusion that macroeconomics no longer exists as a separate subdiscipline.

3 See also chapter 3 for a general discussion on the relation between Lucas' monetary models of the business cycle and older monetarist models.

4 This is not the case when we want to study the individualistic foundations for the notions of the natural rate of output and of competitive equilibrium.

5 Of course, an economist may describe Robinson Crusoe's behaviour by means of the theoretical concept of shadow prices. The only point I want to make here is that in a Robinson Crusoe economy there are no such observable things as prices which have to be explained.

6 Note that the Keynesian phenomenon of 'involuntary unemployment' is explained in a 'non-Keynesian' way: the market imperfection is found on the supply side and not in deficiencies in aggregate demand.

7 The paradox here is that models that argue for the importance of coordination failures for an understanding of market processes do not go far enough: these papers themselves assume a form of coordination without explaining it.

8 There is some experimental literature that shows that in *repeated* coordination games (of the Bryant type) players' strategies will form a Nash equilibrium after some stage (see, e.g., Van Huyck *et al.* 1990). This literature is, however, not directly related to the issue under discussion, because Bryant's model is a one-shot game model. Moreover, it is not at all clear what causes a Nash equilibrium to result in the experimental setting. It might very well be that the participants in the experiment share some norms that help them converge towards a Nash equilibrium (for an alternative view, see Crawford 1991).

9 In the next chapter I will bring a specific model in the coordination failures literature more in line with MI. There, I will also deal with the issue of government policy.

10 With regard to some of the models (e.g. the efficiency–wage model) this statement should be slightly modified. I have argued that these models do not *intend* to provide macroeconomics with individualistic foundations.

11 As this study focuses upon mainstream economics I do not go into these issues. The interested reader is referred to a text such as Dow (1985).

10 RATIONALIZABLE ANIMAL SPIRITS

1 Of course, an exception has to be made for the efficiency–wage model, because many versions of this model are in line with MI.

2 See also the previous chapter.

3 Bryant (1987) also gives a non-Nash game theoretic formulation of a Keynesian model.

4 A more general specification of a subsistence level only complicates the mathematics without modifying the results in any essential way.

5 The introduction of fixed costs only complicates the mathematics without modifying the results in any essential way.

6 The reader is referred to chapter 7 for a discussion on the question of whether an inverse demand function can be taken as an unproblematic concept from the point of view of MI.

7 This assumption is not made because of its truthfulness but instead because I want to emphasize that the Keynesian results obtained in this chapter do not depend on some form of irrationality on the part of the firms. Hence, the assumption can be regarded as an *even if* assumption (see also chapter 4).

8 The numerator of this expression is always positive, because maximal output y^{max} equals α. Thus, the whole expression is positive if firms produce more than the subsistence level 1.

9 The expression for $p'(y)$ is always negative, because of the conditions $\alpha > 1$ and $0 < \gamma < 1$.

10 Using some algebra and equations (10.6) and (10.7) gives

$$(y - 1)(-\gamma y + \alpha \gamma - y + \gamma y + 1 - \gamma) + \gamma(1 - \alpha)y_i = 0$$
$$\Rightarrow (y - 1)[1 - y + \gamma(\alpha - 1)] - \gamma(\alpha - 1)y_i = 0$$
$$\Rightarrow (y - 1)^2 = \gamma(\alpha - 1)(y^e_{-i} - 1)$$
$$\Rightarrow y_i = 1 - y^e_{-i} \pm \sqrt{\gamma(\alpha - 1)(y^e_{-i} - 1)}.$$

It is easy to verify that only the + part of the above expression is associated with profit maximization.

11 These values are obtained by requiring that $y_i > 1$ for $\sum_{j \neq i} y^e_j = 1$.

12 See Kiyotaki (1988) for a similar case.

REFERENCES

Agassi, J. 1960. Methodological Individualism. *British Journal for Sociology* 11: 144–70.

———. 1975. Institutional Individualism. *British Journal for Sociology* 26: 144–55.

Allen, R.G.D. 1967. *Macroeconomic Theory.* London: Macmillan.

Arrow, K.J. 1959. Towards a Theory of Price Adjustment, in M. Abramovitz (ed.). *The Allocation of Economic Resources.* Stanford: Stanford UP.

———. 1968. Economic Equilibrium, in *International Encyclopedia of the Social Sciences.* London: Macmillan and Free Press: 376–86.

Arrow, K.J. and G. Debreu 1954. Existence of an Equilibrium for a Competitive Economy. *Econometrica* 22: 265–90.

Arrow, K.J. and F.H. Hahn 1971. *General Competitive Analysis.* Amsterdam: North-Holland.

d'Aspremont, C., R. Dos Santos Ferreira and L. Gérard-Varet 1990. On Monopolistic Competition and Involuntary Unemployment. *Quarterly Journal of Economics* 105: 895–919.

Aumann, R. 1976. Agreeing to Disagree. *Annals of Statistics* 4: 1236–9.

———. 1987. Correlated Equilibrium as an Expression of Bayesian Rationality. *Econometrica* 55: 1–18.

Azariadis, C. and J. Stiglitz 1983. Implicit Contracts and Fixed-Price Equilibria. *Quarterly Journal of Economics* 98 (supplement): 1–22.

Backhouse, R. 1991. The Neo-Walrasian Research Program in Macroeconomics, in N. de Marchi and M. Blaug (eds). *Appraising Economic Theories: Studies in the Methodology of Scientific Research Programs.* Aldershot: Edward Elgar.

Balzer, W. *et al.* (eds). 1984. *Reduction in Science.* Dordrecht: Reidel.

Barro, R. 1977. Unanticipated Money Growth and Unemployment in the United States. *American Economic Review* 67: 101–15.

Basu, K. 1991. A Characterization of the Class of Rationalizable Equilibria of Oligopoly Games, mimeo, Princeton University.

Bénassy, J.-P. 1975. Neo-Keynesian Disequilibrium Theory in a Monetary Economy. *Review of Economic Studies* 42: 502–23.

———. 1982. *The Economics of Market Disequilibrium.* New York: Academic Press.

————. 1986. On Competitive Market Mechanisms. *Econometrica* **54**: 95–109.

Bernheim, D.B. 1984. Rationalizable Strategic Behavior. *Econometrica* **52**: 1007–28.

————. 1986. Axiomatic Characterizations of Rational Choice in Strategic Environments. *Scandinavian Journal of Economics* **88**: 473–88.

Bicchieri, C. 1987. Rationality and Predictability in Economics. *British Journal for the Philosophy of Science* **38**: 501–13.

————. 1988. Common Knowledge and Backward Induction: A Solution to the Paradox, in M. Vardi (ed.). *Theoretical Aspects of Reasoning About Knowledge*, Los Altos: Morgan Kaufman.

————. 1992. Reply to Janssen and Rosenberg, in N. de Marchi (ed.). *Post-Popperian Methodology of Economics; Recovering Practice*. Boston: Kluwer.

Binmore, K. 1988. Modelling Rational Players I and II. *Economics and Philosophy* **3**: 179–214 and **4**: 9–55.

Blanchard, O. and N. Kiyotaki 1987. Monopolistic Competition and the Effects on Aggregate Demand. *American Economic Review* **77**: 647–66.

Blaug, M. 1980. *The Methodology of Economics*. Cambridge: Cambridge UP.

Boland, L. 1979. A Critique of Friedman's Critics. *Journal of Economic Literature* **17**: 503–22.

————. 1982. *The Foundations of Economic Method*. London: Allen and Unwin.

Börgers, T. 1992. Iterated Elimination of Dominated Strategies in a Bertrand–Edgeworth Model. *Review of Economic Studies* **59**: 163–76.

Börgers, T. and M. Janssen 1991. On the Dominance Solvability of Large Cournot Games. UCL Discussion Paper #91–21. London.

Branson, W. 1979. *Macroeconomic Theory and Policy* (2nd edition). New York: Harper & Row.

Bray, M. 1983. Convergence to Rational Expectations Equilibrium, in R. Frydman and E. Phelps (eds). *Individual Forecast and Aggregate Outcomes*. Cambridge: Cambridge UP.

Brodbeck, M. 1958. Methodological Individualisms: Definition and Reduction. *Philosophy of Science* **25**: 1–22.

Bryant, J. 1983. A Rational Expectations Keynes Type Model. *Quarterly Journal of Economics* **98**: 525–9.

————. 1987. The Paradox of Thrift, Liquidity Preference and Animal Spirits. *Econometrica* **55**: 1231–5.

Causey, R. 1977. *Unity of Science*. Dordrecht: Reidel.

Christ, C. 1968. A Simple Macroeconomic Model with a Government Budget Constraint. *Journal of Political Economy* **76**: 53–67.

Clower, R.W. 1965. The Keynesian Counterrevolution: A Theoretical Appraisal, in F. Hahn and F. Brechling (eds). *The Theory of Interest Rates*. London: Macmillan.

Coddington, A. 1976. Keynesian Economics: The Search for First Principles. *Journal of Economic Literature* **14**: 1258–73.

————. 1983. *Keynesian Economics: The Search for First Principles*. London: Allen and Unwin.

Coleman, J.S. 1986. Social Theory, Social Research and a Theory of Action. *American Journal of Sociology* **91**: 1309–35.

REFERENCES

———. 1990. *Foundations of Social Theory*. Cambridge, MA: Harvard UP.

Cooper, R. and A. John 1988. Coordinating Coordination Failures in Keynesian Models. *Quarterly Journal of Economics* 103: 441–63.

Crawford, V. 1991. An Evolutionary Model of Van Huyck, Battalio and Beil's Experimental Results on Coordination Games. *Games and Economic Behaviour* 3: 25–59.

Daal, J. van. 1980. Money Illusion and Aggregation Bias. *De Economist* 128: 86–93.

Daal, J. van and A. Merkies 1984. *Aggregation in Economic Research*. Dordrecht: Reidel.

———. 1988. The Problem of Aggregation of Individual Economic Relations: Consistency and Representativity in a Historical Perspective, in W. Eichhorn (ed.). *Measurement in Economics*. Heidelberg: Physica-Verlag.

Deaton, A. and J. Muellbauer 1980. *Economics and Consumer Behavior*. Cambridge: Cambridge UP.

Debreu, G. 1959. *Theory of Value*. New Haven, CT: Yale UP.

———. 1974. Excess Demand Functions. *Journal of Mathematical Economics* 1: 15–21.

Diamond, P. 1982. Aggregate Demand Management in Search Equilibrium. *Journal of Political Economy* 40: 881–94.

Dow, S. 1985. *Macroeconomic Thought: A Methodological Approach*. Oxford: Basil Blackwell.

Drazen, A. 1987. Reciprocal Externality Models of Low Employment. *European Economic Review* 31: 436–43.

Drèze, J. 1975. Existence of an Equilibrium with Price Rigidity and Quantity Rationing. *International Economic Review* 16: 301–20.

Dubey, P. 1982. Price–Quantity Strategic Market Games. *Econometrica* 50: 111–26.

Ees, H. van and H. Garretsen 1990. The Right Answers to the Wrong Question? An Assessment of the Microfoundations Debate. *De Economist* 138: 123–45.

Elster, J. 1983. *Sour Grapes: Studies in the Subversion of Rationality*. Cambridge: Cambridge UP.

Evans, G. 1983. The Stability of Rational Expectations in Macroeconomic Models, in R. Frydman and E. Phelps (eds). *Individual Forecast and Aggregate Outcomes*. Cambridge: Cambridge UP.

Fisher, F. 1983. *Disequilibrium Foundations of Equilibrium Economics*. Cambridge: Cambridge UP.

Friedman, J.W. 1991. *Game Theory with Applications to Economics* (2nd edition). Oxford: Oxford UP.

Friedman, M. 1968. The Role of Monetary Policy. *American Economic Review* 58: 1–17.

Frydman, R. 1982. Towards An Understanding of Market Processes: Individual Expectations, Learning and Convergence to Rational Expectations Equilibrium. *American Economic Review* 72: 652–68.

Frydman, R., G. O'Driscoll and A. Schotter 1982. Rational Expectations of Government Policy: An Application of Newcomb's Problem. *Southern Economic Journal* 79: 311–19.

Frydman, R. and E. Phelps (eds). 1983. *Individual Forecast and Aggregate*

REFERENCES

Outcomes: Rational Expectations Examined. Cambridge: Cambridge UP.
Gale, D. 1983. *Money: In Disequilibrium.* Cambridge: Cambridge UP.
Garretsen, H. and M.C.W. Janssen 1989. Two Fallacies of Composition in a Keynesian OLG Model. *Research Memorandum no. 317,* Department of Economics, University of Groningen.
Geanakoplos, J. and H. Polemarchakis 1986. Walrasian Indeterminacy and Keynesian Macroeconomics. *Review of Economic Studies* 53: 755–79.
Gibbard, A. and H. Varian 1978. Economic Models. *Journal of Philosophy* 75: 664–77.
Gorman, W. 1953. Community Preference Fields. *Econometrica* 21: 63–80.
Grandmont, J.-M. 1985. On Endogenous Competitive Business Cycles. *Econometrica* 53: 995–1045.
——. 1987. Distribution of Preferences and the Law of Demand. *Econometrica* 55: 155–61.
Green, H. 1964. *Aggregation in Economic Analysis.* Princeton: Princeton UP.
Guesnerie, R. 1989. An Exploration of the Educative Justifications of the Rational Expectations Hypothesis. Paris, mimeo.
Gul, F. 1989. Rational Strategic Behavior and the Notion of Equilibrium. Stanford University, mimeo.
Haavelmo, T. 1944. The Probability Approach to Econometrics. *Econometrica* 12 (supplement): 1–144.
Hahn, F.H. 1978. On Non-Walrasian Equilibria. *Review of Economic Studies* 45: 1–18.
Hands, D.W. 1985. Karl Popper and Economic Methodology. *Economics and Philosophy* 1: 83–99.
Hart, O. 1982. A Model of Imperfect Competition with Keynesian Features. *Quarterly Journal of Economics* 97: 109–38.
——. 1986. Imperfect Competition in General Equilibrium: An Overview of Recent Work, in K. Arrow and S. Honkapohja (eds). *Frontiers of Economics.* New York: Basil Blackwell.
Hausman, D. 1981. *Capital, Profits and Prices: An Essay in the Philosophy of Economics.* New York: Columbia UP.
Heller, W. 1986. Coordination Failure under Complete Markets with Applications to Effective Demand, in W. Heller, R. Starr and D. Starret (eds). *Essays in Honour of K.J. Arrow* vol. 2: Equilibrium Analysis. Cambridge: Cambridge UP.
Henderson, J. and R. Quandt 1980. *Microeconomic Theory: A Mathematical Approach.* New York: McGraw-Hill.
Henocq, C. and H. Kempf 1984. Aggregation Quasi Parfaite par Convergence. *Revue Economique* 35: 911–27.
Hicks, J. 1937. Mr. Keynes and the Classics: A Suggested Interpretation. *Econometrica* 5: 147–59.
——. 1939. *Value and Capital.* Oxford: Clarendon Press.
——. 1965. *Capital and Growth.* Oxford: Oxford UP.
Hildenbrand, W. 1983. On the 'Law of Demand'. *Econometrica* 51: 997–1019.
Hoffstadter, D. 1979. *Gödel, Escher, Bach.* New York: Penguin Books.
Hoogduin, L. and J. Snippe 1987. Uncertainty In/Of Macroeconomics: An Essay on Adequate Abstraction. *De Economist* 135: 429–41.
Hoover, K. 1988. *The New Classical Macroeconomics.* Oxford: Basil Blackwell.

———. 1991. Scientific Research Program or Tribe? A Joint Appraisal of Lakatos and the New Classical Macroeconomics, in N. de Marchi and M. Blaug (eds). *Appraising Economic Theories: Studies in the Methodology of Scientific Research Programs*. Aldershot: Edward Elgar.

Jackson, F. and Ph. Pettit 1992. In Defense of Explanatory Ecumenism: *Economics and Philosophy* 8: 1–21.

Janssen, M.C.W. 1989. Individualistic Foundations for General Equilibrium Theory: A Consideration of Some Game Theoretic Approaches. *Recherches Economiques de Louvain* 55 (4): 425–46.

———. 1991a. The Alleged Necessity of Microfoundations. *Journal of Macroeconomics* 13: 619–39.

———. 1991b. What is this Thing Called Microfoundations? *History of Political Economy* 23: 687–712.

———. 1992. Undominated Strategies in a Multimarket Bertrand Model. *Discussion Paper* 9211/G. Erasmus University Rotterdam.

Janssen, M.C.W. and T. Kuipers 1989. Stratification of General Equilibrium Theory: A Synthesis of Reconstructions. *Erkenntnis* 30: 183–205.

Jevons, W.S. 1879. *The Theory of Political Economy* (2nd edition). London: Macmillan.

Johansen, L. 1972. *Production Functions, An Integration of Micro and Macro, Short Run and Long Run.* Amsterdam: North-Holland.

Journal of Economic Theory, symposium issue on Non-cooperative Approaches to the Theory of Perfect Competition (1980).

Kemeny, J. and P. Oppenheim 1956. On Reduction. *Philosophical Studies* 7: 6–19.

Keynes, J.M. 1936. *The General Theory of Employment, Interest and Money.* London: Macmillan.

King, R. and C. Plosser 1984. Money, Credit and Prices in a Real Business Cycle Model. *American Economic Review* 74: 363–80.

Kirman, A. 1983. On Mistaken Beliefs and Resultant Equilibria, in R. Frydman and E. Phelps (eds). *Individual Forecast and Aggregate Outcomes.* Cambridge: Cambridge UP.

———. 1989. The Intrinsic Limits of Modern Economic Theory: The Emperor has no Clothes. *Economic Journal* 99 (supplement): 126–39.

Kiyotaki, N. 1988. Multiple Expectational Equilibria under Monopolistic Competition. *Quarterly Journal of Economics* 103: 695–713.

Klein, L. 1946a. Macroeconomics and the Theory of Rational Behavior. *Econometrica* 14: 93–108.

———. 1946b. Remarks on the Theory of Aggregation. *Econometrica* 14: 303–12.

Kreps, D. 1990. *A Course in Microeconomic Theory.* Hemel Hempstead: Harvester Wheatsheaf.

Kuhn, T. 1970. *The Structure of Scientific Revolutions.* Chicago: Chicago UP.

Kuipers, T.A.F. 1984. Utilistic Reduction in Sociology: The Case of Collective Goods, in W. Balzer *et al.* (eds). *Reduction in Science.* Dordrecht: Reidel.

———. 1990. Reduction of Laws and Concepts, in J. Brzezinski *et al.* (eds). *Idealization.* Poznan Studies in the Philosophy of Science 16: 241–76.

Kydland, F. and E. Prescott 1982. Time to Built and Aggregate Fluctuations. *Econometrica* 50: 1345–70.

REFERENCES

Lakatos, I. 1978. *The Methodology of Scientific Research Programs: Philosophical Papers vol. 1.* J. Worall and G. Curie (eds). Cambridge: Cambridge UP.

Latsis, S. 1976. Situational Determinism in Economics. *British Journal for the Philosophy of Science* 23: 207–45.

Leijonhufvud, A. 1968. *On Keynesian Economics and the Economics of Keynes.* New York: Oxford UP.

———. 1976. Schools, Revolutions and Research Programs, in S. Latsis (ed.). *Method and Appraisal in Economics.* Cambridge: Cambridge UP.

Lewbell, A. 1987. Distribution Conditions for the Absence of Aggregate Money Illusion. Brandeis University, mimeo.

Lindbeck, A. and D. Snower 1987. Efficiency Wages versus Insiders and Outsiders. *European Economic Review* 31: 407–16.

Lindenberg, S. 1987. Diepte en Modelbouw (in Dutch). *Kennis en Methode* 11: 91–101.

Long, J.B. and C. Plosser 1983. Real Business Cycles. *Journal of Political Economy* 91: 39–69.

Lucas, R. 1972. Expectations and the Neutrality of Money. *Journal of Economic Theory* 4: 103–24.

———. 1973. Some International Evidence on Output Inflation Tradeoffs. *American Economic Review* 63: 326–34.

———. 1976. Econometric Policy Evaluation: A Critique, in K. Brunner and A. Meltzer (eds). *The Phillips Curve and Labor Markets.* Amsterdam: North-Holland.

———. 1977. Understanding Business Cycles, in K. Brunner and A. Meltzer (eds). *Stabilization of the Domestic and International Economy.* Amsterdam: North-Holland.

———. 1978. Unemployment Policy. *American Economic Review* 68: 353–7.

———. 1981. *Studies in Business Cycling Theory.* Cambridge, MA: MIT Press.

———. 1987. *Models of Business Cycles.* Oxford: Basil Blackwell.

Lucas, R. and L. Rapping 1969. Real Wages, Employment and Inflation. *Journal of Political Economy* 55: 721–54.

Lydall, H. 1968. *The Structure of Earnings.* Oxford: Clarendon Press.

McCallum, B. 1979. Rational Expectations and Macroeconomic Stabilization Policy. *Journal of Money, Credit and Banking* 12: 716–46.

Machlup, F. 1963. Micro- and Macro-Economics, in F. Machlup (ed.). *Essays on Economics Semantics.* London: Prentice Hall.

Malinvaud, E. 1972. *Lecture Notes in Microeconomic Theory.* Amsterdam: North-Holland.

Mankiw, N. and P. Romer 1991. *New Keynesian Economics vols 1 and 2.* Cambridge, MA: MIT Press.

Marchi, M. de and M. Blaug (eds). 1991. *Appraising Economic Theories; Studies in the Methodology of Scientific Research Programs.* Aldershot: Edward Elgar.

Marshall, A.W. and I. Olkin 1979. *Inequalities: Theory of Majorization and its Applications.* New York: Academic Press.

Mas-Colell, A. 1980. Noncooperative Approaches to the Theory of Perfect Competition: Presentation. *Journal of Economic Theory* 22: 121–35.

May, K. 1946. The Aggregation Problem for a One Industry Model. *Econometrica* 14: 285–98.

———. 1947. Technological Change and Aggregation. *Econometrica* **15**: 51–63.

Milgrom, P. and J. Roberts 1990. Rationalizability, Learning and Equilibrium in Games with Strategic Complements. *Econometrica* **58**: 1255–77.

Mongin, P. 1991. Les Anticipations Rationelles et la Rationalité: Examen de quelques Modèles d'Apprentisage. *Recherches Economiques de Louvain* **57**: 319–47.

Moulin, H. 1979. Dominance Solvable Voting Schemes. *Econometrica* **47**: 1337–51.

———. 1984. Dominance Solvability and Cournot Stability. *Mathematical Social Sciences* 7: 83–102.

———. 1986. *Game Theory for the Social Sciences.* New York: New York UP.

Muth, J. 1961. Rational Expectations and the Theory of Price Movements. *Econometrica* **29**: 315–35.

Muysken, J. 1979. *Aggregation of Putty-Clay Production Functions.* Unpublished PhD Dissertation, Groningen.

Nagel, E. 1961. *The Structure of Science.* London: Routledge and Kegan Paul.

Nataf, A. 1948. Sur la Possibilité de Construction de Certains Macromodèles. *Econometrica* **16**: 232–44.

Nau, R. and K. McCardle 1990. Coherent Behavior in Noncooperative Games. *Journal of Economic Theory* **50**: 424–44.

Nelson, A. 1984. Some Issues Surrounding the Reduction from Macroeconomics to Microeconomics. *Philosophy of Science* **51**: 573–94.

———. 1989. Average Explanations. *Erkenntnis* **30**: 23–42.

———. 1992. Human Molecules, in N.B. de Marchi (ed.). *Post-Popperian Methodology of Economics; Recovering Practice.* Boston: Kluwer.

Neumann, J. von and O. Morgenstern 1944. *Theory of Games and Economic Behavior.* New York: John Wiley.

Nickles, Th. 1973. Two Concepts of Intertheoretic Reduction. *The Journal of Philosophy* **70**: 181–201.

Novshek, W. 1985. Perfectly Competitive Markets as the Limits of Cournot Markets. *Journal of Economic Theory* **35**: 72–82.

Olson, M. 1965. *The Logic of Collective Action.* Cambridge, MA: Harvard UP.

Pareto, V. 1896. *Cours d'Economie Politique vol. ii.* Lausanne: Librairie de l'Université.

Patinkin, D. 1956. *Money, Interest and Prices.* New York: Harper & Row.

Pearce, D. 1984. Rationalizable Strategic Behavior and the Problem of Perfection. *Econometrica* **52**: 1029–50.

Peeters, M. 1987. A Dismal Science: An Essay on New Classical Economics. *De Economist* **135**: 442–65.

Pokropp, F. 1972. *Aggregation von Produktionsfunktionen,* Lecture Notes in Economics and Mathematical Systems. Berlin: Springer-Verlag.

Popper, K. 1972. *Objective Knowledge.* London: Routledge and Kegan Paul.

Pu, S. 1946. A Note on Macroeconomics. *Econometrica* **14**: 299–302.

Quirk, J. and R. Saposnik 1968. *Introduction to General Equilibrium Theory and Welfare Economics.* New York: McGraw-Hill.

Reder, M. 1982. Chicago Economics: Permanence and Change. *Journal of Economic Literature* **20**: 1–38.

Roberts, J. and A. Postlewaite 1976. The Incentives of Price-Taking Behavior in

Large Exchange Economies. *Econometrica* **44**: 115–27.

Rosenberg, A. 1976. *Microeconomic Laws: A Philosophical Analysis*. Pittsburgh: University of Pittsburgh Press.

——. 1983. If Economics isn't a Science: What is it? *Philosophical Forum* **14**: 296–314.

Roy, S. 1989. *Philosophy of Economics: On the Scope of Reason in Economic Inquiry*. London: Routledge.

Rubinstein, A. 1982. Perfect Equilibrium in a Bargaining Model. *Econometrica* **50**: 97–109.

Ruffin, R.J. 1971. Cournot Oligopoly and Competitive Behaviour. *Review of Economic Studies* **38**: 493–502.

Samuelson, P.A. 1948. *Economics*. New York: McGraw-Hill.

Sargent, T. and N. Wallace 1975. Rational Expectations, the Optimal Monetary Instrument and the Optimal Money Supply Rule. *Journal of Political Economy* **83**: 241–54.

Schaffner, K. 1967. Approaches to Reduction. *Philosophy of Science* **34**: 137–47.

Schelling, T. 1960. *The Strategy of Conflict*. Cambridge, MA: Harvard UP.

——. 1978. *Micromotives and Macrobehavior*. New York: Norton.

Schlicht, E. 1985. *Isolation and Aggregation in Economics*. Berlin: Springer-Verlag.

Sen, A. 1976. Rational Fools. *Philosophy and Public Affairs* **6**: 317–44.

Sensat, J. 1988. Methodological Individualism and Marxism. *Economics and Philosophy* **4**: 189–219.

Shubik, M. 1973. Commodity Money, Oligopoly, Credit and Bankruptcy in a General Equilibrium Model. *Western Economic Journal* **11**: 24–38.

——. 1975. The General Equilibrium Model is Incomplete and Inadequate for the Reconciliation of Micro and Macroeconomic Theory. *Kyklos* **28**: 545–73.

Simon, H. 1963. Comment. *American Economic Review* **53**: 229–31.

Sims, C. 1980. Comparison of Interwar and Postwar Business Cycles: Monetarism Reconsidered. *American Economic Review* **70**: 250–9.

Sklar, L. 1967. Types of Intertheoretic Reduction. *British Journal for the Philosophy of Science* **18**: 109–24.

Snippe, J. 1986. Varieties of Rational Expectations: Their Differences and Relations. *Journal of Post Keynesian Economics* **8**: 427–37.

Sonnenschein, H. 1972. Market Excess Demand Functions. *Econometrica* **40**: 549–63.

Stoker, T.M. 1984. Completeness, Distribution Restrictions and the Form of Aggregate Functions. *Econometrica* **52**: 887–907.

Sugden, R. 1991. Rational Choice: A Survey of Contributions from Economics and Philosophy. *Economic Journal* **101**: 751–86.

Tan, T. and S. Werlang 1988. The Bayesian Foundations of Equilibrium Concepts. *Journal of Economic Theory* **45**: 370–91.

Theil, H. 1954. *Linear Aggregation of Economic Relations*. Amsterdam: North-Holland.

Van Huyck, J., R. Battalio and R. Beil 1990. Tacit Coordination Games, Strategic Uncertainty and Coordination Failures. *American Economic Review* **80**: 234–48.

Varian, H. 1984. *Microeconomic Analysis* (2nd edition). New York: Norton.

——. 1987. Microeconomics, in J. Eatwell, M. Milgate and P. Newman (eds). *The New Palgrave. A Dictionary of Economics, vol. 1.* London: Macmillan.

——. 1992. *Microeconomic Analysis* (3rd edition). New York: Norton.

Vroey, M. de 1990. The Base Camp Paradox: A Reflection on the Place of Tatonnement in General Equilibrium Theory. *Economics and Philosophy* 6: 235–53.

Walliser, B. 1989. Instrumental and Cognitive Rationality. *Theory and Decision* 27: 7–36.

Weintraub, E.R. 1979. *Microfoundations.* Cambridge: Cambridge UP.

——. 1985. *General Equilibrium Theory: Studies in Appraisal.* Cambridge: Cambridge UP.

Weitzman, M. 1982. Increasing Returns and the Foundations of Unemployment Theory. *Economic Journal* 92: 787–804.

Wolff, P. de 1941. Income Elasticity of Demand, a Microeconomic and a Macroeconomic Interpretation. *Economic Journal* 51: 140–5.

Yellen, J. 1984. Efficiency–Wage Models of Unemployment. *American Economic Review* 74: 200–5.

Zandvoort, H. 1986. *Models of Scientific Development and the Case of NMR.* Dordrecht: Reidel.

AUTHOR INDEX

Agassi, J. 27
Allen, R.G.D. 4
Arrow, K.J. 4, 15, 42, 51, 82, 107, 109, 111–14, 117, 129, 153, 168, 177n
d'Aspremont, C. 163
Aumann, R. 29, 38, 39
Azariadis, C. 53

Backhouse, R. 179n
Balzer, W. 22
Basu, K. 128
Bénnassy, J.-P. 49, 117, 119
Bernheim, D.B. 33, 38, 126, 128
Bicchieri, C. 12, 36, 37, 107, 178n
Binmore, K. 178n
Blanchard, O. 53
Blaug, M. 26, 179n
Boland, L. 13, 14, 180n
Börgers, T. 123, 128, 129
Branson, W. 4
Bray, M. 132
Brodbeck, M. xvi
Bryant, J. 63, 64, 89, 154–6, 183n, 184n

Causey, R. 22
Christ, C. 158
Clower, R.W. 48, 158
Coddington, A. 47, 179n
Coleman, J.S. xiv, 10, 19, 25, 107, 111, 118
Cooper, R. 53, 54, 167
Crawford, V. 183n

Daal, J. van 74, 76, 180n
Deaton, A. 180n
Debreu, G. 4, 42, 51, 82–4, 107, 113, 134, 137, 149, 153
Dow, S. 183n
Drazen, A. 167
Drèze, J. 49
Dubey, P. 139

Ees, H. van 7
Elster, J. 11, 14
Evans, G. 139

Fisher, F. 182n
Friedman, J. 113
Friedman, M. 46, 50, 51, 180n
Frydman, R. 132, 149, 182n

Gale, D. 44
Garretsen, H. 7, 89
Geanakoplos, J. 66
Gibbard, A. 57, 64
Gorman, W. 76
Grandmont, J.-M. 66, 84
Green, H. 94, 95
Guesnerie, R. 183n
Gul, F. 37, 39

Haavelmo, T. xv, xvi, 59
Hahn, F.H. 46, 52, 53, 112, 117, 177n
Hands, D.W. 14
Hart, O. 53, 63, 119
Hausman, D. 179n

Heller, O. 162
Henderson, J. 3
Henoq, C. 101
Hicks, J. 44, 72, 109
Hilderbrand, W. 84-7, 95, 96, 99, 100
Hoffstadter, D. 100
Hoogduin, L. 14
Hoover, K. 51, 179n
Huyck, J. van 183n

Jackson, F. 178n
Janssen, M.C.W. 82, 124, 128, 129, 179n, 182n
Jevons, W.S. 72
Johansen, L. 74
John, A. 53, 54, 167

Kemeny, J. 22
Kemf, H. 101
Keynes, J.M. xix, 5, 28, 44, 49, 87, 154, 156, 157, 160, 161, 183n
King, R. 16, 179n
Kirman, A. 83, 132
Kiyotaki, N. 53, 184n
Klein, L. 72, 74, 75, 78-81
Kreps, D. 5
Kuhn, T. 41
Kuipers, T.A.F. 18, 19, 21, 23, 182n
Kydland, F. 51, 151

Lakatos, I. 42, 157
Latsis, S. 14
Leijonhufvud, A. 7, 48
Lewbell, A. 180n
Lindbeck, A. 152
Lindenberg, S. 19, 24
Long, J.B. 51, 151
Lucas, R. xiv, xv, xix, 49-51, 64, 148-50, 158, 159, 183n
Lydall, H. 99, 102

Machlup, F. 3
Malinvaud, E. 6, 7, 71, 80
Mankiw, N. 52, 155
Marchi, M. 179n
Marshall, A.W. 102
Mas-Colell, A. 119
May, K. 74, 77, 78, 80, 81, 82, 181n

McCallum, B. 131, 142
McCardle, K. 39
Merkies, A. 74, 76
Milgrom, P. 165
Mongin, P. 132
Morgenstern, O. 29, 30, 136
Moulin, H. 27, 38
Muellbauer, J. 180n
Muth, J. 131, 134, 138
Muysken, J. 74

Nagel, E. 18, 21
Nataf, A. 74-6, 81, 94
Nau, R. 39
Nelson, A. 4, 22, 79, 81
Neumann, J. von 29, 30, 136
Nickles, T. 22
Novshek, W. 125

Olkin, I. 102
Olson, M. 17, 19-22, 24, 25, 82, 85, 95
Oppenheim, P. 22

Pareto, V. 181n
Pearce, D. 38
Peeters, M. 47
Pettit, P. 178n
Phelps, E. 132
Plosser, C. 16, 51, 151, 179n
Pokropp, F. 76, 180n
Polemarchakis, H. 66
Popper, K.R. 16
Postlewaite, A. 119
Prescott, E. 51, 151
Pu, S. 74, 77, 78, 80-2, 93, 181n

Quandt, R. 3
Quirk, J. 6, 7

Rapping, L. 50
Reder, M. 46
Roberts, J. 119, 165
Romer, D. 52, 155
Rubinstein, A. 182n
Ruffin, R.J. 125

Samuelson, P.A. 44
Saposnik, R. 6, 7

Sargent, T. 50
Schaffner, K. 22
Schelling, T. 27, 39
Schlicht, E. xv, 74, 84, 93
Sen, A. 11, 65, 177n
Sensat, J. 15
Shubik, M. 119, 157
Simon, H. 180n
Sims, C. 51
Sklar, L. 22
Snippe, J. 14, 131
Snower, D. 152
Sonnenschein, H. 83, 84
Stiglitz, J. 53
Stoker, T.M. 97
Sugden, R. 179n

Tan, T. 38
Theil, H. 180n

Varian, H. 5, 57, 64, 117, 119, 180n

Wallace, N. 50
Walliser, B 12
Weintraub, E.R. 7, 43, 179n
Weitzman, M. 53
Werlang, S. 38
Wolff, P. de 180n

Yellen, J. 53, 153

Zandvoort, H. 148, 156

SUBJECT INDEX

agent: individual agent 10, 11, 13, 43, 83, 139, 176; representative agent 15, 16, 61–3, 71, 75, 84, 92, 93, 177n; Robinson Crusoe 16, 51, 64, 139, 151, 152, 183n
animal spirits 160, 167
auctioneer 112–14, 121, 129, 182n
autonomy xvi, 59

classical dichotomy 47, 51, 52
common knowledge 29, 33, 38, 122, 134, 150, 174, 178n
competition 52–4, 59, 78, 79, 119, 122–5, 129, 168; Bertrand competition 119, 122, 123; Cournot competition 119, 124–9
coordinating device 139, 155, 175, 176, 182n
coordinating failure 54, 168, 183n
core 108, 114–19, 129

equilibrium 5–7, 41–4, 99–122; competitive 49, 107, 108, 110–14, 117, 118, 121–4, 126, 128, 129, 153, 175, 181n, 183n; correlated 38; Cournot-Nash 53, 125–9, 181; general equilibrium analysis (GEA) 5, 7–9, 41–3, 48–50, 52, 107, 147, 148, 157–9, 177n, 179n; Nash 31–5, 37, 38, 53, 108, 113, 120, 122, 123, 130, 139, 142, 155, 161, 165–71, 175, 176, 183n
expectations 12–14, 131–4, 136–43, 147–54, 156, 157, 160–2, 167, 173

explanation 14–27, 58–64, 178n

form: extensive form of a game 30, 31, 33, 34; normal form of a game 30, 31, 33, 35, 36, 124
function: demand function 86, 96, 100, 101, 113, 123, 125, 126, 128, 163; market outcome function 120, 121, 126

game theory 27–31, 33–7, 119–26, 128, 129, 174–6; cooperative game 30, 114, 115; Cournot game 125, 126, 128; game of perfect information 33, 178n; sequential game 33

hydraulic conception (of macroeconomics) 44, 45, 57

income distribution 84–8, 94–103, 181n
individualism xiii, xv, 10, 14, 27, 58, 71, 147, 167, 174; institutional individualism 27; methodological individualism (MI) xiii–xvi, 26–30, 35, 36, 79, 93, 108–14, 147, 174, 175, 177n, 183n, 184n; psychological individualism 14
institution xiii, 14, 15, 35, 155
intentionality 118, 152, 153
Invisible Hand 112, 155

law 21–4; *ceteris paribus* law 58; ideal gas law 17, 95; law of

demand 85, 111; law of supply
and demand 15, 111, 112;
AD-law 103–5, 182

macroeconomics xiii, xvi–xix, 3–9,
44–9, 156, 157, 160, 175, 183n;
new classical 49–52, 147–51; new
Keynesian 52–4, 152–4
market clearing 49, 52, 107, 110,
114, 149, 153, 181n, 182n
market failure 168
methodology xvii
microeconomics xiii, xvii, xix, 3–9,
16, 26, 27, 71
model: Arrow–Debreu model (ADM)
4, 5, 42–4, 46, 48, 52, 54, 82,
107, 108, 110, 111, 113, 114,
118, 125, 129, 158, 181n, 182n;
efficiency wage model 152, 153,
183n, 184n; Lucas' model 149,
150
money illusion 91, 92

Olson's hypothesis 17, 19–22, 24, 25,
85

philosophy: philosophy of science 22,
41; mathematical political
philosophy xvii, xviii, 58, 65, 66,
177n
policy xiv, xv, 46, 47, 50–3, 57, 60,
93, 168–73, 177n
preference ordering 11, 13, 135, 136
price: explanation of 111–25; price
mechanism 45; relative price 4,
41, 53, 142
programme xiv, 9, 19, 35, 42–50, 52,
64, 107, 147, 156–9; descriptive
42; explanatory 44; guide 156–8;
supply 156–8

rationality 12–16, 27–9; cognitive
rationality 12, 13, 27, 29, 34, 44,
151; extra-rational xviii, 137,
175; group rationality 115, 116,
118, 129; individual rationality
39, 115, 131, 134, 138, 139, 142,
150; instrumental rationality 12,
13, 29, 37, 43; rationalizable
expectations 140, 161; rational

expectations (REH) 12, 50, 51,
61, 131–3, 136–43, 147, 149,
152–4, 156, 160
reduction 21–4, 26, 27, 177
reduction scheme 85, 87, 89, 91, 95,
108, 113, 117, 120, 123, 129,
153, 181n; aggregation step 22,
24, 71, 96, 123; application step
22, 87, 89, 114, 117, 118, 120,
123, 125, 153; approximation
step 22, 117, 118, 125, 126,
180n; correlation step 118, 125;
identification step 18, 181n
relationships: aggregate xiv, xv, xvii,
xviii, 10, 15–21, 27, 44–6,
71–102; empirical xvii, 42–5,
57–63, 67, 158, 179n; individual
xv, 73, 75–7, 82, 90, 91, 93–5,
102; probabilistic xviii, 95, 100–2

situational determinism 14
stability: of relations xv, 47, 178n;
rationalizable strategies 128, 140,
141
strategy 30–32, 34–49, 54, 119,
122–4, 127, 137, 161, 166, 171,
172, 176; iteratively undominated
strategies (IUS) 32, 35, 38–40,
108, 122–30, 139, 172, 175;
rationalizable strategies 32, 127,
165, 166, 168, 169, 171

theory: General Theory (Keynes')\u00a05,
39, 160; kinetic theory of gases
(KTG) 17, 85, 179n; theory of
value 4, 5
transitions: macro-to-micro transition
xiv, 25, 26, 35, 36, 177n;
micro-to-macro transition xiv, 25,
26, 62, 63, 177n

uncertainty: endogenous uncertainty
12, 27, 151, 160, 173, 176;
fundamental uncertainty 157, 160
unemployment xiii, xiv, 7, 15, 45, 46,
48, 49, 66, 153, 154; involuntary
unemployment 45, 49, 53, 66,
153, 183n; underemployment 53,
154; natural rate of
unemployment 15, 46